Threatened Birds of Odisha

Threatened Birds of Odisha

Asad R. Rahmani and Manoj V. Nair

Edited by

M.R. Maithreyi

Maps prepared by

Noor I. Khan

Layout and design by

V. Gopi Naidu and

Sanchita Kadge

Supported by

OXFORD

Oxford University Press, Walton Street, Oxford OX2 6DP
Oxford, New York,
Athens, Auckland, Bangkok,
Cape Town, Chennai, Dar-es-Salaam,
Delhi, Florence, Hong Kong, Istanbul,
Karachi, Kolkata, Kuala Lumpur, Madrid, Melbourne,
Mexico City, Mumbai, Nairobi, Paris,
Singapore, Taipei, Tokyo, Toronto,
and associated companies in
Berlin, Ibadan

Recommended citation:
Rahmani, A.R. and Nair, M.V. (2012) *Threatened Birds of Odisha*
Indian Bird Conservation Network, Bombay Natural History Society, Royal Society for the Protection of
Birds, and BirdLife International. Oxford University Press, New Delhi. Pp. 196

Consultant Editor: M.R. Maithreyi
Layout and design: V. Gopi Naidu and Sanchita Kadge
Maps: Noor I. Khan

© IBCN: Bombay Natural History Society, 2015
IBCN, c/o BNHS, Hornbill House, Shaheed Bhagat Singh Road, Mumbai — 400 001, India
Telephone: 0091-22-22821811, Fax: 0091-22-22837615
Email: ibabnhs@gmail.com and bnhs@bom4.vsnl.net.in
Websites: <www.ibcn.in> <www.bnhs.org>

Bombay Natural History Society is registered in India under the Bombay Public Trust Act 1950: F244 (Bom)
dated July 6, 1953

ISBN : 9780199466504

Proceeds from the sale of this book will go to the Indian Bird Conservation Network

Front Cover: Pale-capped Pigeon by Ramki Sreenivasan
Back Cover: Indian Skimmer by Dhritiman Mukherjee

Available from
IBCN, c/o BNHS, Hombill House, Shaheed Bhagat Singh Road, Mumbai — 400 001, India
Telephone: 0091-22-22821811, Fax: 0091-22-22837615
Email: ibabnhs@gmail.com and bnhs@bom4.vsnl.net.in
Websites: <www.ibcn.in> <www.bnhs.org>

Processed by

CONTENTS

NEAR THREATENED

🟥 CRITICALLY ENDANGERED   🟥 ENDANGERED

🟨 VULNERABLE   🟩 NEAR THREATENED

PREFACE

O disha is the ninth largest state of India. In the geographical area of 1,55,707 sq. km, the total recorded forest area is 58,136 sq. km. Out of the 1,303 bird species reported from India, nearly 524 species are found in the state. Every year, BirdLife International, UK, brings out an updated list of globally Threatened species of birds for IUCN. The 2014 list, on which this book is largely based, has 172 species of globally Threatened and Near Threatened categories in India. Out of it, 43 are found in Odisha. Three species, Great Indian Bustard, Pink-headed Duck and Greater Adjutant are now extinct in Odisha. There are still some chances to find Spoon-billed Sandpiper and Forest Owlet in Odisha.

In 2012, Bombay Natural History Society published a comprehensive book on *Threatened Birds of India* by Asad R. Rahmani. Later on the need was felt to publish state-wise books about Threatened bird species, as they would be more relevant, useful, and easily accessed by the forest department and other agencies at state level, where most of the conservation action is decided and implemented. This is the sixth book in this series.

In this book, we try to describe all the globally Threatened and Near Threatened species which are still found in the state. The major species are described in detail, while marginal species which have limited historical and present records are briefly dealt with. The book follows the list of globally Threatened and Near Threatened bird species published by BirdLife International in 2014. BirdLife regularly updates the list for International Union for Conservation of Nature (IUCN). This book provides comprehensive information about six Critically Endangered species, four Endangered species, 11 Vulnerable species, and 21 Near Threatened species which have been reported from Odisha and which need conservation attention.

We have given general recommendations in the Introduction chapter and also specific recommendations under each species. We hope that our book will generate interest among decision makers, researchers, students, teachers, and civil society at large. If the status of threatened birds improves, we will be satisfied that our attempt has not gone in vain.

With its low price and easy accessibility in the state, we hope that it will be used by forest officers, decision makers, researchers and birdwatchers for the protection of birds and their habitats. We also hope that the book will generate more interest in birdwatching.

Asad R. Rahmani
Manoj V. Nair

SHRI BIKRAM KESHARI ARUKHA
MINISTER
Forest & Environment,
Partilamentary Affairs, Odisha

Office   : (0674) 2536930
                   2322185
Res.   :   2536795
Assembly :   2539024
D.O. No..................../MFEPA

Bhubaneswar

MESSAGE

Supporting a wide range of habitats from aquatic to terrestrial ecosystems, Odisha boasts of an incredible biological diversity. The state is also home to more than 500 avian species.

We derive many ecological and social benifits from birds. As one of the important members of our ecosystem, birds play many roles such as predators, pollinators, scavengers, seed dispersers and biological indicators. Migratory species link ecosystem processes and fluxes that are separated by great distances and times.

Even though the state has declared six Important Bird Areas (IBAs) such as Chilika, Bhitarkanika, Chandaka-Dampara, Similipal, Satkosia and Sunabeda Wildlife Sanctuary to protect and conserve the birds, still many dangers loom large, threatening many species of birds.

The current publication "Threatened Birds of Odisha" is an attempt to offer the exact status of those species of birds that are in danger due to several anthropogenic and natural factors. I am sure this book will help to generate awareness on this threatened and very important group of fauna of Odisha. It will also help to highlight the need to protect and conserve such species in Odisha.

I hope this book will serve the objective of enhancing people's interest in protection and conservation of the birds in Odisha.

I congratulate Odisha Biodiversity Board for such a laudable endeavour and wish the book all success.

B. K-

(BIKRAM KESHARI ARUKHA)

Upendra Nath Behera, IAS
Development Commissioner-cum-
Additional Chief Secretary
Government of Odisha
Planning & Coordination Deptt.
Bhubaneswar-751 001, Odisha

Pnone : (+91-674) 2536882
Fax: (+91-674) 2536792
e-mail : dcplg@nic.in

26th September, 2015

MESSAGE

O disha is famous for its temples, sea beaches, diverse people and cultures, and natural beauty. Nearly 7 per cent of India's total forest area is found in Odisha. The protected areas (PA) constitute 10.37% of the total forest area. There are 19 wildlife sanctuaries and two national parks in the state, constituting 5.36% of the total area of the state under PA network. There are three notified tiger reserves (Similipal, Satkosia and Sunabeda), three elephant reserves (Mayurbhanj, Sambalpur and Mahanadi), one biosphere reserve (Similipal) and two Ramsar sites (Chilika and Bhitarkanika). In addition, there are many community reserves such as Balipadar-Bhetnoi Blackbuck area in Ganjam district. There are eight important bird and biodiversity areas identified in the State and there could be more.

Odisha is blessed with diverse flora and fauna: 86 species of mammals, 524 species of birds, 131 species of reptiles, 27 species of amphibians and more than 600 species of fishes (marine and fresh water) have been recorded from the State. Unfortunately, some of these species are threatened with extinction but we do not have up to date information about their status and distribution, which is the first step in planning conservation action.

This book attempts to address this gap in terms of threatened birds of Odisha by providing updated information on eight Critically Endangered, five Endangered, eleven Vulnerable and 22 Near Threatened species which has been recorded from the state. In addition, vital information for the birds which need maximum conservation attention in the state of Odisha is also provided. The authors have tried to do an extensive literature survey, reach out to knowledgeable and experienced birdwatchers and ornithologists, and supplemented these with data from their own field work to compile this very useful source of information. It is hoped that this hand book will be an important tool in the hands of managers and researchers alike to ensure that our threatened birds are better conserved and posterity. The effort of Odisha Biodiversity Board to commission such studies on various faunal and floral groups is indeed praiseworthy.

(Upendra Nath Behera)

SHASHI PAUL
MEMBER SECRETARY
ODISHA BIODIVERSITY BOARD

FOREWORD

Odisha Biodiversity Board (OBB) is committed to highlight the conservation status of lesser known groups of plants and animals and threatened species in the state so that awareness among the masses can be generated, and help and cooperation from all corners is received for their conservation. Without involvement of all the sections of society it is not possible to conserve the biodiversity of the state which is our ecological security for future.

The state of Odisha, due to its strategic location and broad range of ecosystems, supports rich diversity of flora and fauna. Among the faunal diversity, Odisha is home to over 500 species of birds which includes both residential and migratory ones. On one hand having such a rich avian diversity is a matter of pride for the state but at the same time this confers a huge responsibility on the managers and all other stakeholders to conserve it sustainably. This has emerged as a great challenge for all of us.

OBB in collaboration with National Biodiversity Authority and Bombay Natural History Society has undertaken the work of present publication titled as "Threatened Birds of Odisha". This work is an indicator of the conservation status of avian fauna in our state. The authors have made an attempt to provide information on the diversity, distribution, ecology and conservation status of 46 species of birds of Odisha that are categorised under Critically Endangered (CR), Endangered (EN) and Vulnerable (VU) following the IUCN criteria.

It is hoped that this work will create awareness and highlight the need for conservation of these threatened avian members of the state and pave the ways for further studies.

(SHASHI PAUL)

ACKNOWLEDGEMENTS

This book would not have been possible without the constant support of Shri Shashi Paul, IFS, Member Secretary, Odisha Biodiversity Board who not only helped us get funds but also provided generous encouragement. A special word of gratitude to Shri R.K. Sharma, IAS, who was the Principal Secretary, Forest and Environment Department and the Chairperson of the Odisha Biodiversity Board during the time of commissioning of this project, for having graciously accepted the proposal to produce this book.

Heartfelt thanks are also due to Shri U.N. Behera, IAS, Addl. Chief Secretary, Shri J.D. Sharma, IFS, PCCF, Odisha, Shri S.S. Srivastava, IFS, PCCF (Wildlife) and Chief Wildlife Warden, Odisha; Shri Sidhant Das, IFS, Addl.PCCF, Dr D. Swain, IFS, Shri Sandeep Tripathy, IFS, Dr A.K. Mahapatra, IFS, Shri S. Panda, IFS, CCF (Wildlife); Shri H.S. Bisht, IFS, Field Director, Similipal Tiger Reserve, Shri H.S. Upadhyaya, IFS, Shri A.K. Nayak, IFS, Field Director, Satkosia Tiger Reserve, Shri D. Biswal, IFS, Dr M. Biswal, IFS, Dr P.R. Karat, IFS and Shri Raghu Prasad, IFS for their encouragement and support. Shri Ajit Pattnaik, IFS and Shri G. Rajesh, IFS are also gratefully acknowledged for sharing their experience on the birds of Chilika. Much-needed field support was provided by senior field officers of various important Protected Areas as well as Forest Divisions of the state – we express our gratitude to Shri A. Misra, Shri A. Pattnaik, Shri B.K. Acharya, Shri. K.K. Swain, Shri K.L. Purohit and Shri S.K. Panda. We would be failing in our duty if we do not mention the encouragement and support of the retired Senior Research Officers of the Odisha Forest Department – late Dr C.S. Kar, Dr. L.A.K. Singh and Dr S. Kar. Dr L.N. Acharjyo was a source of inspiration and valuable historical information.

Any work on the ornithology of Odisha would be incomplete without the mention of the work of Dr U.N. Dev, the veteran ornithologist of the state and we are grateful to him for kindly sharing his vast experience and insights. Our sincere thanks are also due to the senior conservationists and birdwatchers of the state such as Prof. B.K. Behura, Prof. Mohanty-Hejmady, Prof. S.K. Datta, Shri N.K. Bhujabal, Mrs Monalisa Bhujabal, Shri Gahar Abedin, Dr Biswajit Mohanty, Shri Ramesh Jhankar, Dr Siba Parida, Dr B. Pandav, Shri S. Pradhan and Shri A. Pradhan. Birdwatching as a hobby in Odisha has grown by leaps and bounds over the past few years by the stellar effort of a few dedicated and committed bird lovers and experts. We would like to put on record the selfless help rendered by Mrs Panchami Manoo Ukil, Mr Shakti Nanda and Shri Siddharth Mohanty in this regard. Their colleagues, Ms Swetashree Purohit, Shri B. Padhee and

Shri Avinash Khemka were most generous in sharing many of their observations and photographs.

Experts like Dr Pratyush Mohapatra, Shri Aditya Panda, Vivek Sarkar, Dr Satyaranjan Mishra, Shri Satyesh Naik, Shri P.K. Dhal, Shri Partha Patra, Shri Durgesh Singh, Shri Chandan Jani, Shri Himanshu Palei, Commander Subash Das, Shri Udayan Behera and Dr Gopi G.V. were generous with their time and unstintingly shared their checklists and trip reports. Special thanks to Shri Bijay Das of Dangmal and Madhu Behera of Mangalajodi.

We would like to thank Tim Inskipp for his amazingly detailed work – the Checklist and Bibliography of the Birds of Odisha, available online – which has been of tremendous help in gleaning less-known records.

Ramki Sreenivasan is gratefully thanked for the use of his image for the cover, and Dhritiman Mukherjee for the back cover.

In BNHS, we want to thank Ms M.R. Maithreyi for editing the text, Ms Sanchita Kadge and Mr Gopi Naidu for layout and design, and Mr Noor Khan for preparing the maps. Our gratitude to Mr Homi Khusrokhan, President, BNHS, Dr Ashok Bhagwat, Hon. Secretary, Mr E.A. Kshirsagar, Hon. Treasurer, and Dr Deepak Apte, Director, and all the members of the Governing Council for their support. Among our colleagues at BNHS, we would like to thank Mr Sachin Kulkarni, Dr Raju Kasambe, Mr Abhijit Malekar, Ms Varsha Chalke, Ms Vibhuti Dedhia, Mr Divyesh Parikh, Mr M.G. Mathews, Ms Nirmala Barure, Mr Siddhesh Surve, Mr Asif Khan, Mr Vandan Jhaveri, and Ms Sonali P. Vadhavkar. We are very thankful to Khagolam Institute of Georeferencing - Kalyan.

We wish to thank the following persons for contributing their excellent photographs for the making of this book: Mr Dhritiman Mukherjee, Mr Abrar Ahmad, Mr Bhasmang Mehta, Mr Gobind Sagar Bhardwaj, Mr Ramki Srinivasan, Mr Saleel Tambe, Mr Shashank Dalvi, Mr Vinayak Yardi, Dr Dharmendra Khandal, Mr Rishad Naoroji, Mr Niranjan Sant, Mr Veer Vaibhav Mishra, Mr P.M. Lad, Dr K.S. Gopi Sundar, Mr Sunil Singhal, and Mr Yogendra Shah.

We would like to thank BirdLife International and Royal Society for the Protection of Birds (RSPB), both based in UK, for their unstinted support to this book. In BirdLife International, the first name that comes to mind is that of Dr Nigel Collar whose contribution to the study of Threatened birds of the world is well-known. We thank BirdLife International CEO Ms Patricia, Dr Richard Grimmett, Dr Mike Crosby, Dr Stuart Butcher, Dr A.J. Stattersfield, Dr Richard Thomas and Mr Joe Taylor. In RSPB, we would like to acknowledge the support of Dr Mike Clarke, CEO, Dr Tim Stowe, Mr Chris Bowden, Ms Cristi Nozawa and Mr Ian Barber.

INTRODUCTION

O disha (17° 47'–22° 34' North and 81° 22'–87° 29' East), the ninth largest state in India located along the east coast, has a geographical area of 1,55,707 sq. km, which constitutes about 4.7% of the land area of the country. The north of the state is bounded by Jharkhand and West Bengal, east by the Bay of Bengal, southeast by Andhra Pradesh and the west by Chhattisgarh. The state can be divided into four distinct physiographic regions namely Northern Plateau, Eastern Ghats, Central Tableland and Coastal Plains. The prominent rivers flowing through the state are the Mahanadi, Brahmani, Baitarani, Subarnarekha, Budhabalanga and Rushikulya. With a length of 853 km, the Mahanadi is the one of the largest rivers of the Indian subcontinent. The state is divided into 30 administrative districts. The vast and varied topography, altitudinal variation from sea level up to nearly 2000 msl, a coastline of about 480 km, several large and perennial rivers and a variety of habitat types ranging from mangrove forests, brackish lagoons to semi-evergreen forests—all this in the confluence of two major biogeographic provinces of India namely the Eastern Ghats and Chhotanagpur Plateau—make Odisha an exceptionally rich repository of biodiversity.

The Eastern Ghats in Odisha is unique as it has faunal and floral elements of both Western Ghats and northeast India, besides those of the Deccan Plateau and Gangetic Plains

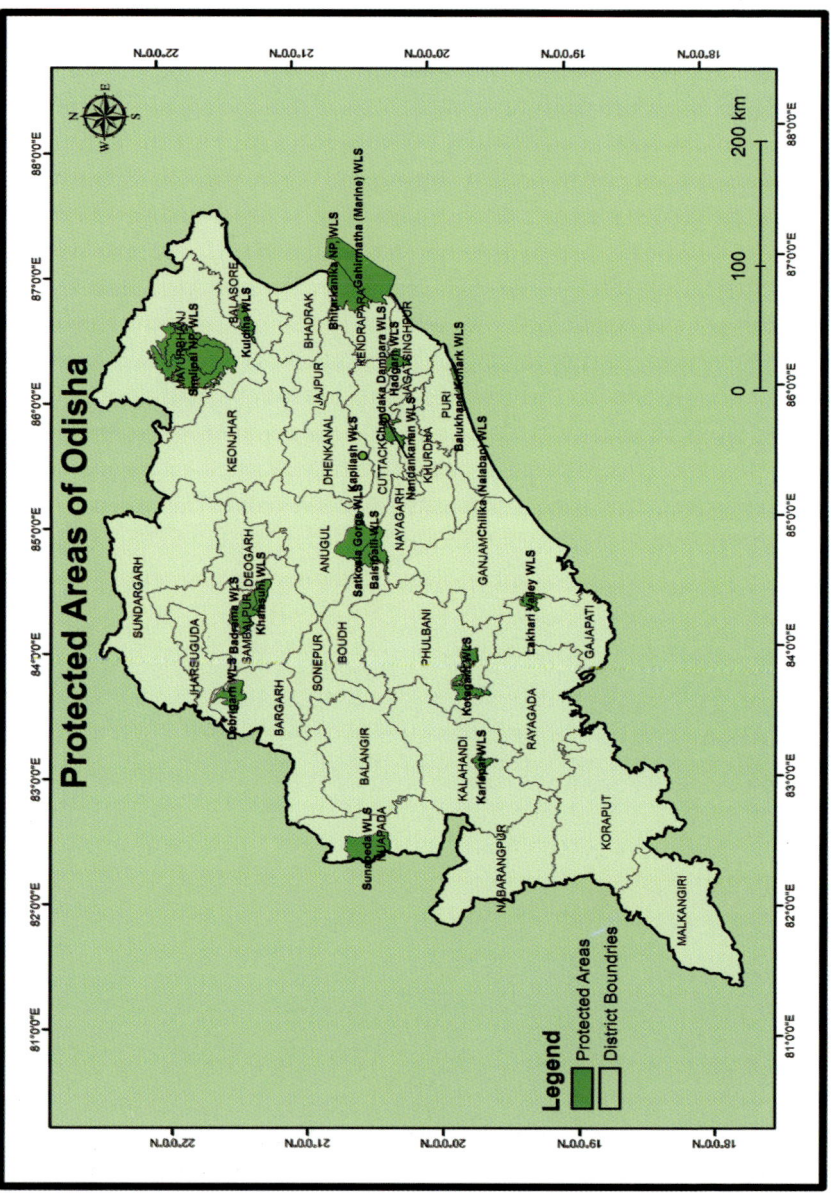

Protected Areas of Odisha

Courtesy: GIS Cell, Wildlife Institute of India

Legend
Protected Areas
District Boundries

Biogeographically, the state falls in three zones viz. Deccan Peninsula (Chotanagpur and Eastern Highlands), Lower Gangetic Plain (7B) and East Coast (8B) (Rodgers *et al.*, 2000). Meher-Homji (2001) has recognised three phytogeographic regions in the state, i.e., Deccan Plateau, Eastern Ghats and Coastal Plains. The state is underlain largely by Precambrian rocks. The geological formations reflect a complex of igneous, metamorphic and sedimentary rocks with alluvial and coastal alluvial plains, each giving rise to distinct soil types which range from alluvial (coastal and riverine types) to lateritic and black cotton.

The total length of the coastline in Odisha is about 480 km. The rivers of Odisha form deltas on the coast, such as Bhitarkanika formed by the Brahmani and Baitarni rivers (Anon. 1992). Brackish water lagoons are also seen among which Chilika Lake, spanning an area of over 1,165 sq. km, is the largest along the east coast of India. Chilika Lake is a Ramsar site and a globally important waterfowl congregation area. The pear-shaped lagoon is about 64.5 km long and its width varies from 5 km to 20 km. It is connected to the sea by a 35-km-long narrow outer channel. In Chilika, there are several islands located in and around the lagoon covering an area of 223 sq. km. The major islands are Kalijai, Barakuda, Ghantasila, Chadhelihaga and Nalabana (Patnaik 2000).

The climate is generally hot and humid. The temperature ranges from 20 °C to 41 °C, with the western districts experiencing higher mean annual temperatures. Precipitation is mainly during the Southwest monsoon (June to September) and to a lesser degree during the Northeast monsoon (September–December). The mean annual rainfall of the state ranges from 1,200 mm to 1,600 mm. The coastal area is highly prone to periodical cyclones.

Odisha is an agricultural state with over 76% of its people dependent on farming for their livelihood. The major crops are rice, pulses, oil-seeds, jute, sugarcane, coconut and turmeric. The total population is 36.7 crores of which 86% is rural. The tribal population is 22%. The population density is 297 persons per sq. km (Ministry of Environment and Forests 1999; Forest Survey of India 2001).

Vegetation and Forest Types

As per Champion and Seth (1968) and Panigrahi (1983), the vegetation of Odisha comes under five types: (i) Odisha Semi-evergreen Forests (ii) Tropical Moist Deciduous Forests (iii) Tropical Dry Deciduous Forests (iv) Central Indian Hill Forests and (v) Littoral and Tidal Swamp Forests. However, considering the physical features and agro-climatic conditions, the state can be divided into four distinct regions as follows:

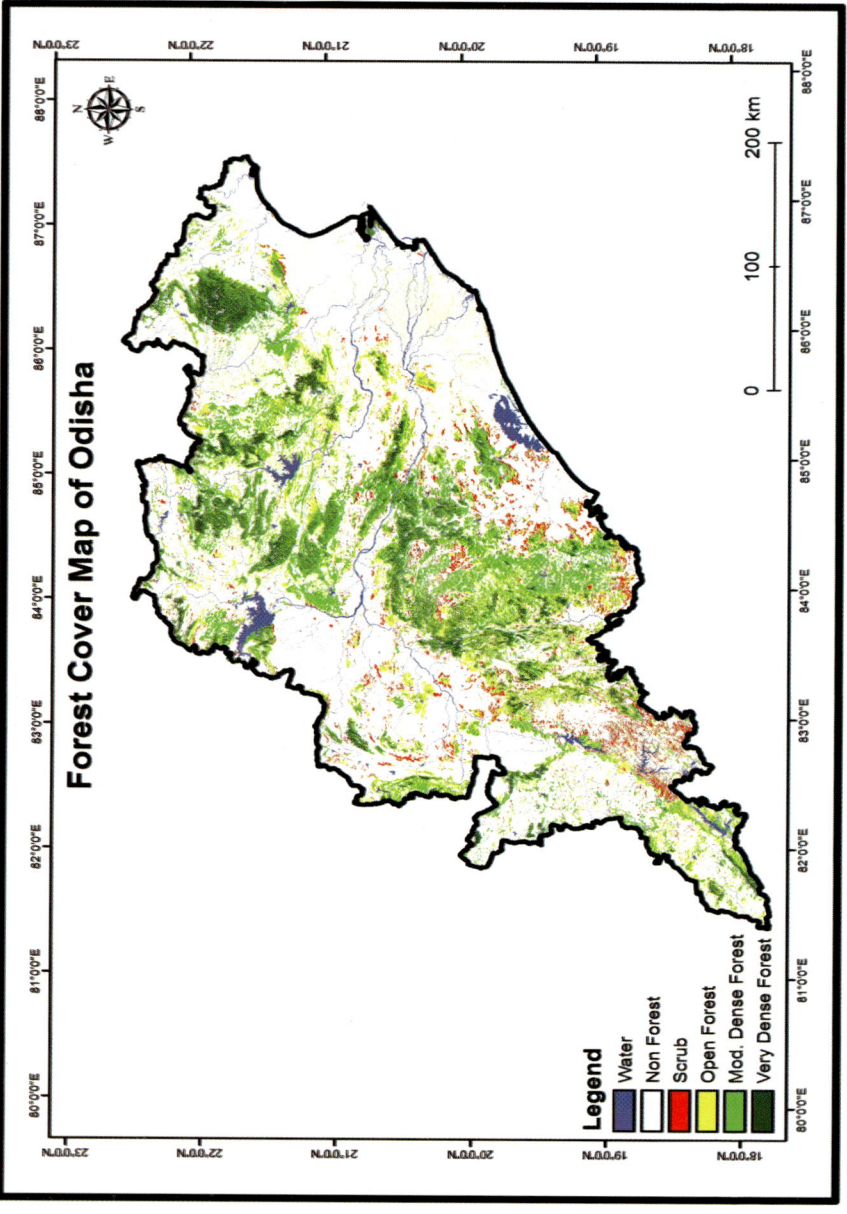

Forest Cover Map of Odisha

Legend
- Water
- Non Forest
- Scrub
- Open Forest
- Mod. Dense Forest
- Very Dense Forest

Threatened Birds of Odisha

Odisha has a variety of forest types

a. **The Northern Plateau**

This region is a continuation of the Chotanagpur plateau and includes the districts of Mayurbhanj, Keonjhar, Sundargarh, and portions of Angul, Jajpur, Deogarh and Sambalpur districts. The main rivers are the Brahmani, Baitarni, Salandi and Budhabalanga. The Northern Plateau constitutes 23% of the total area of the state. The predominant forest type is Sal-dominated Moist Deciduous, though dense Semi-evergreen patches also occur in parts of Similipal in Mayurbhanj. The average altitude is about 600 msl going upto 1,000 msl in the peaks of Meghasani and Khairiburu in Similipal.

b. **The Central Region**

This consists of the districts of Bolangir, parts of Dhenkanal, Boudh and Cuttack, Bargarh and parts of Sambalpur districts. The main rivers are the Mahanadi and tributaries such as the Ib, Jira, Ong and Tel. The main forest types are Moist and Dry Deciduous. The average elevation is about 300 msl except at Gandhamardan hills which is 810 msl.

c. **The Eastern Ghats**

Covering the districts of Malkangiri, Rayagada, Koraput, Kalahandi, Phulbani and parts of Ganjam, Khurda, Nayagarh and Gajapati districts, this is the largest region and includes about 36% of the total area of the state. The

Montane grasslands, dense mangrove and long coastline with mudflats provide habitat to various types of birds

area is mainly hilly with about 300–450 msl elevation, rising up to the high hills of the Eastern Ghats above 1000 msl such as Deomali, Mahendragiri and Singaraj. The forest type is predominantly Moist Deciduous with patches of Semi-evergreen and grasslands. Main rivers are the Mahanadi, Bansadhara and Nagabali. Many interesting species have been recorded from this region (Majumdar 1988).

d.   The Coastal Plains

This region covers the districts of Cuttack, Puri, Balasore and parts of Ganjam. Most of the area is taken up by rice paddy and human habitations though unique habitat elements like mangrove forests, salt marshes and sand dunes also can be seen. The important rivers are the Mahanadi and its tributaries, the Brahmani, Baitarni, Devi, Rushikulya and Budhabalanga. Important wetlands for waterfowl such as the Chilika Lake and Bhitarkanika are situated here.

Odisha harbours an estimated number of 3,100 species of vascular plants (angiosperms and pteridophytes). Among the lower group of plants, 45 species of bryophytes and 35 species of lichens have so far been reported from the state (Dash 2012, Upreti 1993). Similarly, 102 species of mushrooms have been reported from Odisha. The state is credited with 125 orchid species, about 12%

Threatened Birds of Odisha

of the total diversity of the country. Of the 125 species of Indian mangrove flora (39 mangroves and 86 mangrove associates), Odisha ranks the highest among all states with a total of 101 species (Kathiresan, 2010).

Protected Area Network and Biodiversity

Of the total geographical area of 1,55,707 sq. km, the total recorded forest area is 58,136 sq. km (Forest Survey of India 2013). Of the state's total geographical area, 34.91 per cent is covered with forests. This works out to be about 6.89 per cent of India's total forest area. The protected areas (PAs) constitute 10.37% of the total forest area. There are 19 wildlife sanctuaries and two national parks in the state, constituting 5.36 % of the total area of the state under PA network. However, there is a marked absence of PAs in the southern districts of Koraput and Malkangiri in the biodiversity-rich areas of the Eastern Ghats and this gap has to be addressed by the policy makers in future to safeguard these extremely crucial wildlife habitats. Similipal is the only Biosphere Reserve in Odisha and was declared by the Government of India due to its vast biodiversity and rich natural heritage (Mohanty *et al.* 2002). Apart from the aforementioned 19 protected areas scattered across the state, there are many habitats and landscapes

MANOJ NAIR

Numerous streams and rivers originate from the forests of Odisha, providing good habitat for species such as Grey-headed Fish-eagle

Mixed species colonial nesting birds at herony of Bhitarkanika

outside the PA network holding exceptional biodiversity values and providing incalculable ecosystem services to the people of the state. Few examples are Barbara, Gupteswar and Pradhanpat Reserved Forests, Deomali, Mahendragiri, Malayagiri and Gandhamardan hills, and wetlands such as Anshupa lake and Ghodahada reservoir.

Odisha's unique location in peninsular India has blessed it with an interesting and rich assemblage of floral and faunal diversity. The fauna of the state is diverse and has been documented by several workers. Eighty-six species of mammals, 524 species of birds, 131 species of reptiles, 27 species of amphibians and more than 600 species of fishes (marine and fresh water)

Important Bird and Biodiversity Areas in Odisha		
IBA site codes	IBA site names	IBA criteria
IN–OR–01	Bhitarkanika Wildlife Sanctuary	A1, A4ii
IN–OR–02	Chandka–Dampara Wildlife Sanctuary	A1, A3, A4ii
IN–OR–03	Chilika Lake and Wildlife Sanctuary	A1, A4i, A4iii
IN–-OR–04	Mangala Jodi	A1, A4i, A4iii
IN–OR–05	Satkosia Gorge Wildlife Sanctuary	A1, A3
IN–-OR–-06	Similipal National Park	A1, A3
IN–-OR–-07	Sunabeda Wildlife Sanctuary	A1, A3
IN–-OR–-08	Hirakud Reservoir	A1, A4iii

Threatened Birds of Odisha

The 1,100 sq. km Chilika Lake is the largest lagoon in India, connected to sea with a 35-km-long anastomosing channel. More than a million birds are found in Chilika, particularly in Nalabana Bird Sanctuary and Mangalajodi. Sometimes 15,000 to 20,000 Black-tailed Godwits are seen in Mangalajodi

have been recorded from the state. The invertebrate faunal composition has been poorly documented. However, the state is home to over 250 species of butterflies, 102 species of odonates, 48 species of marine molluscs, 12 species of blattaria, 14 species of dermaptera, 31 species of isoptera, 32 species of land molluscs, 48 species of nematodes and 46 species of oligochaetes (ZSI 1993; Dutta 1990; Dutta 1997; Dutta and Acharjyo 1997; Dutta and Ahmed 1989; Dutta and Mohanty-Hejmadi 1993; Murthy 1987).

The mammalian fauna is diverse, with almost all the large and smaller mammals of central India being found here, including Leopard *Panthera pardus*, Tiger *Panthera tigris*, Indian Fox *Vulpes bengalensis*, Wild Dog *Cuon alpinus*, Ratel or Honey Badger *Mellivora capensis*, Fishing Cat *Felis viverrina*, Four-horned Antelope *Tetracerus quadricornis*, Gaur *Bos gaurus*, Sambar *Rusa unicolor* and Chital *Axis axis*. Worthy of mention is the globally unique melanistic Tiger population of Similipal and the recent discoveries of a population of Oriental Small-clawed Otter *Aonyx cinerea* and Stripe-necked Mongoose *Herpetes vitticollis* from the state, the former thought to be discontinuously distributed

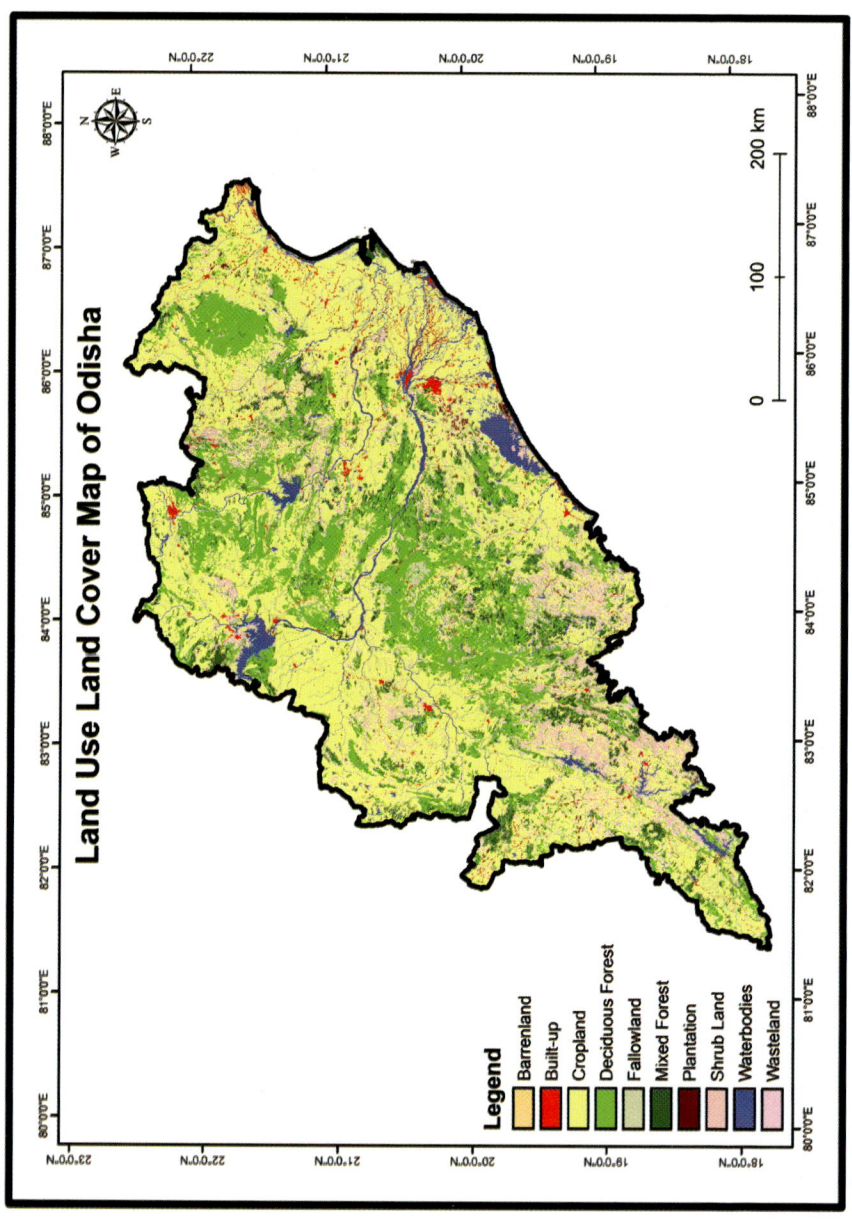

Land Use Land Cover Map of Odisha

Legend

- Barrenland
- Built-up
- Cropland
- Deciduous Forest
- Fallowland
- Mixed Forest
- Plantation
- Shrub Land
- Waterbodies
- Wasteland

Courtesy: GIS Cell, Wildlife Institute of India

200 km

100

0

Threatened Birds of Odisha

in Northeast India and Western Ghats and the latter thought to be confined to the Western Ghats. Among reptiles, Odisha is the only state with all three Indian crocodilians, and the largest population of Saltwater Crocodile *Crocodilus porosus* and Water Monitor lizard *Varanus salvator*. Further, the Odisha coast is known for the world's largest rookery of Olive Ridley Sea Turtle. There are three mass nesting beaches of the Olive Ridleys: the Gahirmatha coast, along with Devi and Rushikulya river mouths (Kar 2000). There are eight species of sea turtles in the world, of which four are known to occur in the coastal areas of Odisha: Olive Ridley *Lepidochelys olivacea*, Hawksbill *Eretmochelys imbricata*, Leatherback *Desmochelys coriacea* and Green Sea Turtle *Chelonia mydas*. Although four species are found in the state, the confirmed nesting of only one species, the Olive Ridley, is known so far (Dash and Kar 1990).

PROTECTED AREAS

The Protected Area Network in Odisha consists of one National Park (Bhitarkanika), one proposed National Park (Similipal) and nineteen wildlife sanctuaries, covering an area of 8352.19 sq. km which constitutes 5.36% of the geographical area of the state. There are three notified Tiger Reserves (Similipal, Satkosia and Sunabeda), three Elephant Reserves (Mayurbhanj, Sambalpur and Mahanadi), one Biosphere Reserve (Similipal) and two Ramsar sites (Chilika and Bhitarkanika). In addition, a Community Reserve to protect the endangered Blackbuck has been proposed in Balipadar-Bhetnoi in Ganjam district.

IBAS IN ODISHA

In 2004, Islam and Rahmani (2004) had identified seven IBAs. One more has been added since then (Nair *et al.* 2014; Rahmani *et al.* 2015) but more are likely to be present. We do not have enough data to identify sites that would qualify the international IBA criteria developed by BirdLife International (unpublished). The same criteria are followed all over the world for identification of IBAs.

AVIFAUNA

The bird life in Odisha is very rich, with 524 species reported till now (Inskipp 2014), including historical records, primarily those by Valentine Ball (Ball, 1876, 1877, 1878). Because of its biogeographical location, the avifauna has a curious mixture of various elements. The Similipal hills appears to have biogeographical affinities to the Northeast and therefore has populations of some birds that

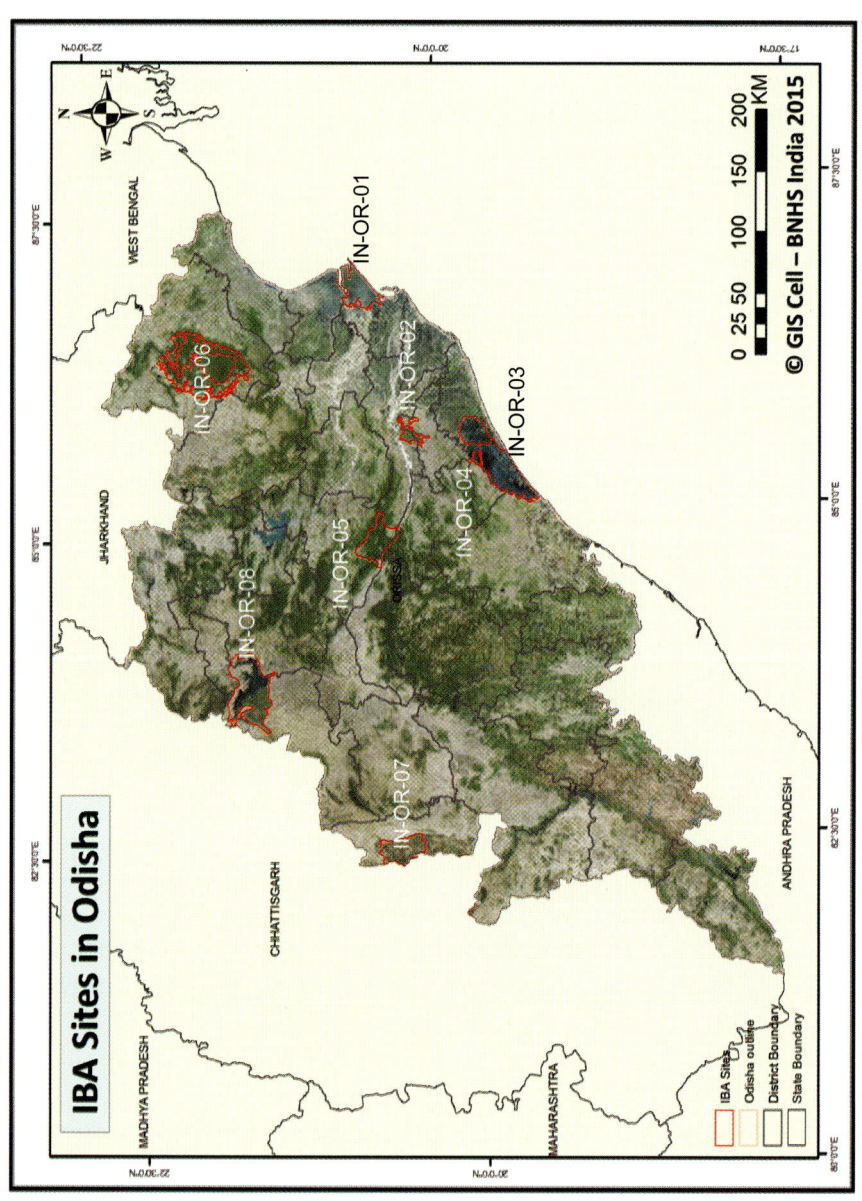

IBA Sites in Odisha

Threatened Birds of Odisha

List of extant threatened birds of Odisha with IBA site codes

CRITICALLY ENDANGERED	
White-rumped Vulture *Gyps bengalensis*	IN-OR-01, 02, 05, 06, 07
Long-billed Vulture *Gyps indicus*	IN-OR-01, 02, 05, 06, 07
Red-headed Vulture *Aegypius calvus*	IN-OR-02, 06
Baer's Pochard *Aythya baeri*	IN-OR-01, 03
Spoon-billed Sandpiper *Eurynorhynchus pygmeus*	IN-OR-03 (old record)
Forest Owlet *Heteroglaux blewitti*	No confirmed record

ENDANGERED	
Egyptian Vulture *Neophron percnopterus*	No record from IBAs
Lesser Florican *Sypheotides indicus*	No recent records
Spotted Greenshank *Tringa guttifer*	IN-OR-01
Black-bellied Tern *Sterna acuticauda*	IN-OR-01

VULNERABLE	
Lesser White-fronted Goose *Anser erythropus*	IN-OR-03, 08
Lesser Adjutant *Leptoptilos javanicus*	IN-OR-01, 03
Pallas's Fish-Eagle *Haliaeetus leucoryphus*	IN-OR-01, 03, 08
Greater Spotted Eagle *Clanga clanga*	IN-OR-01, 06, 08
Indian Spotted Eagle *Clanga hastata*	IN-OR-01, 02, 04
Sarus Crane *Grus antigone*	Not found in any IBA
Great Knot *Calidris tenuirostris*	IN-OR-01, 03
Indian Skimmer *Rynchops albicollis*	IN-OR-01, 03, 05, 08
Pale-capped Woodpigeon *Columba punicea*	IN-OR-02, 06
Bristled Grassbird *Chaetornis striatus*	IN-OR-05, 06
Green Munia *Amandava formosa*	IN-OR-06,

NEAR THREATENED	
Ferruginous Duck *Aythya nyroca*	IN-OR-03
Falcated Duck *Marcea falcata*	IN-OR-03, 08
Spot-billed Pelican *Pelecanus philippensis*	IN-OR-01, 03, 04, 08
Oriental Darter *Anhinga melanogaster*	IN-OR-01, 03, 04, 08
Painted Stork *Mycteria leucocephala*	IN-OR-01, 03, 04, 08
Black-necked Stork *Ephippiorhynchus asiaticus*	IN-OR-01, 03
Black-headed Ibis *Threskiornis melanocephalus*	IN-OR-01, 03, 04, 08
Great Thick-knee *Esacus recurvirostris*	IN-OR-01, 03, 05
River Lapwing *Vanellus duvaucelli*	IN-OR-02, 03, 05, 07, 08
Eurasian Curlew *Numenius arquata*	IN-OR-01, 03, 04, 05, 08
Black-tailed Godwit *Limosa limosa*	IN-OR-01, 03, 04, 08
Asian Dowitcher *Limnodromus semipalmatus*	IN-OR-03
River Tern *Sterna aurantia*	IN-OR-03, 04, 05, 08
Cinereous Vulture *Aegypius monachus*	Not reported from any IBA
Pallid Harrier *Circus macrourus*	IN-OR-03, 04
Grey-headed Fish-eagle *Ichthyophaga ichthyaetus*	IN-OR-06
Red-headed Falcon *Falco chicquera*	IN-OR-06, 07
Laggar Falcon *Falco jugger*	IN-OR-03
Brown-winged Kingfisher *Pelargopis amauroptera*	IN-OR-01
Malabar Pied Hornbill *Anthracaceros coronatus*	IN-OR-05, 06
Alexandrine Parakeet *Psittacula eupatria*	Mainly outside IBAs
Mangrove Pitta, *Pitta megarhyncha*	IN-OR-01

Protected Area Network in Odisha

S.No.	Name of P A	Area (km²)	District
1.	Bhitarkanika National Park	145	Kendrapara and Bhadrak
2.	Similipal National Park (Proposed)	845.70	Mayurbhanj
3.	Bhitarkanika Wildlife Sanctuary	672	Kendrapara
4.	Balukhand-Konark Wildlife Sanctuary	71.72	Puri
5.	Baisipalli Wildlife Sanctuary	168.35	Nayagarh
6.	Badrama Wildlife Sanctuary	304.03	Sambalpur
7.	Chilika (Nalabana) Wildlife Sanctuary	15.53	Puri
8.	Chandaka-Dampara Wildlife Sanctuary	175.79	Khurda and Cuttack
9.	Debrigarh Wildlife Sanctuary	346.91	Bargarh
10.	Gahirmatha Marine Sanctuary	1435	Kendrapara and Bhadrak
11.	Hadgarh Wildlife Sanctuary	191.06	Keonjhar
12.	Khalasuni Wildlife Sanctuary	116	Sambalpur
13.	Kuldiha Wildlife Sanctuary	272.75	Balasore
14.	Nandankanan Wildlife Sanctuary	4.26	Khurda
15.	Similipal Wildlife Sanctuary	2306.61	Mayurbhanj
16.	Sunabeda Wildlife Sanctuary	600	Nuapada
17.	Satkosia Gorge Wildlife Sanctuary	795.52	Angul, Boudh, Cuttack, Nayagarh
18.	Karlapat Wildlife Sanctuary	147.66	Kalahandi
19.	Lakheri Valley Wildlife Sanctuary	185.87	Gajapati
20.	Kotgarh Wildlife Sanctuary	399.05	Kandhamal
21.	Kapilash Wildlife Sanctuary	125.50	Dhenkanal

MANOJ V. NAIR

Satkosia Gorge Wildlife Sanctuary is one of the main wintering habitats of Indian Skimmer

Community conservation work is best exemplified by the people of Mangalajodi where many former bird trappers now take people for birdwatching. In Brahmakumei, villagers have taken the initiative to protect a large patch of forest

are known only in the Himalaya and southern Assam hills such as Collared Falconet *Microhierax caerulescens*, Pale-capped Woodpigeon *Columba punicea*, Abbot's Babbler *Malacocincla abbotti*, Grey Treepie *Dendrocitta formosae* and Pale-footed Bush Warbler *Cettia pallidipes*. The State also possibly forms the southernmost limit of several Himalayan/Northeastern species such as Lineated Barbet *Megalaima lineata*, Thick-billed Pigeon *Treron curvirostra*, Grey-headed Woodpecker *Picus canus*, Large Yellownape *Picus flavinucha* and Fulvous-breasted Woodpecker *Dendrocopos macei*. Further, Odisha has many discontinuously distributed species such as the Little Spiderhunter *Arachnothera longirostra*, Dollarbird *Eurystomus orientalis*, Great-eared Nightjar *Lyncornis macrotis*, Rufous-bellied Eagle *Lophotriorchis kienerii*, Black Baza *Aviceda leuphotes*, Jerdon's Baza *Aviceda jerdoni* (Ripley *et al*. 1985).

Among the Critically Endangered species, the White-rumped Vulture *Gyps bengalensis* and Long-billed Vulture *G. indicus* are still present in the state in highly depleted numbers. Birds such as the Great Indian Bustard *Ardeotis nigiriceps* and Lesser Florican *Sypheotides indica* were found earlier but there is no recent

Bagaghana heronry in Bhitarkanika is one of the largest heronries of India, famous for Asian Openbill

MANOJV NAIR

The IBA Programme of BirdLife International aims to identify, monitor, and protect a global network of Important Bird Areas (IBAs) for the conservation of the world's birds and other biodiversity. BirdLife Partners take responsibility for the IBA Programme nationally, with the BirdLife Secretariat taking the lead on international aspects and in some priority non-Partner countries. As of 2013, more than 12,000 sites in some 200 countries and territories have been identified as Important Bird Areas.

Important Bird Areas are sites of international significance for the conservation of birds and their habitats at the global, regional, and sub-regional level. The selection of IBAs is a particularly effective way of identifying conservation priorities. IBAs are key sites for conservation, small enough to be conserved in their entirety and often already part of a protected area network (BirdLife International undated).

A site is recognised as an IBA only if it meets certain criteria based on the occurrence of key bird species that are vulnerable to global extinction or whose populations are otherwise irreplaceable. The IBA programme aims to fill the gaps in knowledge and further understanding about the conservation of these sites and their avifaunal diversity.

An IBA must be amenable to conservation action and management. The IBA criteria which are applicable globally are as follows:

A1: Sites holding globally threatened bird species of global conservation concern.

A2: Sites having restricted range bird species, i.e., bird species with a historic breeding range up to 50,000 sq. km in the world.

A3: Sites having biome restricted bird species, i.e., bird species representing distinct habitat types.

A4: Sites having large congregations of birds.

What is the significance of IBAs?

For conservation

- IBAs help identify priority sites for conservation action.
- IBAs provide the framework to monitor and manage sites of global conservation significance.
- IBAs provide decision makers with high quality information needed to formulate national conservation strategy and implement international agreements.
- IBA programme helps develop national and local capacity for biodiversity conservation.

For communities

- IBAs help meet daily subsistence needs of communities for food, fuel, fodder, and other natural resources.
- IBAs are a source of livelihood for many communities who harvest minor forest produce for sale in local markets.
- IBAs are a part of distinct indigenous cultures and a repository of traditional knowledge resources.

For climate change

- IBAs play an important biological role as carbon sinks, thereby reducing the amount of CO_2 in the atmosphere.
- IBAs help mitigate the impact of extreme weather events such as drought, flash floods, and cyclones by acting as a buffer for human habitations.
- IBAs help climate change affected communities cope by providing water, food, and building material for temporary shelters.

record (Rahmani and Manakadan 1990). The Greater Spotted Eagle *Clanga clanga*, Pallas's Fish-Eagle *Haliaeetus leucoryphus,* Wood Snipe *Gallinago nemoricola*, Bristled Grass-Warbler or Grassbird *Chaetornis striatus*, Green Munia *Amandava formosa*, and Great Knot *Calidris tenuirostris* are some of the Threatened species found in some IBAs.

IUCN RED LIST SPECIES OF ODISHA

Unfortunately, there has been an increasing rise in the number of globally red-listed bird species in India, both in the Threatened and Near Threatened categories. BirdLife International (2014), the agency that prepares Red List of Birds for IUCN, has listed a total of 174 bird species in India. This includes 17 Critically Endangered, 19 Endangered, 54 Vulnerable, 81 Near Threatened and three Data Deficient species. Out of these, eight Critically Endangered species have been reported from the state. This includes Pink-headed Duck *Rhodonessa caryophyllacea* that is probably extinct in India (world?), and the Great Indian Bustard *Ardeotis nigriceps* that is extinct in Odisha but survives in very small numbers in Maharashtra, Andhra, Gujarat and Rajasthan. Although we do not have any confirmed record of Forest Owlet from the state, it probably survives in some unsurveyed remote areas, bordering Chhatisgarh.

Among the Endangered species, seven species were initially listed by us but we have definite and relatively recent records of only three species (Spotted Greenshank *Tringa guttifer*, Egyptian Vulture *Neophron percnopterus* and Black-bellied Tern *Sterna acuticauda*). For the rest of the species, either the records are 100 years old (e.g. Lesser Florican *Sypheotides indicus*) or unconfirmed (e.g. Saker Falcon *Falco cherrug cherrug*). Some species, for example Masked Finfoot *Heliopais personatus*, may be found in Bhitarkanika mangroves but more rigorous surveys are required.

Eleven Vulnerable species are found in Odisha, most of them with recent records. We only have unconfirmed records of two species: Eastern Imperial Eagle *Aquila heliaca* and Yellow-throated Bulbul *Pycnonotus xantholaemus*, so we are not including them in the book.

Twenty-two bird species found in Odisha can be considered Near Threatened, according to IUCN criteria. All are fairly common and some are quite widely distributed in suitable habitats.

For 11 species, the IBAs and protected areas of Odisha are highly important for survival.

THREATENED BIRDS FOR WHICH ODISHA MAY BE IMPORTANT

White-rumped Vulture *Gyps bengalensis* Critically Endangered

This species has been reported in the Bhitarkanika Wildlife Sanctuary (Pandav 1996), Sambalpur, north of Mahanadi and south of Mahanadi (Ball 1878). It has been reported in five IBAs but is likely to be present in more areas.

Long-billed Vulture *Gyps indicus* Critically Endangered

This Critically Endangered species has been reported in the Bhitarkanika Wildlife Sanctuary (Pandav 1996) and Similipal (Rahmani and Prakash 2000). It has also been reported in the same five IBAs as the earlier noted species but appears to be much more widespread despite a massive decline in recent years. Recent information suggests that small populations exist near Badgaon and Bonei in Sundergarh district, Anandpur in Keonjhar and Bamra in Sambalpur district.

Spoon-billed Sandpiper *Eurynorhynchus pygmeus* Critically Endangered

During studies conducted by the Bombay Natural History Society at Chilika, this species was seen (Hussain *et al.* 1984, Mohapatra and Hussain 1988, Hussain 1991). Later, Acharya and Kar (1996) also recorded it from the Nalbana Island (part of Chilika Lake). In the winter of 2001–2002, up to 200 were reported from Chilika but later this report was proved to be a case of mistaken identity. Although there is no recent record of this bird in Chilika Lake, there are chances that a few individuals may winter in the mudflat and shoreline of this vast Lake.

Indian Skimmer *Rynchops albicollis* Vulnerable

Historically, this species have been seen in "a large flock consisting of skimmers and terns", on the Mahanadi river (Ball 1876, 1878) and thought to be resident (D'Abreu 1935). Tikarpara in Satkosia Gorge Wildlife Sanctuary and Barunei River Mouth in Bhitarkanika WLS are regular wintering sites for this species. Intensive surveys along the undisturbed sandbanks of the Mahanadi during summer might result in discovering small breeding populations.

Pale-capped Woodpigeon *Columba punicea* Vulnerable

In the past, this northeastern bird was reportedly seen in the Similipal hills of Mayurbhanj at an elevation of about 600–900 m (Jayakar 1967), and also in the Chandaka Dampara Sanctuary, and near Bhubaneswar (Jayakar 1967). However, recent studies have confirmed a very good population in Similipal Tiger Reserve as well as a few other sites and it is highly likely that Odisha is a stronghold of this Vulnerable species.

Green Munia *Amandava formosa* **Vulnerable**

Many parts of southern Odisha have reported sightings of this Vulnerable species. Karlapat Sanctuary in Kalahandi district, Kotagarh Wildlife Sanctuary in Kandhamal district and hill slopes of Koraput district seem to harbour scattered populations of this poorly known bird.

River Tern *Sterna aurantia* **Near Threatened**

River tern *Sterna aurantia* has been uplisted to Near Threatened category because increasing human disturbance and dam construction projects are expected to cause a moderately rapid population decline over the next three

There are three nesting areas of Olive Ridley Turtle in Odisha but the main is Gahirimata where more than a million females come for nesting some years

generations (BirdLife International 2014). Sathiyaselvam and Balachandran (2007) reported a large breeding colony of River Tern from Nalabana island on Chilika Lake. Number of nests observed by them were 540 (2002), 476 (2003) and 304 (2004).

Spot-billed Pelican *Pelecanus philippensis* **Near Threatened**

This species has been reported from various parts of the state in the Asian Waterfowl Census (BirdLife International 2001) over the years. It is listed from Ghodahada (Ghodahad) Dam, Bhitarkanika Wildlife Sanctuary, Cuttack district (Kar 1991, Pandav 1996); Dhulianali dam, Manpur, Chilika lake, and breeding (recorded as "pelicans", but presumably, is this species), ("Vagrant" 1868, Hussain *et al.* 1984, Johnson *et al.* 1993), at Kalijai (Sect. 6), at Nalaban (Nalban, Nalabana)

Black-bellied Tern *Sterna acuticauda* is a Near Threatened species and nests on remote islands in large rivers. It is threatened by numerous human-related factors

Sanctuary, and at Satpada, Bhetanai Haja, Ongaito lake, Kanhei-nala, Mukundadev Sagar, Pachi Cherugu Girisola, Mari tank, Singipur (Singpur), Jagannath Sagar, Badabandha Puduni and Balimela (BirdLife International 2001).

Mangrove Pitta *Pitta megarhyncha* Near Threatened
Bhitarkanika National Park has an excellent population of this habitat specialist species which is found only in the dense mangrove patches and is possibly a globally significant site for this species. It has also been recently discovered to be breeding here, the first record for India.

Brown-winged Kingfisher *Pelargopsis amauroptera* Near Threatened
This mangrove specialist kingfisher has a good breeding population in Bhitarkanika National Park and the park is possibly one of its global strongholds.

THREATS AND CONSERVATION ISSUES
Being a state which is in a high trajectory of economic growth, habitat alteration and destruction by changing land use is possibly the most important threat facing the avifauna of Odisha. Reclamation of wetlands for industrial development and real estate business is a very real threat facing several such fragile ecosystems. Mushrooming of prawn *gherries* and aquaculture ponds

in coastal habitats is a case in point. The deleterious byproducts of increasing industrialization such as air and water pollution also have their own impact in reducing the inherent quality of the natural areas. The coastal ecosystem of the state and its diverse habitats are threatened by problems of erosion, siltation, pollution, flooding, salt water intrusion, cyclones, storm surges, artificial lighting, over-fishing, changing land and sea use and overall increase in human settlements (Kar 2000).

Odisha is one of the most mineral-rich states of India with much of its mineral wealth being situated in densely forested and biodiversity-rich habitats. Hence, there is an ever present danger of exploitation and consequent impacts. For that matter, even seemingly benign activities such as promotion of nature-based tourism, if unregulated, can have deleterious impacts on precious breeding bird habitats. Uncontrolled boating activities for tourists in rivers and lakes have also been seen to cause major disturbance to both resident birds and migratory waterfowl. Hence it is imperative that virgin forest and wetland areas are opened for visitors only after careful consideration and thought.

Though on a rapid path to prosperity, Odisha still continues to have about 32% of its population below the poverty line (http://www.odisha.gov.in/pc/download/economic_survey 2014-2015.pdf). Most of these people belong to the

Mangrove Pitta *Pitta megarhycha* has been recently found breeding in the mangroves of Bhitarkanika

MANOJ V. NAIR

Threatened Birds of Odisha

tribal communities living in forested landscapes and necessarily have to depend on forests for their livelihood, thus exerting a continuous biotic pressure on the forests for fuel wood, timber and minor forest produce. Poaching of birds, especially waterfowl, for selling to roadside eateries has of course reduced over time in intensively protected areas such as Chilika and Mangalajodi, but still continues to persist in some interior pockets. However, pervasive small scale trapping of birds for own consumption by certain tribal communities still takes its toll, especially on some birds such as quails, francolins, Red Junglefowl *Gallus gallus murghi*, spurfowls and even hornbills. Trapping and killing of birds by marginal farmers to prevent crop loss, though not a major threat, has also been noticed in some areas.

Illegal trapping of wild birds for pet bird trade is also a significant threat, with the most affected species being three species of parakeets, Common Hill-myna *Gracula religiosa*, four species of munias, two species of bulbuls and two species of mynas also being marginally affected. Trapping of large owls such as Brown Fish Owl *Ketupa zeylonensis* and Spot-bellied Forest Eagle-owl *Ketupa nipalensis* and their sale at unbelievably high prices, ostensibly for black magic rituals has also been on the rise.

Apart from the above mentioned threats which are anthropogenic, there are natural factors too, which impact birds and their habitats. Situated in the cyclone-prone east coast of India with a coastline of over (485 km), Odisha has always been vulnerable to natural disasters such as tropical cyclones, hurricanes and recurrent floods. The supercyclone that occurred in 1999 was exceptionally severe and caused widespread damage in the coastal districts, literally destroying important components of bird habitats such as tall mature trees used for nesting and roosting and fruit trees which were an important food source. The state was again subjected to a very severe cyclonic storm 'Phailin' on the 12 September 2013 where wind speed of over 200 km/hr was reported, again causing widespread damage to bird habitats, especially in the coastal districts of Ganjam and Puri. Massive tree falls were also reported from several protected areas, some located inland too, such as Similipal Tiger Reserve and Satkosia Gorge Tiger Reserve.

Proliferation of alien invasive species could also be an important factor responsible for reduction of habitat quality and therefore the number of birds inhabiting them. The insidious spread of Water Hyacinth *Eichhornia crassipes* in various waterbodies, taking over of natural vegetation by unpalatable weeds such as *Parthenium* sp., *Eupatorium* sp. and *Mikenia* sp. are glaring examples of this.

Illegal trapping of waterbirds occurs in some remote wetlands. Large nets can be seen in this picture

MANOJ V. NAIR

General Recommendations

The following recommendations on conservation of birds in Odisha are generic in nature. They are not comprehensive but are only indicative and are aimed at flagging some important points for the benefit of various stakeholders involved in bird conservation.

1) Apart from the Mid-winter Waterfowl census which is being conducted annually in most Forest Divisions, a census for targeted threatened bird species should be taken up on an annual basis involving experts in all PAs and IBAs.

2) Systematic surveys are required in the Eastern Ghats of Odisha, especially in the districts of Kalahandi, Kandhamal, Ganjam, Koraput and Malkangiri.

3) A state-wide survey of all heroneries should be taken up. Many of these, in which even threatened species nest, are being protected by local villagers. Their efforts should be recognized and encouraged. The respective Honorary Wildlife Wardens can play a key role in this and other bird conservation-related activities.

4) Traditional nesting trees of large raptors such as White-bellied Sea Eagle are also well-known among local people. These should be mapped and monitored on a long-term basis.

5) Capacity building workshops for the frontline staff of the Forest Department on bird identification, monitoring and conservation should be held regularly.

6) Long-term and short-term research on threatened bird species of the state should be promoted by the Government of Odisha. This could be by a Small Grants Programme by the Wildlife Wing or by the Odisha Biodiversity Board.

7) The ongoing bird ringing/banding programme at Chilika may be expanded to other sites such as Hirakud with the help of professionals from BNHS and other organisations.

8) There is vast potential for identification and nomination of more IBAs in the state. Methodical collection of data from such sites will help in providing adequate justification for the required IBA criteria. Some potential sites are Barbara-Dhuanali RFs, PPL Wetlands, Anshupa lake, Karlapat WLS etc.

9) Non-protected IBAs should be protected under the Wildlife Protection Act as sanctuaries or conservation/community reserves.

10) Studies on the impact of pesticides on birds should be started with the help of Sálim Ali Centre for Ornithology and Natural History (SACON) as they have been doing such studies. Local universities should be involved.

11) Ban on veterinary use of diclofenac should be implemented fully with the help of vets and para-vets. Regular monitoring of carcasses for diclofenac should be taken up by BNHS, WII, and other institutions in collaboration with the forest department.

12) Latest technology such as satellite tracking, DNA sampling, use of unmanned aerial vehicles (UAV) or Conservation Drone should be used for research and management.

13) Regular monitoring of species for which Odisha is important such as Pale-capped Woodpigeon, Mangrove Pitta, Brown-winged Kingfisher, Green Munia etc. should be started with appropriate funding mechanism.

14) Citizen Science Programmes aimed at monitoring of common birds such as House Sparrow, Magpie Robin, Black Kite, Barbets etc., should be initiated involving civil society groups and conservation NGOs.

15) Although the Forest Department is doing a commendable job of controlling illegal bird trade and poaching in the state, regular raids on identified hotspots needs to be carried out, especially in various underground bird markets around Chilka, Sambalpur and Pipili. An efficient local intelligence-based team needs to be put in place for this.

16) Wetlands, large or small, are the most threatened of all bird habitats in the state. The directive of the Supreme Court regarding protection of ponds/waterbodies from encroachments is a valuable judgement and can be used effectively by enforcement agencies.

17) The process of notifying Eco-sensitive Zones has almost been completed in the state; appropriate bird conservation oriented action points may be included while formulating Zonal Plans.

18) A district-level wetland atlas based on remote sensing data and a perspective plan for conservation of the wetlands should be made for every district. A district wetland committee should be made active and made the nodal body to take up conservation of these waterbodies. Local village wetland management committees may be constituted to look after the wetlands.

19) An award could be instituted for individuals/organisations doing outstanding work on various threatened species to encourage such work.

20) A biennial newsletter of threatened species could be published and made available in the public domain, which includes data about census if any, habitat, conservation issues, efforts of the state government, and future plan of action.

21) An interpretation centre with interactive models, audio-visual display of threatened birds etc. may be proposed at Nandankanan Zoo for awareness generation among the masses.

REFERENCES

Acharya, S. and Kar, S.K. (1996) Checklist of waders (Charadriiformes) in Chilika Lake, Odisha. *Newsletter for Birdwatchers* 36: 89–90.

Anonymous (1992) Coastal Environment. Remote Sensing Application Mission, SAM/SAC/COM/SN/11/92. Indian Space Research Organisation. Ahmedabad. Pp. 1–114.

Ball, V. (1876) Notes on some birds collected in Sambalpur in Odisha. *Stray Feathers* 4: 231–237.

Ball, V. (1877) Notes on birds observed in the region between the Mahanadi and Godavari rivers. *Stray Feathers* 5: 410–420.

Ball, V. (1878) From the Ganges to the Godaveri. On the distribution of birds, so far as it is present known, throughout the hilly region, which extends from the Rajmehal Hills to the Godaveri valley. *Stray Feathers* 7: 191–235.

BirdLife International (2001) *Threatened Birds of Asia: The BirdLife International Red Data Book.* 2 Vols. BirdLife International, Cambridge, UK.

BirdLife International (2014) IUCN Red List for birds. Downloaded from http://www.birdlife.org

BirdLife International (Unpubl.) *Important Bird Areas in Asia: Project briefing book.* BirdLife International, Cambridge, UK.

Champion, H.G. and Seth, S.K. (1968) *A Revised Classification of Forest Types of India.* Manager of Publication, New Delhi.

D'Abreu, E.A. (1935) A list of the birds of the Central Provinces. *JBNHS.* 38: 95–116.

Dash, M.C. and Kar, C.S. (1990) *Turtle Paradise Gahirmatha* (An Ecological Analysis and Conservation Strategy). M/S. Interprint Publishers, New Delhi. Pp. 300.

Dash, P.K. (2012) Biodiversity of aquatic plants of Similipal Biosphere Reserve, Odisha. PhD. thesis, Utkal University, Odisha.

Dutta, S.K. (1990) Ecological natural history and conservation of herpetofauna of Orissia, India. *Tiger Paper* 17: 20–28.

Dutta, S.K. (1997) Herpetofaunal assessment of northeastern Odisha with special reference to Similipal. Pp. 92–104. In: Tripathy, P.C. and Patro, S.N. (Eds) *Similipal: A natural habitat of unique biodiversity.* Odisha Environmental Society, Bhubaneswar.

Dutta, S.K. and Acharjyo, L.N. (1997) Further additions to the herpetofauna of Odisha, India. *Cobra* 30: 1–8.

Dutta, S.K. and Ahmed, (1989) Report on a herpetological collection trip to Barbara, Puri district, Odisha. *Hamadryad* 14 (2): 36–37.

Dutta, S.K. and Mohanty-Hejmadi, (1993) Herpetofauna of Odisha and their conservation. *Bihang Newsletter* 1(3): 7–8.

Forest Survey of India (2001) State of Forest Report 2001. Ministry of Environment and Forest, Dehra Dun.

Forest Survey of India (2013) State of Forest Report 2013. Ministry of Environment and Forest, Dehra Dun.

Hussain, S.A. (1991) Bird migration project. Annual report 1990–91. Bombay Natural History Society, Bombay. Pp. 1–101.

Hussain, S.A., Mohapatra, K.K. and Ali, S. (1984) *Avifaunal profile of Chilka Lake: A case for conservation*. Technical Report 4, Bombay Natural History Society, Bombay.

Inskipp, T. (2014) Checklist and bibliography of birds of Odisha, Birds of Odisha Facebook Group.

Islam, Z.A. and Rahmani, A.R. (2004) *Important Bird Areas in India: Priority Sites for Conservation*. Indian Bird Conservation Network, Bombay Natural History Society and BirdLife International, UK. Pp. xviii + 1133.

Jayakar, S.D. (1967) The Purple Wood-Pigeon (*Columba punicea*, Blyth) and the Himalayan Tree Pie *Dendrocitta formosae* Swinhoe) in Odisha. *JBNHS* 64: 109.

Johnson, J.M., Perennou, C. and Crivelli, A. (1993) Towards the extinction of the Spot-billed Pelican (*Pelecanus philippensis*). Pp.92–94. In: Moser, M. and Vessem J van. (Eds) *Wetland and waterfowl conservation in south and west Asia*. IWRB Spec. Publ. No. 25, AWB Publ. no. 85.

Kar, C.S. (2000) Sea-turtles and their habitats in Odisha, India. In: *UNTAMED ODISHA*, Wild Odisha Publ., Pp. 105–122.

Kar, S. (1991) Checklist of birds in the Bhitarkanika Wildlife Sanctuary, Odisha. *Newsletter for Birdwatchers* 31(11 & 12): 3–6.

Kathiresan, K. (2010) Importance of mangrove forests of India, *J. Coast. Env.* 1(1): 11–26.

Majumdar, N. (1988) On a collection of birds from Koraput district, Odisha, India. *Rec. Zool. Surv. India, Misc. Publ. Occas. Pap.* 108.

Meher-Homji, V.M. (2001) Bioclimatology and Plant Geography of Peninsular India. Scientific Publishers, Jodhpur, India.

Ministry of Environment and Forests (1999) Forest Survey of India Report –1999. Government of India, New Delhi.

Mohanty, R.C., Mishra, R.K. and Bal, S. (2002) Phytosociological and Plant Diversity studies of Simlipal Biosphere Reserve. Pp. 16–26. In: *Proceedings of the National Seminar on Conservation of Eastern Ghats,* March 24–26, 2002, Tirupati, Andhra Pradesh,

Mohapatra, K.K. and Hussain, S.A. (1988) Avifauna of Chilika Lake. Pp. 89–95. In: Patro, S.N (Ed) *Chilika, the pride of our wetland heritage*. Odisha Environmental Society, Bhubaneshwar.

Murthy, T.S.N. (1987) Herpetofauna of the Chilika Lagoon, India. *British Herpetol Bulletin* 21: 8–12.

Nayak, A.K., Nair, M.V. and Mohapatra, P.P. (2014) Stripe-necked Mongoose *Herpestes vitticollis* in Odisha, eastern India: a biogeographically significant record. Small Carnivore Conservation, The Journal of the IUCN SSC Small Carnivore Specialist Group, Vol. 51: 71-73.

Pandav, B. (1996) Birds of Bhitarkanika Mangroves, Eastern India. *Forktail* 12: 9–20.

Panigrahi, G. (1983) Vegetational types of Orissa. 43–48. Survey. Souv. 6th All India. Bot. Conf., Utkal University, Bhubaneswar.

Patanaik, A.K. (2000) Conservation of Chilika — An Overview. *Wetlands International* 1: 3–5.

Rahmani, A.R. and Manakadan, R. (1990) The past and present distribution of the Great Indian

Bustard *Ardeotis nigriceps* (Vigors) in India. *JBNHS* 87: 175–194.

Rahmani, A.R. and Prakash, V. (2000) Technical note on the catastrophic decline in vulture populations in India. Unpubl.

Rahmani, A.R., Islam, Z.A. and Kasambe, R. (2015) *Important Bird and Biodiversity Areas of India: Priority Sites for Conservation*. Revised edition. Bombay Natural History Society, Indian Bird Conservation Network, BirdLife International (UK) and Royal Society for the Protection of Birds. Oxford University Press, New Delhi.

Ripely, S.D., Beehler, B.M. and Krishna Raju, K.S.R. (1985) Birds of the Visakhapatnam Ghats, Andhra Pradesh. *JBNHS* 84(3): 540–559 & 85 (1): 90–107.

Rodgers, W.A., Panwar, H.S. and Mathur, V.B (2000) Wildlife Protected Area Network in India: A review (Executive Summary). Wildlife Institute of India, Dehra Dun. Pp. 44.

Sathiyaselvam, P. Balachandran, S. (2007) A large breeding colony of River Tern *Sterna aurantia* in Chilika Lake, Odisha (India). *Indian BIRDS*. 3(2): 65–66.

Upreti, D.K. (1996) Lichen on *Shorea robusta* in Jharsuguda district, Orissa, India. *Flora and Fauna* 2(2): 159–161

'Vagrant' (1868) *Random notes on Indian and Burman ornithology*. Regimental Press, Bangalore.

ZSI (1993) *Fauna of Orissa-State Fauna Series*. Zoological Survey of India, Kolkata.

■ ■ ■

Baer's Pochard *Aythya baeri*
(Radde 1863)

TIM LISEBY

Baer's Pochard *Aythya baeri* is a purely migratory bird in India, arriving by October and departing by March end. Formerly classified as Vulnerable (BirdLife International 2001), it has been upgraded to Critically Endangered owing to an apparent acceleration in the rate of its decline, as observed both in the breeding and wintering grounds (BirdLife International 2014).

Field Characters: Baer's Pochard exhibits slight sexual dimorphism—the male has dark green metallic glossy head, white iris and pale-tipped grey bill, while the female has dark chestnut head and breast without metallic gloss, paler patch at the base of the bill, and dark iris. Breeding male is similar to Ferruginous Duck *Aythya nyroca* except for its head and neck which is dark glossy green, grading into rich rufous-chestnut on the breast. Female is indistinguishable from the female Ferruginous Duck, particularly if not accompanied by male (Ali & Ripley 1987). In flight, wing pattern is like Ferruginous Duck, but white upperwing band does not extend as far onto the outer primaries. Juvenile resembles female, but with more chestnut-tinged head with darker crown and hindneck, and no defined loral patch.

Distribution: Baer's Pochard is a globally Threatened waterfowl. It breeds in eastern Russia, northeast China, and possibly in Mongolia and North Korea, and was recorded on passage or in winter (or as a vagrant) in Mongolia, Japan,

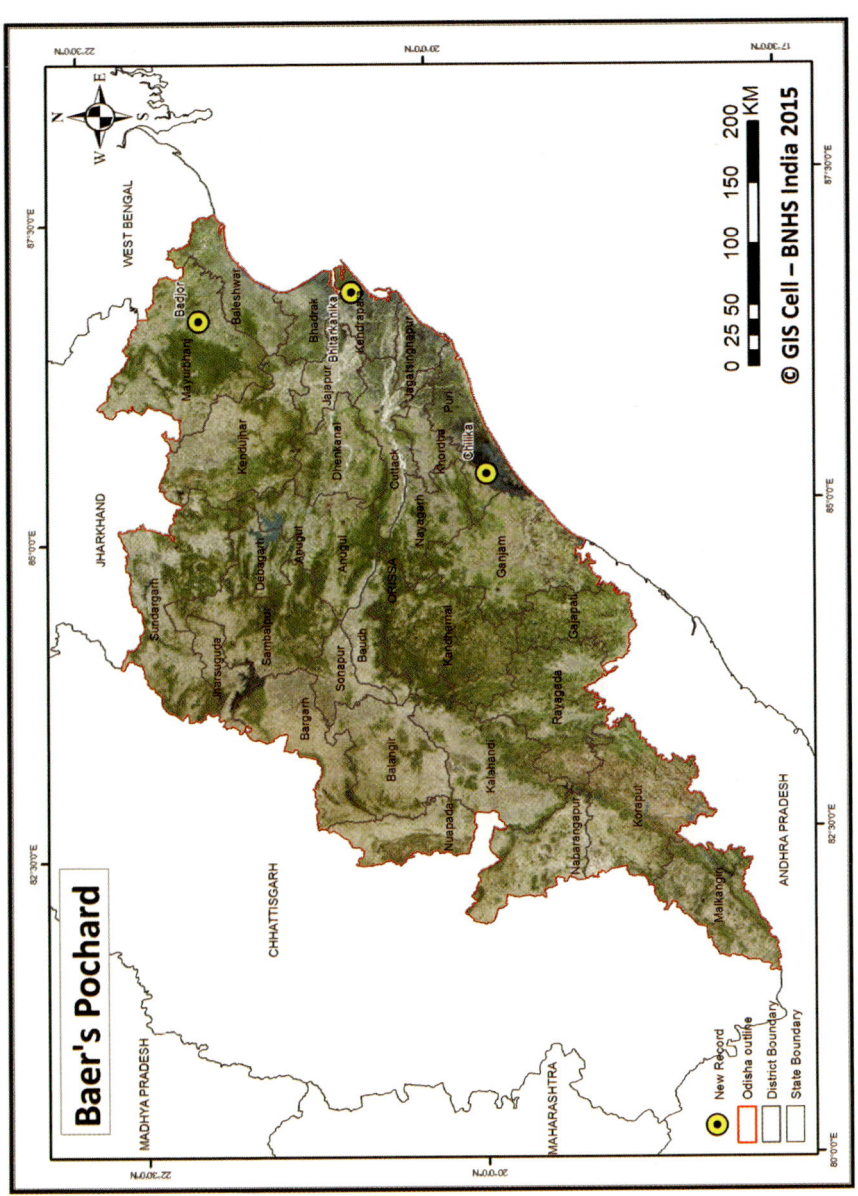

Baer's Pochard

North Korea, South Korea, mainland China, Hong Kong, Taiwan, Pakistan, India, Nepal, Bhutan, Bangladesh, Myanmar, Thailand, Vietnam, and the Philippines (BirdLife International 2001). The main wintering areas appear to be in eastern and southern China, northeast India, Bangladesh, Thailand and Myanmar.

In India, it is an uncommon and erratic winter visitor to Manipur (fairly regularly), Assam and West Bengal. It has been recorded in other states also. For more recent records, see *Duck, Geese and Swans of India*, by Rahmani & Islam (2008). Possibly it is less rare in India than recorded, but easily confused with the Ferruginous Duck or overlooked. Both the species are found together and the females are superficially alike (Ali & Ripley 1987). Recent published records of this species are given by Rahmani (2012).

In Odisha, it is probably a very rare winter visitor. It has been recorded mainly from **Chilika lake**. Dev (2013) reported large numbers from the deep water areas of the lake. A single unconfirmed report has been obtained recently from Badjor, a small reservoir in Mayurbhanj district.

Ecology: In winter, Baer's Pochard is frequently seen in large wetlands including marshes, coastal lagoons and estuaries. It nests on small islands that are densely vegetated with grass, and on migration it uses small lakes and swampy shores, overgrown with reeds and other wetland vegetation. In its wintering grounds, it occurs in marshy wetlands, small pools and ponds, wet paddy fields and sandy islands.

Conservation measures underway: It is protected under the Indian Wildlife (Protection) Act, 1972 and listed in Schedule IV. In India it has been reported from many IBAs and PAs (Rahmani & Islam 2008).

RECOMMENDATIONS

(1) Special emphasis to be paid on identification of waterfowl by frontline staff of the Forest Department engaged in mid-Winter Waterfowl Count.

(2) Regular patrolling along inland waterbodies with waterfowl congregation will act as deterrent to local poaching.

(3) Intelligence gathering and subsequent raids/searches to unearth organised poaching rackets which make use of a network of small-time poachers to supply waterfowl to local eateries and *dhabas*.

Pink-headed Duck *Rhodonessa caryophyllacea*
(Latham 1790)

According to BirdLife International (2014), "This species has not been conclusively seen in the wild since 1935; it was always considered rare, and is likely to have declined severely through a combination of hunting and habitat loss. However, further surveys are needed of remote wetlands in northern Myanmar where there has been a possible recent sighting, and credible local reports were received in 2006. Any remaining population is likely to be tiny, and for these reasons it is treated as Critically Endangered."

The Pink-headed Duck was formerly distributed in the Gangetic Plains from central Uttar Pradesh, east to extreme west Assam, and south to east Odisha. There are records from Bangladesh and Myanmar, but rarely from Nepal. Scattered records from Punjab, Maharashtra, and Andhra Pradesh represent former vagrancy and/or erroneous observations (Rasmussen & Anderton 2005). The last record is of a bird shot in 1935 in Darbhanga in Bihar by C.M. Inglis.

In Odisha, this species was reported from Khorda (Taylor 1887). The only evidence of its occurrence in the state during this century are unconfirmed sight records by veteran ornithologist U.N. Dev who claims to have seen the Pink-headed ducks a few times in various areas in Khurda in the early 1940s. According to him, rampant hunting in the late 19th and early 20th centuries was the main cause of the decline of this beautiful species. Also responsible, of course, was habitat loss with the gradual conversion of many wetlands into agricultural land.

Due to the absence of any recent record, this species can be considered extinct in Odisha.

It is included in Schedule I of the Indian Wildlife (Protection) Act, 1972. It is also listed in CITES Appendix I and CMS Appendix II. Since 2003, BirdLife International has conducted searches in Indochina and the Biodiversity and National Conservation Association (BANCA) have conducted five separate searches in Kachin State, Myanmar, following convincing local reports (BirdLife International 2014) but no bird has been found.

White-backed or White-rumped Vulture
Gyps bengalensis (Gmelin 1788)

DHRITIMAN MUKHERJEE

According to BirdLife International (2014) the White-rumped Vulture qualifies as Critically Endangered because it has suffered an extremely rapid population decline primarily as a result of feeding on carcasses of animals treated with the veterinary drug diclofenac.

Field Characters: The White-rumped Vulture is the smallest of all *Gyps* vultures. It weighs 9lb to13lb, measures 89–93 cm in length, and has a wingspan of 210–216 cm.

Distribution: Before the 1990s, the White-rumped Vulture was probably the most abundant vulture of the world, particularly in northern states of India. It was also reported from Pakistan, Bangladesh, Nepal, Bhutan, Myanmar, Thailand, Laos, Cambodia and southern Vietnam, and earlier from southern China and Malaysia, but nowhere as abundant as in India, southern parts of Nepal and the Punjab province of Pakistan. It has been recorded from southeast Afganistan and Iran, where its status is currently unknown. According to BirdLife International (2001), it disappeared from most of Southeast Asia in the early 20th century and the only viable populations in the region are found in Cambodia (Pain *et al*. 2003) and Myanmar (both probably in the low hundreds of individuals). In other countries of Southeast Asia (Malaysia, Laos, Vietnam, Thailand) it disappeared or has become extremely rare mainly due to lack of carcasses of large ungulates,

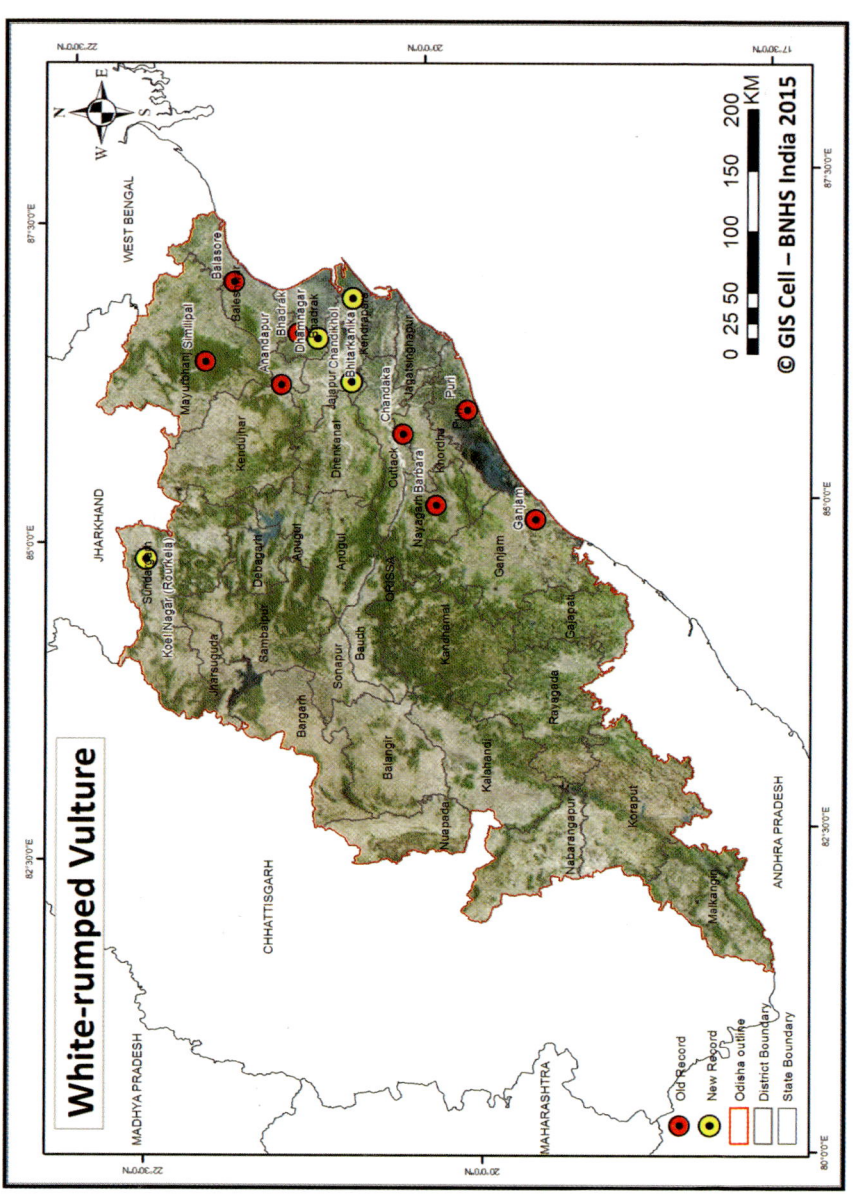

White-rumped Vulture

Threatened Birds of Odisha

both wild and domestic, which are its main food. In Bhutan, it was considered "notably common around the border towns of Phuntsholing and less so around Samdrop Jongkhar" (Bishop 1999). Unlike in south Asia where food for vultures is abundant, in southeast Asian countries, improvements in animal husbandry and extensive poaching of wild ungulates have diminished the food supply of these majestic birds.

As far as Odisha is concern, veteran birdwatchers of the state describe this species as common, especially in the coastal districts of Balasore, Bhadrak, Puri and Ganjam till the late eighties and early nineties. Specific records are from **Similipal TR**, **Anandapur**, **Athmallik**, **Chandaka Sanctuary**, **Chilika lake environs**, **Barbara** RF, **Puri**, and **Bhitarkanika NP**, the latter being a breeding stronghold of this vulture. While Pandav (1997) describes the species as common in Bhitarkanika and mentions it breeding during December and January, Gopi & Pandav (2007) reported the status to be rare and that about 10 individuals were present in Rangadapatia and Barapita forest areas of **Bhitarkanika** during 2005–06. Two nests with two juveniles were also sighted on *Sonneratia apetala* trees in March 2005. However, the population seems to have largely vanished from Bhitarkanika of late (Bijay Das *pers comm*. 2014), indicative of the precipitous decline throughout the state.

Apart from an injured individual rescued from Dhamnagar on July 2, 2011 and which still survives in Nandankanan Zoo, a photographic record of a juvenile on August 26, 2014 near **Koel Nagar**, Rourkela (Satyanarayan Misra, *pers comm*. 2014) and a single sight record along NH-5 near **Chandikhol** by the second author, no recent record exists from the state. Vulture surveys carried out by some Forest Divisions of the state in the recent past also failed to find any surviving population.

Nandankanan Zoo in Bhubaneswar is one of the eight new nodal centres identified for vulture conservation breeding by the Central Zoo Authority. The centre which already has all the requisite infrastructure, is soon to be made functional after a founder population of five pairs of White-rumped vultures from Pinjore, Haryana, or Rani Centre, Assam will be brought here.

Vulture decline: The most catastrophic and rapid decline of the White-rumped Vulture (and other related *Gyps* species) has been seen in south Asia. This decline was first reported in newspapers in mid 1990s and later confirmed scientifically at Keoladeo National Park (Prakash 1999) and all over India (Prakash *et al*. 2003, Prakash *et al*. 2007). Similar steep declines were noticed in Nepal (Baral *et al*. 2005) and Pakistan (Gilbert *et al*. 2006).

For many years, virus-related disease(s) was considered as the likely cause of the massive number of deaths of vultures, but in 2003, a non-steroidal anti-inflammatory drug (NSAID), diclofenac, was identified as the culprit (Oaks *et al*.

2004a; Green *et al*. 2004; Shultz *et al*. 2004; Swan *et al*. 2006b). This drug is used as a pain killer for domestic livestock. If livestock dies within 2–5 days of ingestion of diclofenac and vultures feed on its carcass, they suffer renal failure which causes visceral gout (Oaks *et al*. 2004a; Oaks *et al*. 2004b; Gilbert *et al*. 2006). The *Gyps* species of vultures have disappeared by 97 to 99% during the last 15 years (Prakash *et al*. 2007). As diclofenac is widely used even now, the rate of decline is nearly 50% per annum in the remaining populations (Green *et al*. 2004). Statistical modelling shows that vulture decline at the observed rates can be caused by the contamination of less than 1% of livestock carcasses with levels of diclofenac lethal to vultures. The proportion of adult vultures which die with symptoms of diclofenac poisoning is consistent with that expected if diclofenac is the sole cause of the recent rapid population declines (Green *et al*. 2004; Pain *et al*. 2008).

Ecology: The White-rumped Vulture is a bird of open countryside, avoiding thick forests and wooded hilly areas. As it feeds on large carcasses, it has to find them visually. So it soars regularly on thermals, covering hundreds of square kilometres in a single day. It finds food either directly or by looking at other descending vultures and scavengers.

Since the collapse of the White-rumped Vulture populations from the mid 1990s (still continuing), domestic animal carcasses are now mainly attended by pie dogs, crows, and Cattle Egret (the latter two species feed on maggots and flies). It is presumed that populations of domestic dogs have increased, triggering a scare of rabies in humans.

Threats: The White-rumped Vulture is in real danger of becoming extinct in another 5–10 years if diclofenac is not effectively and completely banned from veterinary use. It has been found that even if less than 1% of the cattle carcass contains a lethal level of diclofenac, the *Gyps* vultures will die at the observed rate (Green *et al*. 2004). In a carcass sampling study conducted from May 2004 to June 2005 across 12 states (Senacha *et al*. 2008) it was found that nearly 10% of the carcasses which should be available to the vultures in the countryside have diclofenac residue enough to kill vultures. Since the official ban on the use of diclofenac in 2006, its residue in the cattle carcasses samples show a decline (about 2% in 2014) but still enough to kill the vultures.

There are some other causes such as inadvertent poisoning from baits placed to kill other species, collision and electrocution injury from kite threads (particularly seen in Gujarat during annual Kite Festival), and chicks falling from nests, but these play a minor role.

Conservation action in place: All three *Gyps* species have been included in Schedule I of the Indian Wildlife Protection Act since 2000. They are listed in CITES Appendix II and CMS Appendix II. BirdLife International and IUCN have listed them as Critically Endangered. In 2004, the IUCN passed BNHS/RSPB/BirdLife-sponsored resolution in its World Congress urging all the range states for effective protection of *Gyps* vultures. An International South Asian Vulture Recovery Plan (Anonymous 2004) has been developed and being implemented in India, Nepal and Pakistan. This Plan suggests establishing a minimum of three captive breeding centres each capable of holding 25 pairs. Captive breeding efforts are ongoing and met with success when two chicks hatched in early 2007 at a breeding centre in Pinjore, Haryana. Conservation breeding centres have been established in Buxa in West Bengal and Rani Reserve Forest near Guwahati in Assam by the RSPB and Bombay Natural History Society in collaboration with the state forest departments.

Conservation measures required: Although the Government of India has officially banned veterinary use of diclofenac and government vets have almost stopped using it, it is widely available in the market and wherever not available, human diclofenac is now increasingly used for veterinary purpose.

a) We recommend that all competent organisations and agencies implement programmes to raise awareness of the problem of diclofenac poisoning of vultures with the general public and especially with groups of interested parties, including farmers, graziers, veterinarians, pharmacists, staff of government and state wildlife and agricultural agencies and religious and other groups which place special value on the continued existence of vultures. The awareness programmes need to be carried out in a decentralized way with the collaborative involvement of government bodies and NGOs as many parts of the coastal zone of the state still have suitable areas which can help in the comeback of the species.

b) A regular programme for monitoring of threatened Vultures in the state is the need of the hour which should be steered by the Forest Department and supported by NGOs across the state. A synchronised count of vultures across the state along with the regular monitoring of nests should be the major components of this important programme. Bhitarkanika Sanctuary should be thoroughly surveyed for vultures. With the surge in birdwatching as a hobby in the state, thanks to social media platforms, Citizen Science initiatives can be taken up by the birding groups to scout the state for any surviving breeding population.

c) We recommend that appropriate authorities undertake thorough evaluation of pharmaceutical drugs likely to be used in place of diclofenac to ensure that they are not also toxic to vultures and other scavengers.

Long-billed Vulture *Gyps indicus*
(Scopoli 1786)

The Long-billed Vulture *Gyps indicus*, sometimes known as Indian Vulture, is classified as Critically Endangered by BirdLife International and IUCN because it has suffered an extremely rapid population decline as a result of feeding on carcasses of animals treated with the drug diclofenac.

Field Characters: A large robust vulture of about 92 cm, with a conspicuous white neck-ruff and a long black neck with pale down feathers (missing in Slender-billed Vulture *G. tenuirostris*).

Distribution: The Long-billed Vulture is a semi-endemic bird of India, with a small population surviving in the Sind Province of Pakistan, near the Indian border. In India is it found from the Gangetic Plain to almost up to Tamil Nadu. Along with White-backed *Gyps bengalensis*, the Long-billed *G. indicus* was one of the most common vultures of India till the 1990s when diclofenac was introduced for veterinary purpose.

Anecdotal evidence and information from senior birdwatchers indicate that though not as common as the White-backed Vulture, this species used to be observed throughout the state till mid-nineties, particularly in parts of western Odisha, where local people report that vultures, possibly of this species, used to nest in cliff ledges along the hill ranges. The two main areas of congregation were **Bargaon** in Sundergarh and **Bamra** in Sambalpur. They were also recorded

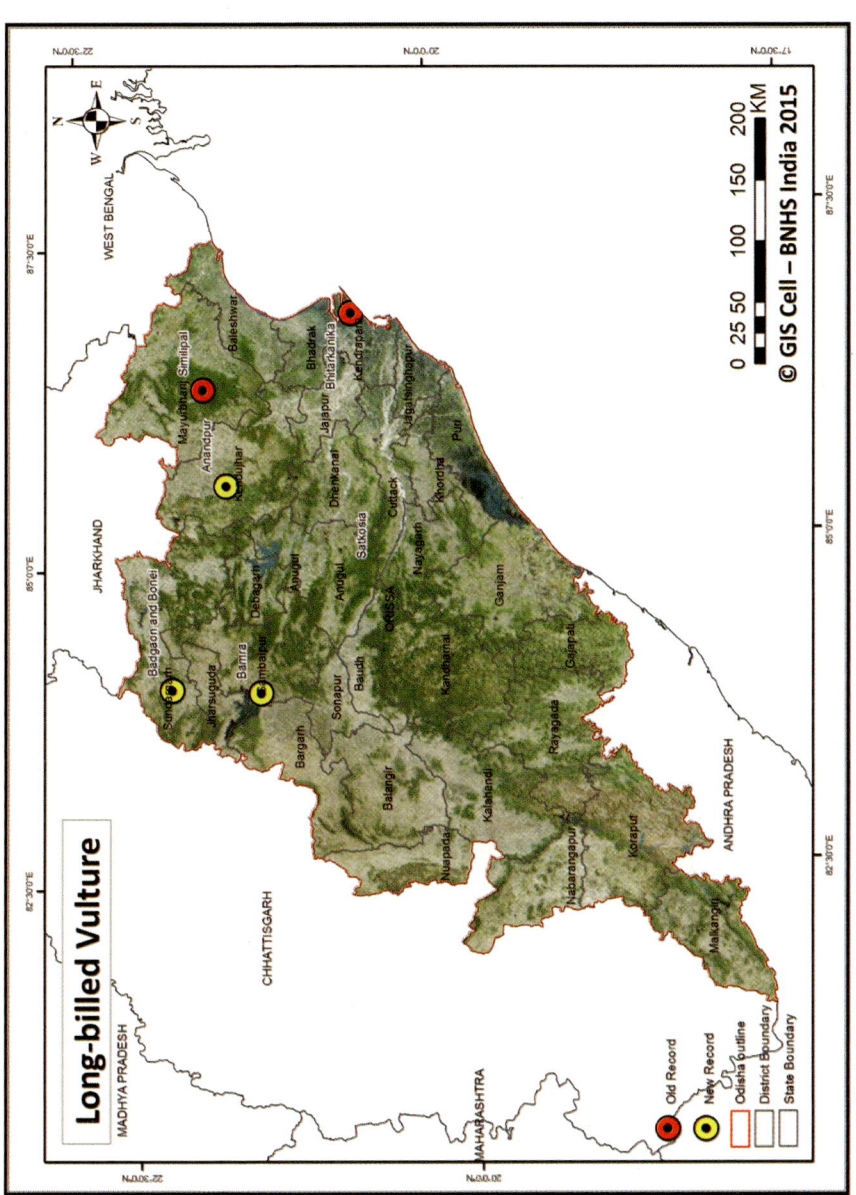

from the outskirts of **Similipal**. Based on the studies in 1990s, Pandav (1997) mentions the status of this species as common in **Bhitarkanika**, while Gopi and Pandav (2007) did not record it there during their study from August 2004 to October 2006.

Apart from an injured individual rescued and brought to Nandankanan Zoo on June 3, 2012 from Sundargarh district and a single photographic record of a solitary bird from **S**atkosia, near Anandapur on August 16, 2014 by Pramod Dhal, no recent record exists from the state. Vulture surveys carried out by some Forest Divisions of the state failed to find any surviving population. However, information from local people suggests that a small population exists near **Badgaon** and **Bonei** in Sundergarh district, **Anandpur** in Keonjhar and **Bamra** in Sambalpur district.

Ecology: Its ecology is not very different from that of White-backed Vultures, as both used to be present in large numbers in the open countryside, sometimes in villages, near cultivated areas, and in lightly wooded areas. Earlier when it was common, it was found near cities and towns, particularly on carcass dumps and slaughterhouses. It is a scavenger and feeds almost entirely on carrion, often with the White-backed Vulture. Unlike White-backed that nest on trees, the Long-billed nests almost exclusively in small colonies on cliffs and ruins. Where cliffs are absent, sometimes they nest on trees. During day time, they roam in a large area of hundreds of square kilometres in search of food, but return to the same cliffs for roosting at night. Nesting colonies are traditional and used year after year, clearly visible due to the white fecal markings below nests.

Threats, Conservation Measure and Recommendations
See White-rumped Vulture

Red-headed or King Vulture *Aegypius calvus*
(Scopoli 1786)

The Red-headed Vulture has suffered an extremely rapid population reduction in recent years, and it is predicted that this trend will continue, probably largely as a result of the birds feeding on carcasses of animals treated with the veterinary drug diclofenac, and perhaps in combination with other causes. For this reason it is classified as Critically Endangered (BirdLife International 2014).

Field Characters: A medium-sized (76–86 cm) vulture, mainly black with bare red head, neck and legs. Thigh patches and ruff are white. The male has yellowish eyes, while the female has dark reddish eyes. In flight, the conspicuous red head and legs, white breast and white patches at the side of the thighs are diagnostic. Besides, the whitish band along the underwing lining is another field character seen in flight. Immature birds are similar to adult, except they are overall brown; head is pink and covered with white down; anterior flank and abdomen are pale brown, posterior flank, abdomen and undertail-coverts are white which is a diagnostic feature of the immature in flight.

Distribution: The Red-headed Vulture found in South Asia has a scarce though widespread distribution in the Indian subcontinent. However, it is absent in Sri Lanka. Historical reports indicate that it was widespread and generally abundant, but it has suffered a population decline and loss of range in recent decades. Its population is likely to be 2,500 and 10,000 across its vast distribution range from

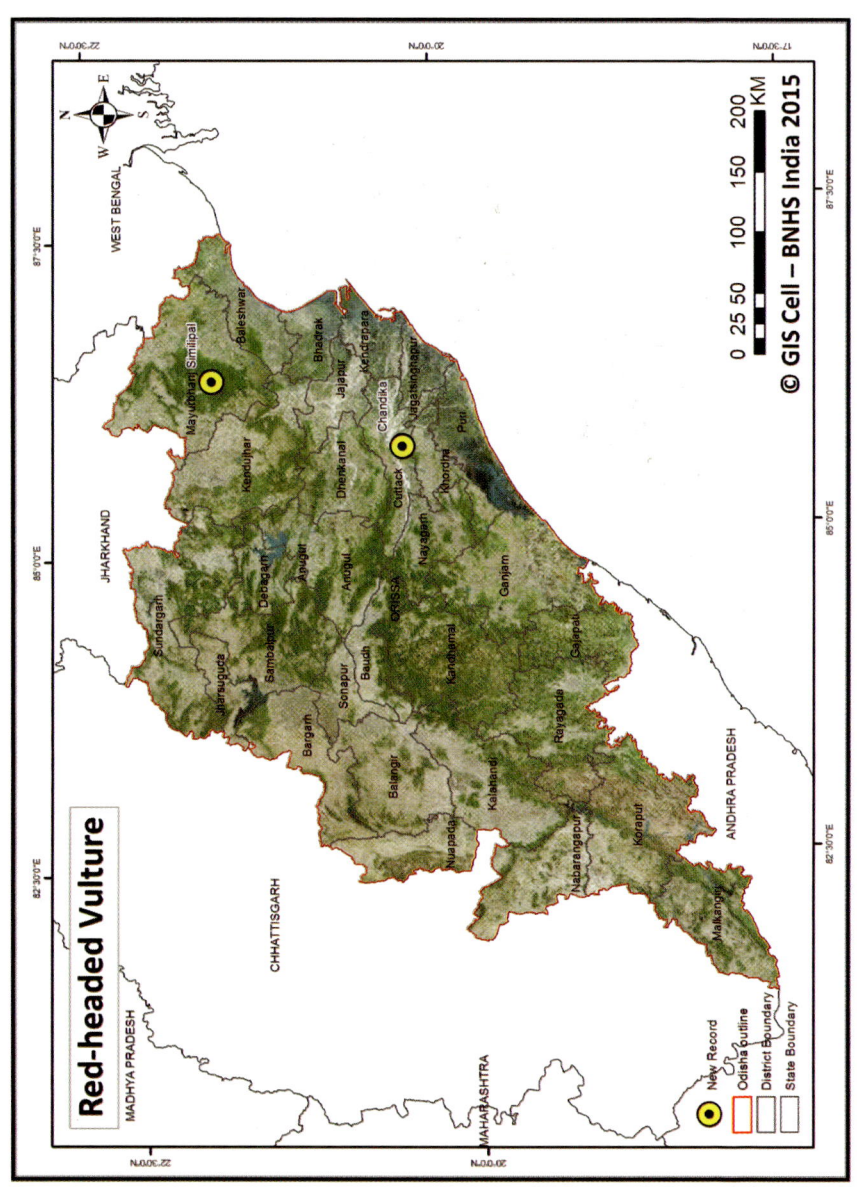

Red-headed Vulture

New Record
Odisha Outline
District Boundary
State Boundary

© GIS Cell – BNHS India 2015

Threatened Birds of Odisha

Pakistan, through India, Nepal, Bhutan, and Bangladesh, eastward to peninsular Malaysia. It possibly occurs in southeast Tibet (China) (BirdLife International 2014). It is rare in Pakistan, Bangladesh, Bhutan, Thailand, Vietnam, China, and Myanmar. There is a small population in Cambodia and Laos.

In India, it was widespread but never common. Recent surveys indicate (Cuthbert *et al*. 2006) that in India it has undergone a rapid population decline and is now rare or absent from some areas. Its recent distribution records from India are given in Rahmani (2012). Here, we describe records from Odisha.

Ball in the 18th century described the status of this vulture in Odisha to be 'not very common but probably occurs throughout the sub-province' (Ball 1878). During the past fifty years, sporadic records exist from the state mainly from **Similipal** Tiger Reserve, where it has been described as rare resident (Anon. 1995) or local migratory (Dev 1986), and a single sight record was made by the second author in 2008. It has also been recorded from **Chandaka** Sanctuary (Rath and Mohanty-Hejmadi 1996). No other recent record exists for the state.

ECOLOGY: The Red-headed Vulture mainly inhabits dry deciduous forest and wooded hills, usually below 2,500 msl. It is found in open countryside and even in the desert. Its large bald head and neck enables it to reach deep into the cavities of a large carcass without soiling its feathers. The nesting season is from December to May; both sexes share parental duties. Incubation period is *c*. 80 days and complete fledging occurs about four months from the date of hatching.

Threats: As it is a shy bird found in low numbers, its decline has not caught the attention of conservationists or the government, unlike the *Gyps* vultures. Though there is currently no direct evidence to link the decline in this species with diclofenac poisoning, the geographic extent and rate of decline are very similar to the decline in the *Gyps* populations for which the impact of diclofenac poisoning is now established. Counts of Red-headed Vultures carried out in 13 Protected Areas in India from 1991–1993 were repeated in 2000, which revealed a significant decline of around 48% (Prakash *et al*. 2003) Maybe its decline is not as rapid in the forested parts of India, as it mainly feeds on wild ungulates (which are not contaminated with diclofenac).

In Southeast Asia, its rapid population decline coincides with the decline of wild ungulates due to extensive poaching and improvement of animal husbandry, leading to lack of its food (BirdLife International 2014, Species Factsheet). However, this species previously had less exposure to the toxin owing to competitive exclusion from carcasses by *Gyps* vultures (Cuthbert *et al*. 2006). With the present decline in *Gyps* vultures, the Red-headed Vulture now has more access to carcasses, particularly the softer visceral organs such as liver and kidneys, which have the highest concentration of diclofenac (Taggart *et al*. 2006).

Veterinary use of diclofenac has been banned in India, Nepal and Pakistan, although it is still in widespread use and is likely to remain so for several years. Recently, the commonly used veterinary drug ketoprofen has been found lethal to *Gyps* vultures (Naidoo *et al.* 2009), and could have the same effect on the Red-headed Vulture. This needs to be tested further.

Poisoned carcasses placed by villagers for revenge killing of large predators such as tigers and leopards also lead to accidental poisoning of vultures. With its already low numbers and slow growth, any further abnormal adult mortality brings the Red-headed Vulture closer to extinction.

Conservation measures underway: The Red-headed Vulture is included in Schedule IV of the Indian Wildlife (Protection) Act, 1972. It is also listed in CITES Appendix II and CMS Appendix II. BirdLife International and IUCN have listed it as Critically Endangered. Nation-wide survey of all species of vultures is being conducted by BNHS, RSPB and IBCN. Conservation breeding efforts have not been done as they are for the Critically Endangered Gyps vultures, and these are urgently needed.

RECOMMENDATIONS

(a) Survey Odisha, specifically Similipal Biosphere Reserve, extensively to identify the location and number of remaining individuals,.

(b) Support the ban on the veterinary use of diclofenac, ketoprofen, and other similar drugs. Promote the immediate adoption of meloxicam as an alternative to diclofenac and ketoprofen.

(c) Test other NSAIDs to identify additional safe alternative drugs to diclofenac and also other toxic ones.

(d) Initiate public awareness and public support programmes along with the programmes for other vulture species.

SAVING ASIA'S VULTURES
FROM EXTINCTION

A consortium Saving Asia's Vultures from Extinction (SAVE) was launched in February 2011 in Delhi and Kathmandu to provide a strategic framework through which the unprecedented problem and threat to South Asian Gyps vultures could be addressed across national boundaries. It provides a clear scientifically based outline of the priorities that need addressing to conserve the most threatened species, and also a recognised channel for supporters to ensure that resources are used to address those priorities.

SAVE consists of six core members: Bird Conservation Nepal, Bombay Natural History Society, International Centre for Birds of Prey (U.K.), National Trust for Nature Conservation (Nepal), the Royal Society for the Protection of Birds (U.K.), and WWF Pakistan, and a growing number of project and research partners including the Indian Veterinary Research Institute. Professor Ian Newton, world renowned raptor expert, agreed to take the chair for the first four years; and there are two main subcommittees that help drive the research, field actions and advocacy that is needed.

Vulture conservation efforts in India are showing the first signs of success thanks to the initiative of the Indian Government (led by the Ministry of Environment and Forests) in banning veterinary formulations of diclofenac in 2006 which has had an important impact in slowing the declines. The breeding programme includes three BNHS-run centres in Haryana, West Bengal and Assam with the support of the respective state government Forest Departments and the Central Zoo Authority is supporting further breeding facilities to extend these efforts at five more zoos. A Regional Steering Committee has been established through an IUCN initiative in 2012 with National Vulture Recovery Committees being set up in each of Pakistan, India, Nepal, and Bangladesh which will be an important forum for delivering the further measures required to conserve vultures in the subcontinent.

A website, www.save-vultures.org provides full details and more information, as well as all key Asian vulture publications available for download, the manifesto, and most importantly a donations button where supporters can help ensure that resources are available to support these vital efforts.

Chris Bowden, SAVE Programme Manager

Great Indian Bustard *Ardeotis nigriceps*
(Vigors) 1831

According to BirdLife International (2014), the Great Indian Bustard (GIB) qualifies as Critically Endangered because of its very small, declining population, which is a result of hunting and continuing agricultural development in its habitats.

Field characters: A large (92–122 cm) brown-and-white bustard with black crown and black wing markings. Male has whitish neck and underparts, with narrow black breast-band. Female is smaller, with greyer neck, without breast-band in non-breeding birds and with broken breast band in breeding birds.

Distribution: The Great Indian Bustard occurs in the Indian subcontinent, with former strongholds in the Thar Desert in the northwest, and the Deccan tableland in the Indian peninsula (Rahmani & Manakadan 1990). It has been extirpated from 90% of its former range and is now principally confined to Rajasthan (*c.* 100–150 birds), with smaller populations (<20 birds) in Andhra Pradesh, Gujarat, Maharashtra and Karnataka. It has completely disappeared from Haryana, Punjab, Uttar Pradesh, Tamil Nadu, and Odisha (Rahmani & Manakadan 1990). Historically, it has been recorded from Sambalpur, south of Mahanadi (Ball 1877, 1878). It is extinct in Odisha.

Ecology: GIB's ecology and behaviour have been extensively studied by Rahmani (1989) and in recent years by Dutta *et al.* (2010). As it is extinct in Odisha, we are not describing its ecology in detail.

Threats: Habitat destruction and conversion, and hunting are the biggest threats to the survival of the Great Indian Bustard. These threats were prevalent earlier too, and resulted in its disappearance from about 90% of its range. Even now, the same factors not only prevail but have increased manifold (e.g., conversion of grasslands). Hunting is a major threat, particularly in the Thar Desert. Mismanagement of bustard grasslands by the Forest Department, along with overall and increasing disturbances to the landscapes are major threats.

Conservation Action: Species recovery plan has been prepared (Dutta *et al*. 2013) and some states have taken action but not enough has been done to arrest the decline of this grand bird.

Spoon-billed Sandpiper *Eurynorhynchus pygmeus* (Linnaeus, 1758)

TUKAI BISWAS

The Spoon-billed Sandpiper is a Critically Endangered bird (BirdLife International 2014) because recent surveys indicate that its population is now extremely small, and undergoing an extremely rapid population reduction. This is because of a number of factors, including habitat loss in its breeding, passage and wintering grounds, which is compounded by disturbance, hunting and the effects of climate change.

Field Characters: It is a small stint (14–15 cm), like Little Stint *Calidris minuta* but with spatulare bill, hence its name. It moves with other stints and small waders, so could be easily missed unless someone is really searching for it. The breeding adult bird has a rufous-orange head, neck and breast with dark brown streaks. It has blackish upperparts with buff and pale rufous fringing. Non-breeding birds which we encounter in India lack rufous and have pale brownish-grey upperparts with whitish fringing to the wing-coverts. The belly, breast and neck are white and legs are black (in all age class). Juveniles are slightly darker with boldly patterned upperpart.

Distribution: The Spoon-billed Sandpiper has a naturally limited breeding range on the Chukotsk peninsula and southwards along the isthmus of the Kamchatka peninsula in northeastern Russia. It is an extremely rare migratory species on the east coast of India.

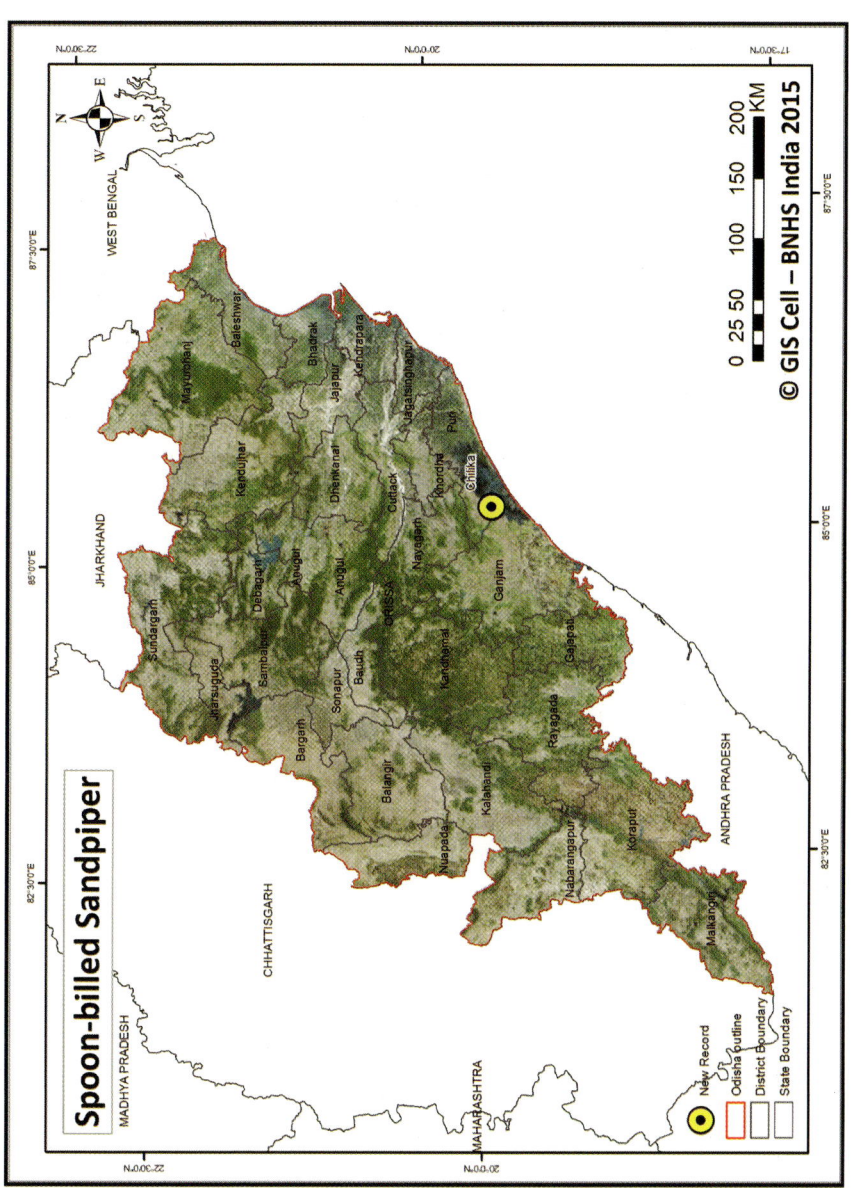

Spoon-billed Sandpiper

The confirmed records from the east coast of India are as follows: One bird was ringed in 1981 at Chilika Lake, (Ali 1981). This is the last authentic record of its occurrence in the Lake. It was neither sighted nor ringed during BNHS studies from 2001 to 2009 (Balachandran *et al.* 2009). However, Dev (2013) mentions that 'quite a few of these birds come to Chilika during winter and are distributed all over the swampy islands'. It has not been reported from any other site in the state. As this bird is found amongst large flocks of other small waders, unless we have photographic evidence, no record can be accepted. For recent records from India, see Rahmani (2012).

Ecology: It has a very specialised breeding habitat, using only lagoon spits with crowberry-lichen vegetation or dwarf birch and willow sedges, together with adjacent estuary or mudflat habitats that are used as feeding sites by adults during nesting (BirdLife International 2014). The species has never been recorded breeding further than 5 km (and exceptionally once, 7 km) from the sea shore. Habitats utilised by the Spoon-billed Sandpiper at Point Calimere and its feeding behaviour have been studied by Sugathan (1985).

It winters on tidal mudflats and saltpans (BirdLife International 2014). In the wintering areas, it has been found to feed and rest with other waders such as Lesser Sand Plover *Charadrius mongolus*, Red-necked Stint *Calidris ruficollis*, Sanderling *Calidris alba* and Common Greenshank *Tringa nebularia*. It can be easily distinguished from other waders when it is feeding on the shallow water by repeated sideways movements of the bill (Khan 2006).

Threats: The greatest threat to the survival of the Spoon-billed Sandpiper is the destruction of its habitat constituting intertidal mudflats during migration in China, Japan and Korea and the wintering grounds in Vietnam, Thailand, Myanmar and Bangladesh. In addition, hunting and trapping of sandpipers in Russia, China, Vietnam, Myanmar, Bangladesh and India are serious and continuing threats. Among several others, such as coastal development, pollution and climate change on stopover sites, the small and large-scale reclamation of intertidal mudflats are recognised as the most serious threats (Zöckler *et al.* 2008).

In recent years, the Spoon-billed Sandpiper has suffered poor productivity, perhaps owing to heavy nest predation, and bad weather, and there are concerns that breeding habitat in the south of its range is no longer suitable owing to climate change (Syroechkovskiy *et al.* 2009). Rapid habitat changes in the wintering areas are also impacting the numbers. Key stopover sites on migration, particularly intertidal wetlands in the Yellow Sea, have been converted for urban and industrial development.

Conservation measures underway: It is listed in the Schedule IV of the Wildlife Protection Act, 1972. In most of the range countries it is legally protected. It is listed under CMS in Appendix II. BirdLife International (2014) and IUCN now list it as Critically Endangered. On the International level, Spoon-billed Sandpiper Recovery Action Plan has been implemented in some regions. An international Spoon-billed Sandpiper Recovery Team was established in 2003, and several research projects in many range countries have started since. Increased international efforts are required to halt the decline of this charismatic sandpiper.

Conservation Strategies: Although there is no targeted hunting or trapping of Spoon-billed Sandpiper, it is caught with other small waders. Hunting of waders and other shorebirds is still very common, particularly outside protected areas. In India, a detailed survey on sites such as Sunderbans (West Bengal), Chilika lake (Orissa), Naupada swamp (Andhra Pradesh) and Point Calimere (Tamil Nadu) should be done.

RECOMMENDATIONS

(a) Detailed survey should be conducted on the east coast starting from Sundarbans to Kerala every year to monitor Spoon-billed Sandpiper population.

(b) Strict control on trapping of waders all along the coast should be implemented and special anti-poaching flying squad should be activated in winter in West Bengal, Odisha, Andhra Pradesh (Telengana) and Tamil Nadu.

Forest Owlet *Heteroglaux blewitti* Hume 1873

MANOJ V. NAIR

This owlet has a tiny, severely fragmented population, and is recently known from less than 10 locations. It is likely to be declining as a result of loss of its Dry Deciduous Forest habitat. Although surveys continue to discover more individuals, the above factors lead to its present classification as Critically Endangered. Further information may warrant its downlisting to a lower category of threat in the future (BirdLife International 2014).

Field Characters: A small owlet *c.* 23 cm, with a rather plain crown, heavily banded wings and tail, and a dark grey-brown crown and nape, faintly spotted with white. Broadly banded, blackish-brown and white wings and tail, with a broad white tail-tip. The breast is dark brown, flanks with broad, prominent barring, rest of the underparts are white. Territorial call is a rather loud, mellow *uwww* or *uh-wuwww*. Calls include hissing *shreeee* or *kheek* and repeated *kwaak* notes, rising and falling in pitch (Ishtiaq *et al.* 2002). For identification see Rasmussen & Collar (1998).

Distribution: The Forest Owlet is endemic to central India. Until its rediscovery in 1997, it was known from only seven specimens collected during the 19th century at four localities in two widely separated areas, northern Maharashtra and southeast Madhya Pradesh/western Orissa (Odisha). Of the seven specimens

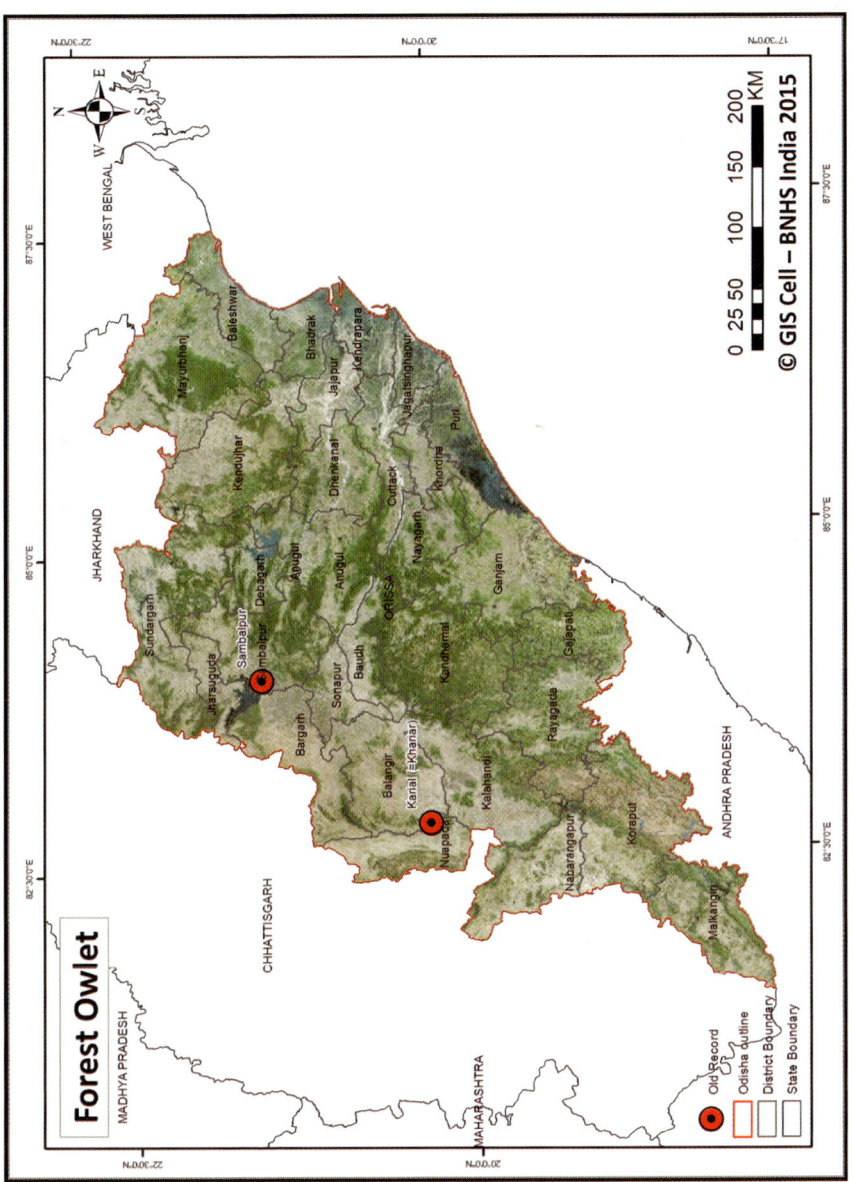

Forest Owlet

Dry Deciduous Forests of Debrigarh Sanctuary could be a potential habitat for the Forest Owlet

collected during the 19th century, one male was collected from Karial (=Khariar), extreme northwestern Odisha by V. Ball (1877), who also reported it from Sambalpur, north of Mahanadi. On November 25, 1997, King & Rasmussen (1998) rediscovered the Forest Owlet in the Tropical Forest of Shahada in Maharashtra. Subsequently, during the surveys conducted by BNHS from June 1998 to June 1999, four nesting pairs of Forest Owlets were recorded in Toranmal Reserve Forest between 400–500 msl. Three of these nests were found at Shahada, while one nest was located in Taloda, about 30 km from Shahada (Ishtiaq & Rahmani 2000a). In a survey conducted from January 28 to February 22, 2000, 25 Forest Owlets were located from two new sites in Maharashtra and Madhya Pradesh along the Satpuda (= Satpura) mountain range. No birds were found in a brief survey of its former eastern range in Orissa (Ishtiaq & Rahmani 2000a). A 12-day survey conducted in 2007, which covered teak-dominated areas of Barbara Reserve Forest, Komna, Sunabeda Sanctuary and adjoining areas of Khariar covering up to the border of Araku Valley in Andhra Pradesh also found no evidence of the bird (Abedin, B. *pers. comm.* 2015; Mehta *et al.* 2007, 2010). The second author during his four year stay in Sambalpur and Bargarh districts from 2009–10 to 2013–14, searched extensively for the bird using callplayback

Threatened Birds of Odisha

but failed to locate it from Debrigarh Sanctuary and parts of Badrama Sanctuary. Considering these facts, the existence of this species within the limits of the state remains doubtful.

Ecology: It appears to be a resident bird of fairly open Deciduous Forests dominated by Teak *Tectona grandis*. Most historical records came from Moist Deciduous Forest or dense jungle, the altitudinal range of which is unclear, although most specimens were collected in plain forest. This suggests that the recent observations from hill slopes may represent birds in suboptimal habitat.

This owlet appears to be quite strongly diurnal and fairly easy to detect, frequently perching on prominent bare branches. Lizards, small rodents, grasshoppers, and nestlings of other birds are all prey (Kasambe *et al.* 2005). It breeds between October and May, laying a clutch of two eggs (Ishtiaq & Rahmani 2005) in the hole of a softwood tree, and can re-lay if its first nesting attempt fails.

For details of its ecology and behaviour, see Ishtiaq & Rahmani (2000a,b 2005) Ishtiaq *et al.* (2002), Jathar & Rahmani (2010), Jathar (2006) and Yosef *et al.* (2010).

Threats: Habitat destruction and modification, and poaching are the biggest threats to the Forest Owlet in its distribution range in other states. Even if the species occurs in Odisha, these factors are likely to operate here as well. In addition, the recent spurt in collection of owls and owlets for illegal trade is also likely to play a crucial role in the decimation of owl populations.

Conservation measures underway: It is included in Schedule I of the Indian Wildlife (Protection) Act, 1972, and in CITES Appendix I and II. Since its rediscovery in 1997, field studies have been conducted on its status, ecology and threats. Interventions have been made in Maharashtra to try and prevent further forest loss at the site of rediscovery.

RECOMMENDATIONS

(a) Though the presence of this bird in Odisha is doubtful, vast stretches of potential Forest Owlet habitat still exist in parts of Nuapara, Kalahandi and Bolangir districts. Coordinated surveys by birdwatchers familiar with the habits of the species, using active search and call playback methods, might yield results.

(b) Awareness campaigns aimed at frontline staff and local tribal people also need to be initiated. Posters with colour images of the birds may be circulated among them in the likely areas. They also may be made to listen to the characteristic calls of the bird so as to aid detection in case of its presence in the area.

Greater Adjutant *Leptoptilos dubius*
(Gmelin 1789)

ASAD R. RAHMANI

This is a marginal species to Odisha so we are not describing it in detail. Greater Adjutant has a wide range in north and northeast India, and Southeast Asia. Its small population is declining very rapidly. For these reasons it is classified as Endangered by IUCN and BirdLife International (2014).

A huge bird (145–150 cm) with a thick, four-sided, wedge-shaped bill and pendulous neck-pouch. It has pinkish naked head, and white neck-ruff. Pale grey greater coverts and tertials contrasting with otherwise dark upperwing are characteristic. In flight, paler underwing-coverts are also characteristic. Juvenile has narrower bill than adult, denser head and neck-down and, initially, all dark wings.

The Greater Adjutant formerly occurred in much of South Asia and continental Southeast Asia, from Pakistan through northern India, Nepal, and Bangladesh to Myanmar, Thailand, Laos, Vietnam, and Cambodia. It is mainly seen in north and northeast India and Bihar. Recently, Rahmani (2012) has described its distribution in India. This bird has been recorded in the state only from Chilika (Dev 2013) . There is no recent report.

Egyptian Vulture *Neophron percnopterus*
(Linnaeus 1758)

BHASMANG MEHTA

The Egyptian Vulture *Neophron percnopterus* is perhaps the most widespread Old World vulture, with isolated resident populations in Cape Verde and Canary Islands off the northwest coast of Africa, north Africa, Ethiopia and east Africa, and isolated populations in Angola and Namibia, southern Europe, the Mediterranean, the Middle East, Central Asia to India and Nepal. In this wide range, it is declining rapidly, therefore BirdLife International (2014) has listed it as Endangered. It is a long-lived, slow breeding bird with very few predators on the adult, therefore any decrease in breeding or increase in adult mortality, as seen in southern Europe (>50% over the last three generations, i.e. 42 years) could spell doom for this species. In India too, where healthy populations were recorded 20 years ago, there has been a sharp decline. BirdLife International (2014) estimates its total world population between 20,000 and 61,000 mature individuals.

Field Characters: The Egyptian Vulture is unmistakable for any other vulture. This small, kite-like vulture has a naked head and short, completely feathered neck. Adult is dirty white with black flight feathers; juvenile is dark with pale vent and tail. The face is bare, yellow in adult and brown in juvenile.

Distribution: The Egyptian Vulture is widely distributed in Africa, southern Europe, the whole of the Middle East, Iran, Afghanistan, Pakistan, India and

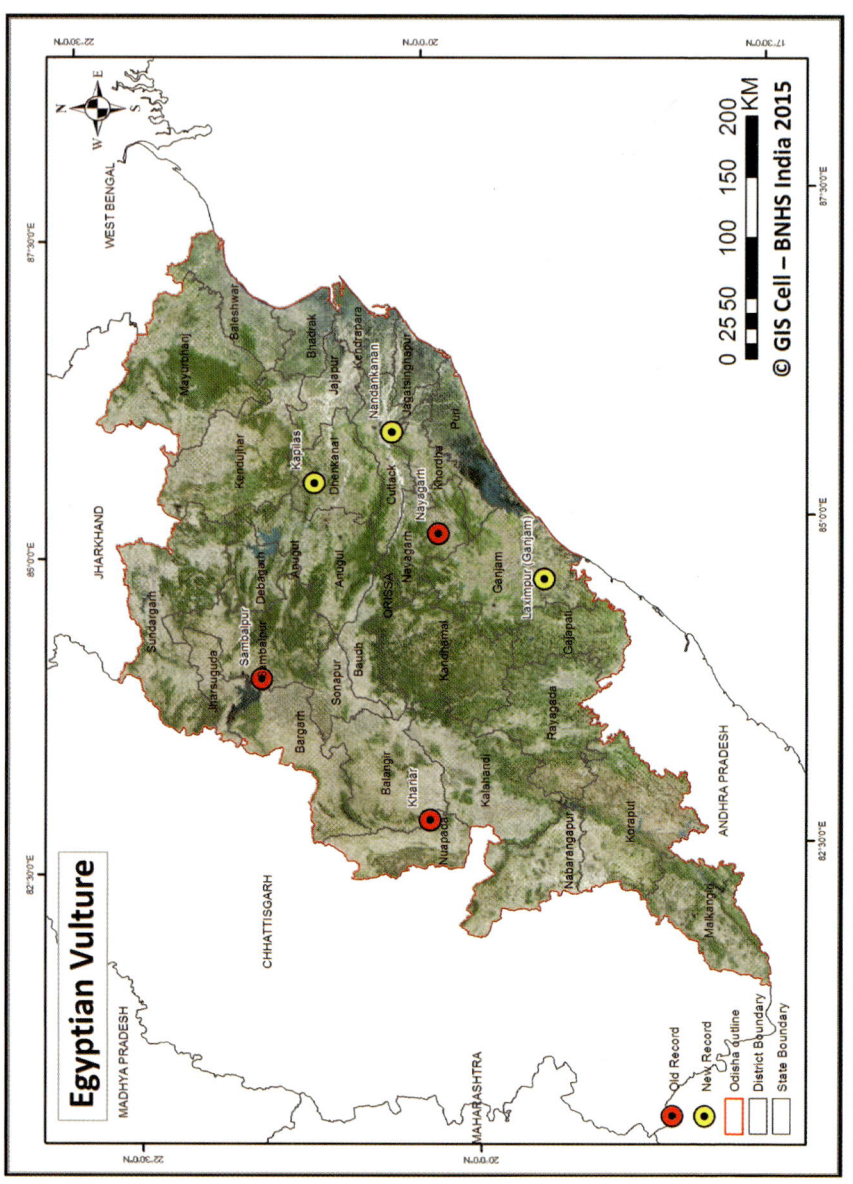

Egyptian Vulture

Threatened Birds of Odisha

Nepal. For population data, see BirdLife International (2014). It is found across India, from the plains to *c.* 2,500 msl, sometimes very close to human habitation, but in decreasing numbers.

Once common in the state, it has been historically recorded from Sambalpur north and south of the Mahanadi, Nayagarh, and Khariar. However, its numbers have dwindled considerably in Odisha and very few recent records exist. Recently a group of 13 birds has been sighted from **Laxmipur** in Ganjam district's Chikiti forest range. The second author have two sight records—one near **Kapilas** and another near **Nandankanan**, both being solitary adult individuals.

Ecology: The Egyptian Vulture is generally seen stalking about around villages and nomad camps in search of carrion, offal, garbage and human excrement. It feeds opportunistically on crickets, frogs and alates of emerging termites as well. Its use of stones as a tool to break Ostrich eggs in Africa is well-known. Its long, narrow beak helps it to tear off small pieces of meat through narrow spaces between the bones of a carcass, where large-beaked vultures cannot reach.

The Egyptian Vulture is usually solitary or found in pairs with juveniles, but on good feeding sites (e.g. Jorber carcass dump, Bikaner), 1,000–2,000 are seen in winter. It roosts singly or in small groups, generally on tall trees, but electric pylons are frequently used where tall trees are absent (e.g., Rann of Kutch). Although it is mostly resident and seen around its usual haunts throughout the year, the northern populations undertake short to long distance migration as conditions become unsuitable during winter. Though it mainly feeds on carrion, it can also kill stranded fish and turtles, and perhaps small prey.

This vulture mainly nests on cliffs, rocky outcrops, ledges of occupied buildings, abandoned forts and ruins and occasionally on tall trees where its preferred nesting habitat is not available. A single egg is laid, and both parents share incubation and chick-rearing duties.

Threats: In its vast distributional range, threats vary from country to country and region to region. In some areas, loss of wild ungulate populations and hence reduced food supply is the main threat, while in some countries antibiotic residues in cattle carcasses could be the major threat. Another threat that was recorded in, but may not be confined to, Bulgaria is avian pox. Death by collision with powerlines is an additional risk in some European countries where the population is small anyway. In India, the annual rate of population decline was 35% during 2000–2003 and the population in 2003 was estimated to be 20% of that in the early 1990s (Cuthbert *et al.* 2006). In India, the main threat could be poisoning by feeding on cattle carcasses contaminated by diclofenac, as observed in *Gyps* vultures. Other NSAIDs used in livestock could be killing these vultures also. Earlier, when *Gyps* vultures were in abundance, they would not allow the Egyptian Vulture to feed on the internal organs of a carcass such as lungs and liver, but now with the near total disappearance of *Gyps* vultures from the Indian subcontinent, the Egyptian Vulture has a greater chance to feed on such internal organs that contain more diclofenac than the muscles and tendons on which this bird fed earlier. Thus the risk of diclofenac poisoning increases in this species.

Conservation measures underway: The Egyptian Vulture is listed in Schedule IV of the Indian Wildlife (Protection) Act, 1972. In India it still occurs in numerous PAs and IBAs. The veterinary use of diclofenac has been totally banned by the Indian Government since 2006. Regular surveys by BNHS, funded by RSPB, are going on in India.

RECOMMENDATIONS

(a) The ban on veterinary use of diclofenac should be implemented in the whole country. Enforcement agencies should ensure that human use of diclofenac is not being put to veterinary use.

(b) Study the impact of other NSAIDs on Egyptian Vulture.

(c) Conduct surveys on a regular basis to study the population trend.

(d) Start an environmental education campaign in rural areas about the importance of vultures.

(e) Conduct ecological and behavioural studies on this species.

(f) Monitor its movement through satellite tracking to map its home range in breeding and non-breeding seasons, and also study the dispersal of juveniles.

Lesser Florican *Sypheotides indicus*
(Miller 1782)

The Lesser Florican qualifies as Endangered because it has a very small, declining population, primarily as a result of loss and degradation of its dry grassland habitat. The rate of decline is predicted to increase in the near future, as pressure on the remaining grasslands intensifies (BirdLife International 2014). It is a marginal species to Uttar Pradesh with only a few recent records.

Distribution: The Lesser Florican is endemic to the Indian subcontinent. It is an irregular local migrant, and also nomadic in the rainy season (southwest monsoon). It was once widespread and common, but now breeds in a few areas in Gujarat, southeast Rajasthan, northwest Maharashtra and western Madhya Pradesh. There is some dispersal to southeast India in the non-breeding season. It was once common in the Terai of Nepal, but now it is rarely seen in the area. It has also been sighted in Pakistan and is a vagrant in Bangladesh. For a review of its former distribution, see Sankaran *et al.* (1992) and BirdLife International (2001).

Historically, Ball (1877) reported it from Sambalpur, south of the Mahanadi. Although there are no recent records of this bird in the state, it is likely that a few might occur in the dry grasslands in parts of western Odisha such as Sohela and Gainslet in Bargarh and in Bolangir districts.

Threats: Earlier, hunting was the main threat as this florican was considered a game bird, but now destruction and deterioration of its grassland habitat is the

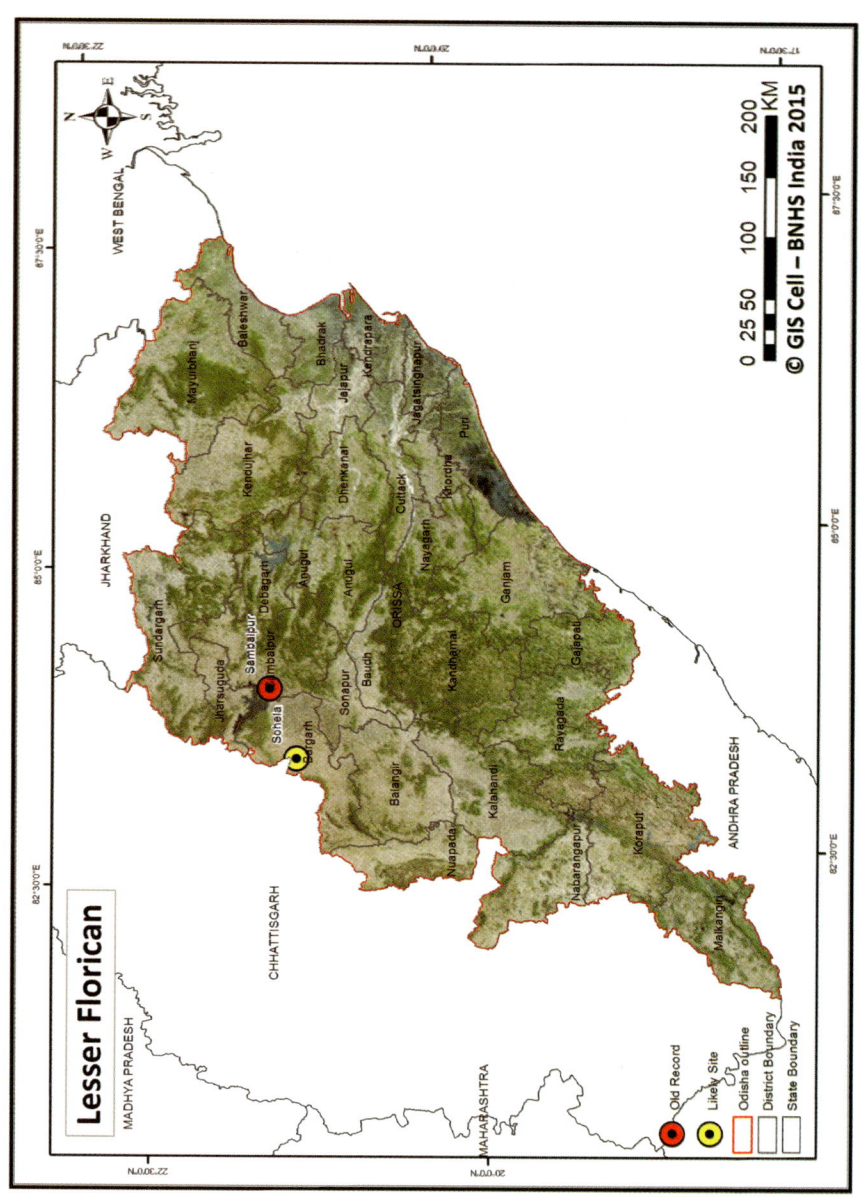

Lesser Florican

WEST BENGAL

JHARKHAND

MADHYA PRADESH

CHHATTISGARH

MAHARASHTRA

ANDHRA PRADESH

ORISSA

Mayurbhanj
Baleshwar
Bhadrak
Jajpur
Kendujhar
Kendrapara
Dhenkanal
Jagatsinghapur
Sundargarh
Debagarh
Anugul
Cuttack
Khordha
Puri
Sambalpur
Jharsuguda
Sonapur
Baudh
Nayagarh
Sohela
Bargarh
Balangir
Kandhamal
Ganjam
Nuapada
Kalahandi
Rayagada
Gajapati
Nabarangapur
Koraput
Makangiri

Old Record
Likely Site
Odisha outline
District Boundary
State Boundary

0 25 50 100 150 200 KM

© GIS Cell – BNHS India 2015

Threatened Birds of Odisha

main threat, although it is still poached by tribals in many areas. In some areas, invasive species such as *Prosopis chilensis* threaten habitat quality.

Conservation measures underway: It is included in Schedule I of the Indian Wildlife (Protection) Act, 1972 and listed in CITES Appendix II. Two sanctuaries were declared in Madhya Pradesh (Sailana in Ratlam and Sardarpur in Jhabua districts) for the Lesser Florican. Good florican habitat is present in Lala and Naliya grasslands in Kutch, and Velavadar National Park in Bhavnagar district, Gujarat. The Rajasthan Forest Department has deployed watchmen and cattle guards in Sonkhaliya area in Ajmer district to protect both Great Indian Bustard and Lesser Florican. There are many private initiatives also, which are quite effective, albeit on a small scale. The Ministry of Environment, Forests and Climate Change (MoEFCC), with the help of BNHS, WWF, WII and state forest departments, has prepared the Lesser Florican Recovery Programme (Dutta *et al.* 2013 and MoEFCC website).

RECOMMENDATIONS

As it is marginal to Odisha, we are not giving detailed recommendations. For more on the species, consult Rahmani (2012). Site-specific recommendations have been made in the Bustard Species Recovery Plan (Dutta *et al.* 2013).

Spotted or Nordmann's Greenshank
Tringa guttifer (Nordmann, 1835)

SAYAM CHOWDHURY

BirdLife International (2014) has listed it as Endangered as it has a very small population which is declining as a result of the development of coastal wetlands throughout its range, principally for industry, infrastructure projects and aquaculture.

Field Characters: It is a medium-sized sandpiper (29–32 cm) with slightly upturned, bicoloured bill and shortish yellow legs. It is distinguished from the Common Greenshank *Tringa nebularia* by shorter yellow legs and heavier bill with pale basal half (Rasmuseen and Anderton 2005). Overall it has a "chunkier outline….presumably caused by the combination of the distinctly shorter legs, slightly smaller size, slightly shorter neck and stouter bill" (Bijlsma and de Roder 1986).

Breeding adults, which we generally do not see in India, are boldly marked, with whitish spots and spangling on blackish upperside, heavily streaked head and upper neck, broad blackish crescentic spots on lower neck and breast and darker lores. In flight, it shows all-white uppertail-coverts and rather uniform greyish tail. Toes do not extend beyond tail tip. It has webbed feet so it might also swim in search of food. Juvenile is browner above than the non-breeding adult, and has whitish notching on scapular and tertial fringes, pale buff wing-covert fringes and faintly brown-washed breast with faint dark streaks on the sides. It has partial webbing between three toes, while the Common Greenshank

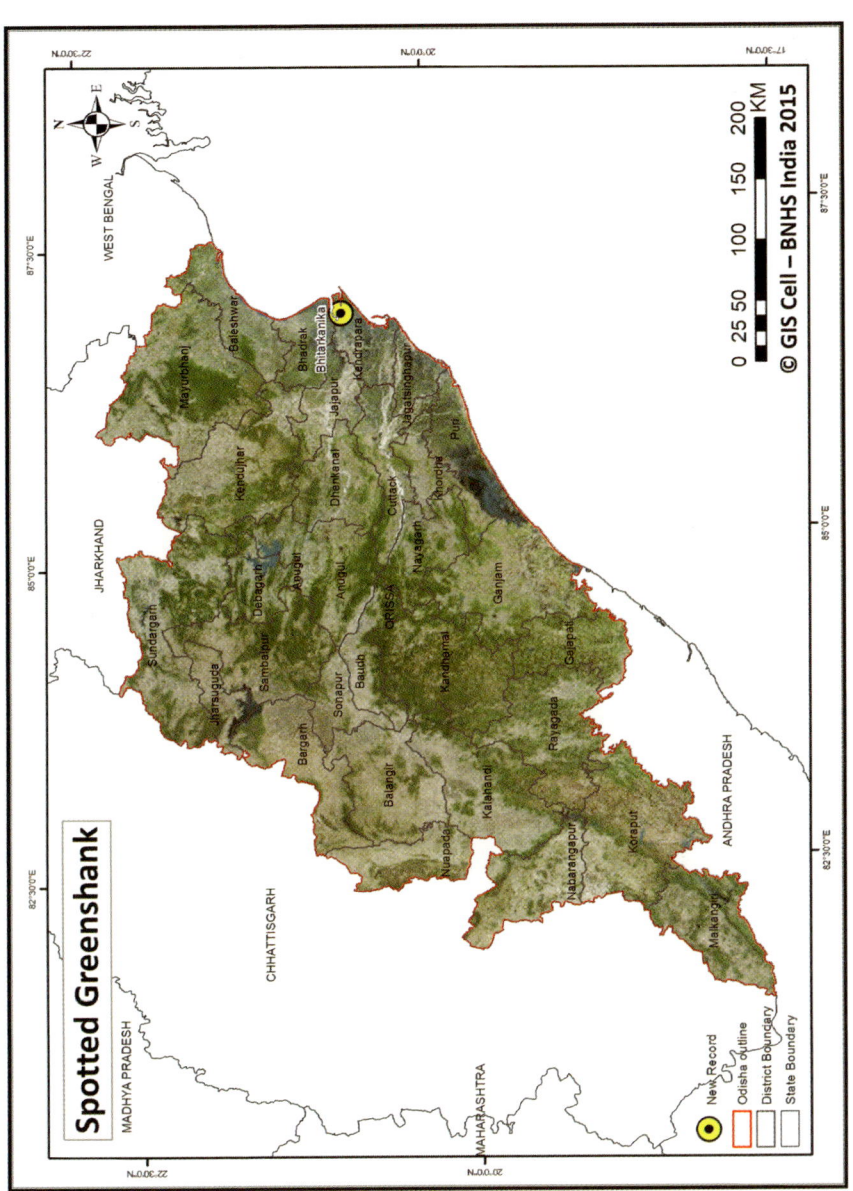

Spotted Greenshank

Tringa nebularia to which it is sometimes confused has webbing only between two toes. Another difference between these two species is that the Nordmann's Greenshank has a pure white underwing and axillaries while the Common Greenshank has finely barred underwing and axillaries.

Distribution: In India it is a rare winter visitor to Assam (Ali and Ripley 1987) but according to Rasmussen and Anderton (2005) records from "India, Nepal, Chagos and Sri Lanka all unconfirmed...and listing from inland Assam (Baker) dubious (as is Baker's report of breeding in Tibet)".

In Odisha, it has only been recorded from **Bhitarkanika** and adjoining areas. Two birds were sighted on January 2003 in Udabali islands adjoining the sea and two birds on December 2005 near Barunei river mouth (Gopi & Pandav 2007).

Ecology: In India it is a rare winter visitor (but see Rasmussen and Anderton 2005) and possibly overlooked and may be less rare than apparent. It is found in grassy meadows near streams, sand and mudflats in the larger rivers and near the sea (Ali and Ripley 1987). Wintering birds also frequent estuaries, coastal mudflats and lowland swamps, and sometimes saltpans and rice-fields.

Threats: As it is a rare winter migrant in India with very few recent records, we cannot do much for this species other than controlling poaching of all waders. BirdLife International (2014) has identified the key threats as development of coastal wetlands throughout Asia for industry, infrastructure and aquaculture, and the degradation of its breeding habitat in Russia by grazing reindeer. Pollution in coastal wetlands, hunting and human disturbance are further threats.

Conservation measures underway: Like most wild birds, it is also protected under the Indian Wildlife Protection Act. It is included in Schedule IV of the Indian Wildlife Protection Act. It is listed in CITES Appendix I and CMS Appendix II.

RECOMMENDATIONS

India is only at the margin of its winter habitat, so no specific measure can be taken. The general measures which India can take is to control all sorts of poaching and trapping, and conduct surveys in the east coast (Assam, West Bengal, Odisha) to find out its wintering status.

Black-bellied Tern *Sterna acuticauda*
Gray 1832

According to BirdLife International (2014), Black-bellied Tern is almost extinct in a large part of its range, but remains locally common throughout the Indian Subcontinent. Since the overall decline may be moderately rapid, it qualifies the species as Endangered, a category to which it was uplisted in 2012. Monitoring is still urgently needed to assess better trends in India.

Field Characters: A small (33 cm) tern with deeply forked tail and deep orange bill. During the breeding season, adult male and female have black cap, white lores, dark grey breast and black belly and vent. Non-breeding birds and immatures have a white belly with streaked crown and black mask. Juveniles are buffy-grey above with blackish marking, lack tail streamers, and the orange bill has a dark tip.

Distribution: The Black-bellied Tern is found at all the major rivers of India, Pakistan, Bangladesh, Nepal, Myanmar, southern China, Thailand, Laos, Cambodia, and Vietnam. In India, it is mainly found in north, east and central India, and is less common in the south. It inhabits major rivers of north, central and eastern India, becoming uncommon in the south where it is a winter migrant. Recently, Rahmani (2012) has produced state-wise records from India.

In Odisha, it is widely distributed though nowhere is it common. It occurs throughout the course of the River Mahanadi, and sporadically along the

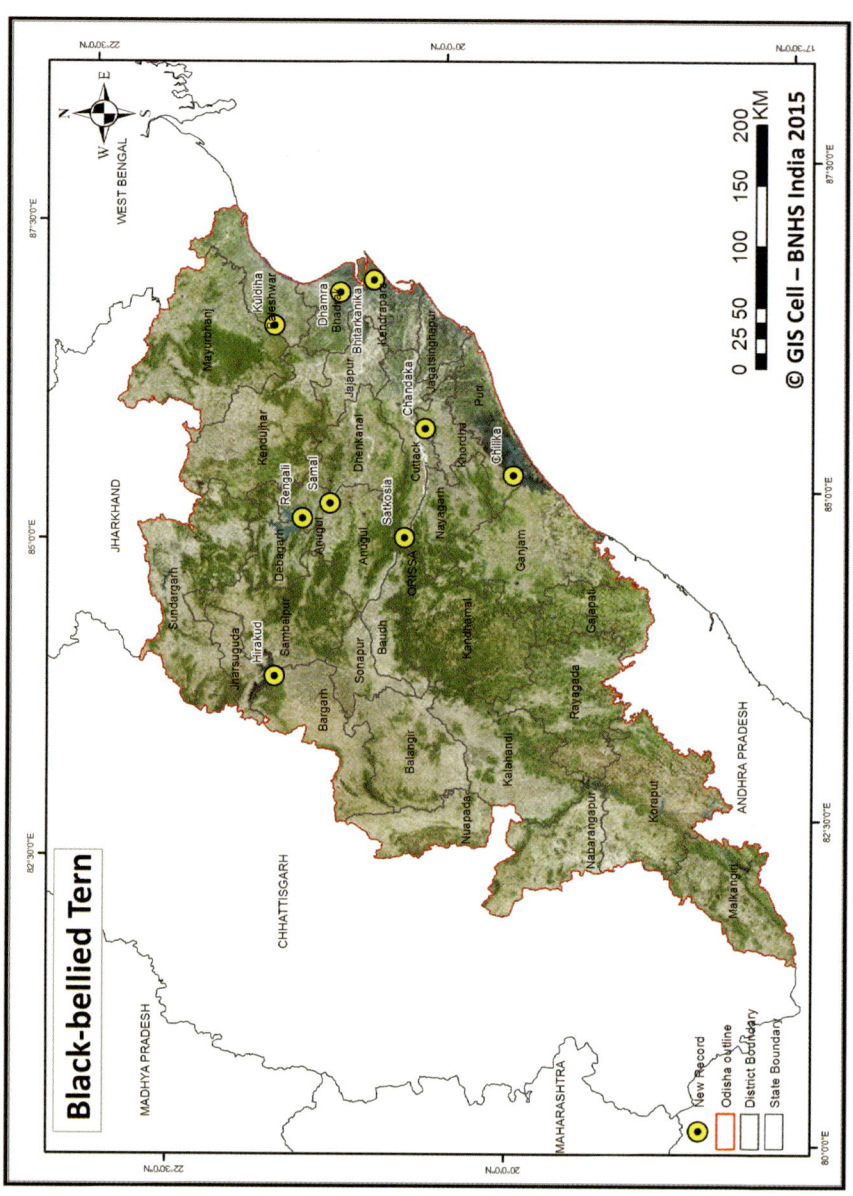

Black-bellied Tern

© GIS Cell – BNHS India 2015

Brahmani, especially where undisturbed sand banks are enclosed by braiding river channels. It is also seen in inland reservoirs during winter. Specific records are from **Chilika**, **Chandaka** (Tiwari *et al.* 2002), **Bhitarkanika** (Pandav 1997; Gopi and Pandav 2007), **Dhamra** estuary (Dutta 2007), Coconut Wheeler islands, **Kuldiha** (Das *et al.* 2010), Samal reservoir near **Talcher** (Palei and Mohapatra 2011), **Rengali** reservoir and the Mahanadi river downstream of **Hirakud** reservoir. Dev (2013) reports it breeding in Chilika, while the second author has observed breeding in sandbanks downstream of **Satkosia Gorge** and isolated islands near Mundali.

Ecology: Essentially an inland and freshwater tern, not found on the sea coast (Ali & Ripley 1987), it inhabits large rivers, foraging methodically over long stretches of placid waters, and resting on riverine islands and sandbanks. It feeds mainly on fish, also insects and crustaceans. It is gregarious and hunts in groups. It breeds colonially in summer (April to June) in the north, and February onwards in the south. The nest is just a scrape in the sand, where two or three eggs are laid. Sometimes the nests are quite far apart, but they are also found in colonies with other terns, Indian Skimmer and pratincoles (del Hoyo *et al.* 1996). Wide nest dispersion is presumably an adaptation to heavy pressure from terrestrial predators, including human beings. Incubation and fledgling periods are not known. The call is a pleasant *krek-krek*, constantly uttered as they fly about. Not much is known about the breeding and feeding ecology.

Threats: These birds face numerous threats, particularly during the breeding season. Most of the large rivers in India have now been dammed and their islands heavily cultivated, leaving not many undisturbed places for these birds to breed. As a result of the construction of dams and utilisation of water (through pumps and pipes) for cultivation or in towns and villages for drinking, there is very little left in the rivers in summer, exposing the riverine islands to threats from terrestrial predators. Although there is not much removal of eggs for food in India, dogs, cats and crows destroy whole colonies. Sudden release of water from dams also washes away eggs and chicks in their nests.

Conservation measures underway: Like most wild birds, it is listed in Schedule IV of the Wildlife (Protection) Act, 1972. It is found in a large number of Protected Areas and Important Bird Areas (Rahmani 2012).

RECOMMENDATIONS

(a)   Study its breeding and feeding ecology, with special emphasis on the threats to its breeding areas.

(b)   Monitor its movement by marking and releasing the birds.

Lesser Adjutant *Leptoptilos javanicus*
(Horsfield, 1821)

MANOJ V. NAIR

BirdLife International (2014) considers Lesser Adjutant as Vulnerable due to its small declining population, particularly as a result of hunting pressure in some countries of its range. Its number is estimated to vary between 6,500 and 8,000.

Field Characters: It is the smallest member of the genus *Leptoptilos*, but still a big bird of 122–129 cm height, weighing about 5 kg (11 lbs), and has a 210 cm wingspan. It is dark grey-black above, white below, with naked head and neck and a dirty yellowish wedge-shaped massive bill. It has sparse hair-like feathers on the naked head and neck, hence its old name Hair-crested Adjutant. Non-breeders have mostly yellowish head and neck skin with vinous-tinged sides and contrasting pale forehead. Breeding males show coppery spots on median coverts, narrow whitish edges to lower scapulars, tertials and inner greater coverts, and redder head sides. Juvenile is duller and less glossy above, with more down on head and neck.

Distribution: The Lesser Adjutant has an extensive range across South and Southeast Asia. It is found all over India, particularly in well-watered tracts but avoids the dry northwest, parts of the peninsula and the Himalaya. Breeding has been recorded from the Terai in Uttar Pradesh and Bihar, Assam, West Bengal,

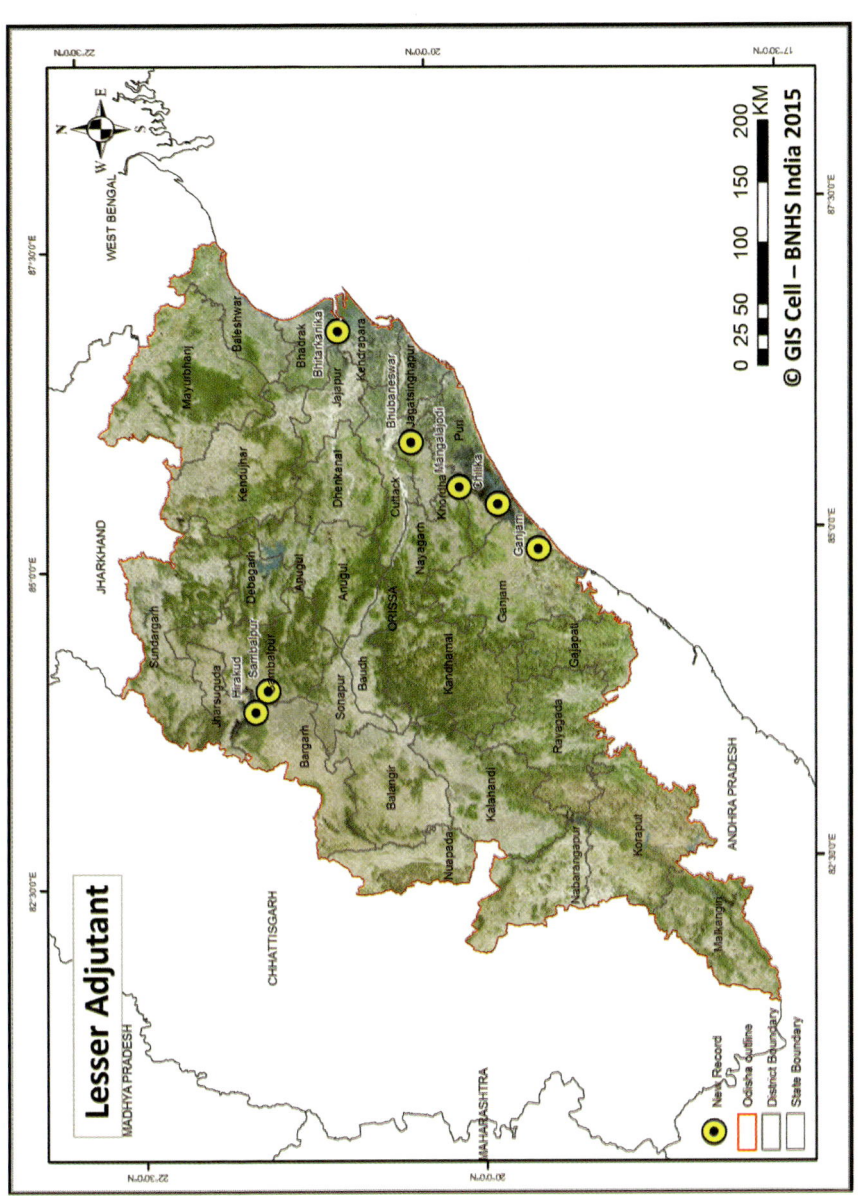

Lesser Adjutant

© GIS Cell – BNHS India 2015

0 25 50 100 150 200 KM

New Record
Odisha Outline
District Boundary
State Boundary

Odisha, Karnataka and Tamil Nadu. Rahmani (2012) has given some records of India.

Dev (2013) terms it a winter visitor to **Chilika**. Sporadic reports exist from **Mangalajodi**, outskirts of **Bhubaneswar**, paddy fields along the NH-5 almost till **Ganjam** and also at **Hirakud** reservoir (Nair *et al.* 2014). The stronghold of the species in the state is undoubtedly **Bhitarkanika** including Satbhaya wetlands where it is a rare resident. Pandav (1997) estimated the total population there to be about 20. The only breeding report from within the state limits is again from **Bhitarkanika** where Gopi and Pandav (2007) recorded a colony of four nests on *Xylocarpus mekongensis* trees near Balijori creek. Nest building activity started in early October and the colony was active till mid-January.

Ecology: The Lesser Adjutant is found in forest pools, shallow open jheels, human-made wetlands, edges of reservoirs, drying roadside pools, mangroves and coastal wetlands, wherever it can get food. It is also found at city dumps but not as much as its larger cousin, the Greater Adjutant, perhaps due to their different food habits.

It nests on tall trees preferably in forests, but wherever it is not molested, as in many places in Assam, nests have been found on roadside avenue trees and even inside towns (e.g., Nagaon). Nesting is either in loose scattered colonies, with sometimes up to eight nests found on a tree, or solitarily. In its vast distribution range, the breeding season varies from area to area. Although, it is solitary or seen in small scattered groups, sometimes 10 to 15 are seen in an area.

Threats and conservation: There are many threats to this species (and other related species), varying from region to region and culture to culture. Fortunately, hunting is not a major threat to this species in India as it is reasonably tolerated by people. It is considered not good to eat and unclean due to its feeding habits. However, intensive fishing decreases its food base and also brings it in direct conflict with humans. Intensive use of pesticides in paddy fields is another indirect threat. Shallow ephemeral wetlands and swamps are still considered wastelands in India and are increasingly coming under large-scale developmental projects.

In India, the Lesser Adjutant is a protected species under Schedule IV of the Wildlife (Protection) Act, 1972. It is found in many Protected Areas/IBAs but most of the nesting colonies, at least in Assam, are outside PAs/IBAs. Such colonies survive mainly due to community protection which should be enhanced and replicated.

RECOMMENDATIONS

Proper survey should be conducted on this species in Odisha to know its distribution and important nesting and feeding sites.

Lesser White-fronted Goose *Anser erythropus*
(Linnaeus 1758)

According to BirdLife International (2014), the Lesser White-fronted Goose is listed as Vulnerable in the IUCN Red List because its key breeding population in Russia has suffered a rapid population reduction and equivalent decline is predicted to continue.

Field Characters: The Lesser White-fronted Goose *Anser erythropus* is closely related to the Greater White-fronted Goose *A. albifrons*. It is small (53 cm), even smaller than some ducks such as the Indian Spot-billed Duck *Anas poecilorhyncha* (61 cm). It has a diagnostic white patch on the forehead, sloping forehead and small head, short pink bill and yellow eye-ring. Overall it is grey-brown, with blotchy black bands on lower breast and belly. Due to its size and characteristic features, it is not difficult to identify. It walks faster than *A. albifrons* and is consequently often found at the front of feeding flocks (BirdLife International 2014). An attractive species, it is often kept in wildfowl collections, from where escapes do occur: individuals seen in summer, or in the company of other feral geese, are likely to be of captive origin.

Distribution: The Lesser White-fronted Goose breeds in taiga and tundra zones of northern Eurasia, from Arctic Europe to northeastern Siberia (Russia), and winters primarily in southeastern Europe, around the Black and Caspian

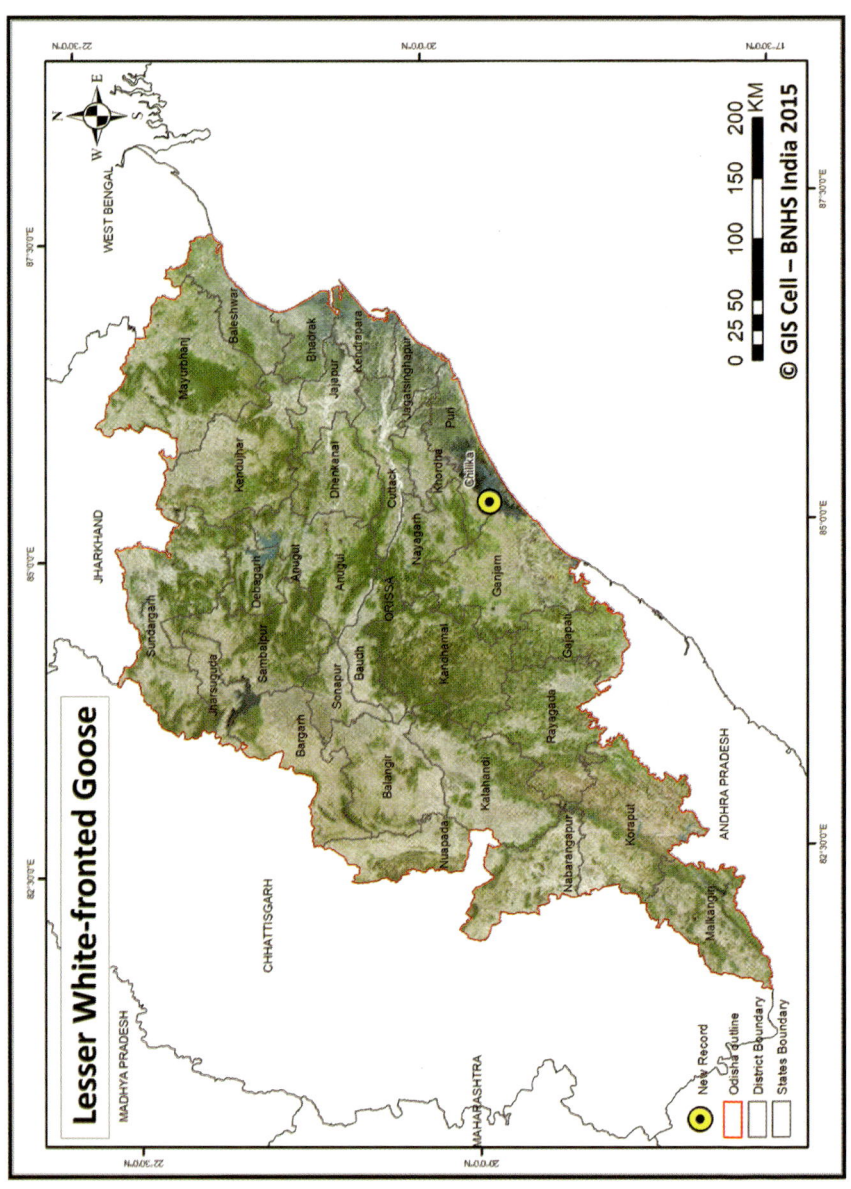

Lesser White-fronted Goose

Threatened Birds of Odisha

seas, at the lower Euphrates in Iraq and in the lowlands of eastern and southern Euphrates. It has been recorded outside the breeding season in Japan, South Korea, mainland China, Taiwan, Pakistan, India and Myanmar, with unconfirmed reports from Bangladesh.

In India, it is a rare and sparse winter visitor. Within the limits of Odisha, this species has only been recorded from **Chilika**. Dev (2013) states that it was once very common in Chilika but has become very rare and sporadically sighted at Nalabana island usually mingled with gaggles of Greylag Geese. The only recent record for this species was that of a pair recorded in the marshes between Sundarpur and Bhusandpur during December 2004 in the **Chilika Lake** (Balachandran *et al*, 2009).

Ecology: As it is a marginal species in the state, we are not describing its ecology in detail. The Lesser White-fronted Goose breeds mainly within the forest zone at the southern edge of the Arctic Circle and in the tall-shrub tundra belt, and after breeding it migrates north to the Arctic coastal lakes to moult. It winters in open treeless tracts, including semi-arid salt steppes, meadows, pastures, and sometimes cropfields, and roosts in reed beds and rushes, or on water or the banks of lakes and rivers; it rarely visits marine waters (Cramp & Simmons 1977).

Threats: Illegal hunting and disturbance to its breeding areas are the biggest threats. In India, it faces the usual threats of hunting, poisoning, drainage of wetlands and pollution.

Conservation measures underway: It is listed in Schedule IV of the Indian Wildlife (Protection) Act, 1972, so hunting and shooting is totally illegal. It is listed in CMS Appendix I and II.

RECOMMENDATIONS

As it is a marginal species to the state, we do not have any specific recommendation. We have to prevent poaching and hunting of all types of ducks and monitor and protect key wetlands.

Greater Spotted Eagle *Clanga clanga*
(Pallas 1811)

DHRITIMAN MUKHERJEE

The Greater Spotted Eagle is a marginal species with few but regular records. BirdLife International (2014) lists it as Vulnerable as it has a small population which appears to be declining owing to extensive habitat loss and persecution.

Field Characters: A very dark eagle of 62–74 cm invariably found near large jheels and wetlands. On perch at close range, the best way to separate it from other *Aquilas* is by its round nostrils and the gape line stopping at the centre of the eye. This facial characteristic is consistently different in all *Aquila* eagles which are sometimes found in the same area in winter. On closer examination, an adult is dark brown (not black) with purplish or maroon sheen on mantle, with slightly paler ventral side. It also has slightly paler flight feathers, with underwing coverts generally darker than flight feathers. Sexes are alike, but female is larger. Juveniles are paler, with back and wings sparsely spotted or streaked with buff or white. Age-related plumage differences are described by Naoroji (2007).

Distribution: In India, the Greater Spotted Eagle winters widely in north and central India and up to Karnataka, Kerala and Tamil Nadu. It breeds in Eastern Europe, Russia and Central Asia, Mongolia and China. Passage or wintering birds are seen in many countries (del Hoyo *et al.* 1994, Ferguson-Lees & Christie 2001). Its wide range appears to be deceptive as it has fragmented populations which

Threatened Birds of Odisha

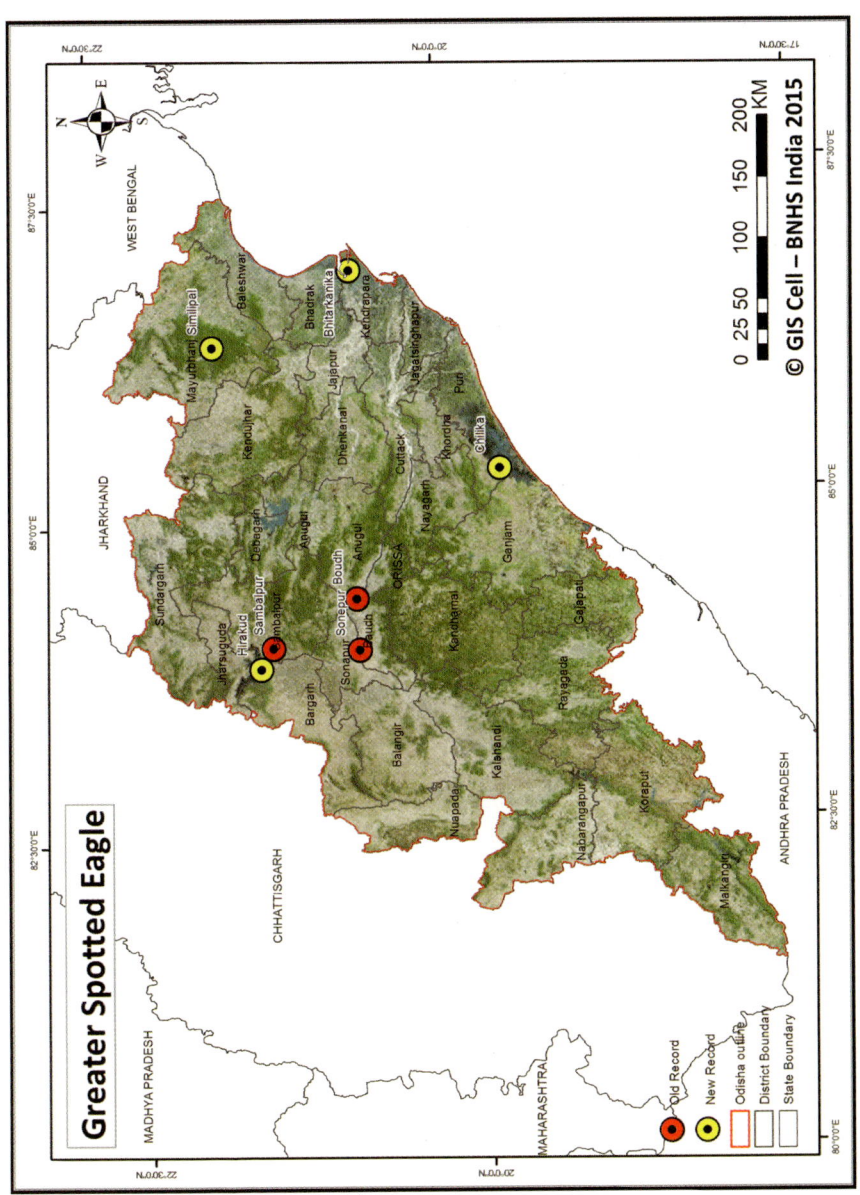

Greater Spotted Eagle

are undergoing an overall decline. Rahmani (2012) has described latest records from different states of India.

In Odisha, historically this raptor has been recorded from **Sambalpur**, **Sonepur** and **Boudh** (Ball 1878). Recent records are from **Similipal**, **Bhitarkanika** (Gopi and Pandav 2007), **Chilika** (Karuthedathu *et al*. 2014) and **Hirakud** reservoir (Nair *et al*. 2014). It is in all probability a scarce winter visitor to the state, though Gopi and Pandav (2007) state that it is an uncommon resident in Bhitarkanika.

Ecology: The Greater Spotted Eagle is invariably found near water where it sits and waits for hours for the right prey. It preys upon waterfowl, particularly the sick and the injured, and chicks from heronries, as seen in Keoladeo National Park. Its diet is very variable. Basic information on its ecology and behaviour are given in del Hoyo *et al*. (1994) and Ferguson-Lees and Christie (2001). Existing information on its ecology in India has been compiled by Naoroji (2007).

Threats and conservation: In India, drainage and degradation of wetlands is the biggest threat to this species, and all waterbirds in general. Like all large birds of prey, the Greater Spotted Eagle is also protected under the Indian Wildlife (Protection) Act, 1972 and listed in Schedule I. It is listed in CITES Appendix II, and CMS Appendix I and II. As it is found in many IBAs/PAs and other sites in India, we will not provide all records as they are too numerous and many records may be based on misidentification.

RECOMMENDATIONS

Protection of wetland habitats will greatly help this species and other Threatened wetland birds. Regular surveys of wetlands will be of great value in identifying important sites for the conservation of the species.

Indian Spotted Eagle *Clanga hastata*
(Lesson 1831)

VINAYAK YARDI

BirdLife International (2014) has listed this species in the Vulnerable category as it is thought to have a small and declining population. However, this statement has to be examined based on recent observations from Karnataka and Kerala. The bird is regularly seen in small numbers over the whole Deccan plateau and a few wetlands in Kerala. This shows that it has a much larger range and perhaps a larger population than hitherto known. Further research on its status in Cambodia and possibly also elsewhere in Southeast Asia may lead to a revised population estimate and a reassessment of its threat status.

Field Characters: A medium-sized, slim eagle with small bill and long gape extending to the middle of the eye, and round nostrils. It is supposed to have the widest gape among all Aquila. Adult birds are drab brown and unspotted, with yellowish brown eyes and often paler brown vent and tarsi. The name Spotted is quite misleading as the adult does not have spots. It has short, broad wings (wingspan 150 cm). In proportion to the Greater Spotted Eagle, the Indian Spotted Eagle has a longer tail. The legs appear longer and thinner due to the tarsi being less thickly feathered, because of which it was also known as Long-legged Eagle. The head is large in relation to body size. First year juveniles have brown eyes and pale flecks on nape (no rufous patch), upper back and wing-coverts, larger pale spots on

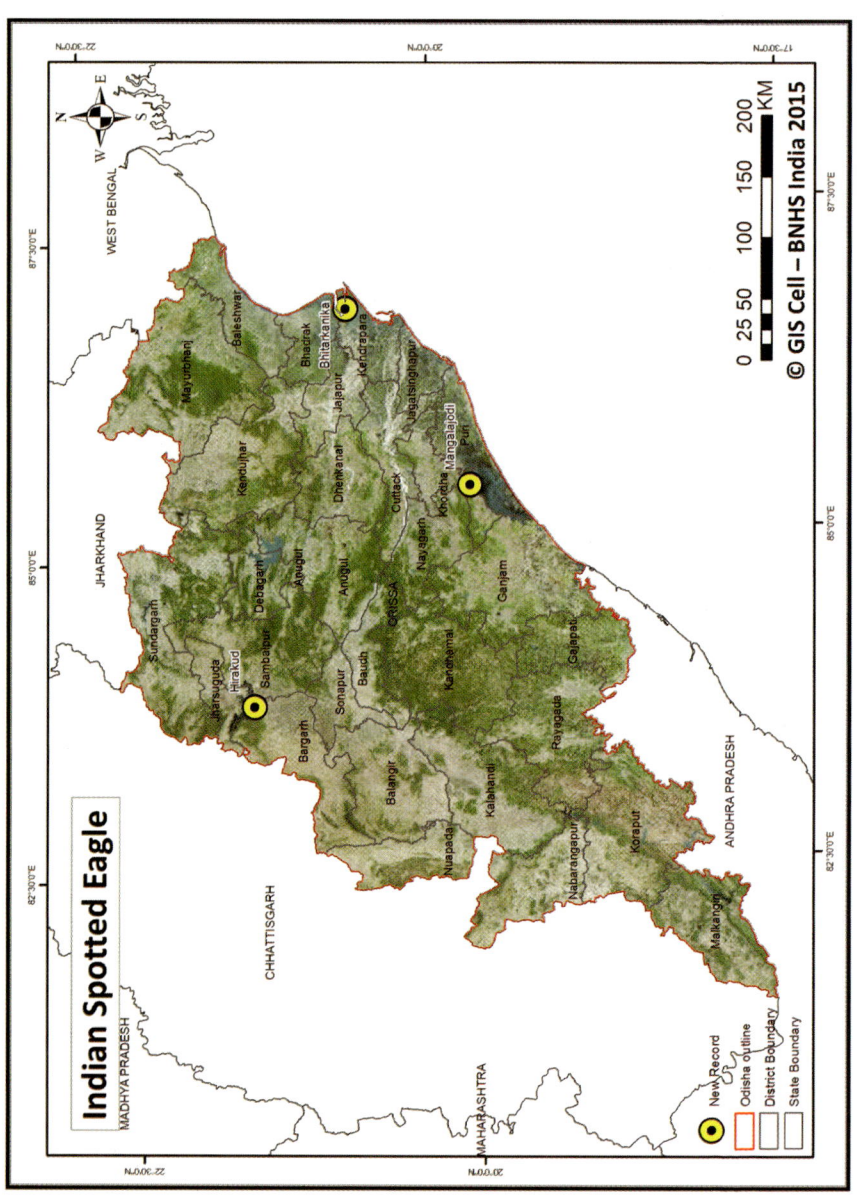

Indian Spotted Eagle

New Record
Odisha outline
District Boundary
State Boundary

© GIS Cell – BNHS India 2015

0 25 50   100   150   200
KM

median coverts and narrow pale tips to tertials, and are often heavily streaked below (Rasmussen & Anderton 2012). For more details of age-related plumage variation, see Naoroji (2007).

Distribution: The Indian Spotted Eagle is a semi-endemic species, chiefly found in India, but also recorded in Pakistan, Nepal, Bangladesh and Myanmar. According to BirdLife International (2014) sighting of *Aquila* in Cambodia almost certainly refers to this species, indicating that a population may persist in the dry deciduous dipterocarp forest mosaic in parts of Indochina.

It is present in drier biotope from north India to central and western regions, and probably there is a separate population in Karnataka, Tamil Nadu and part of Andhra Pradesh. For detailed distribution in India, see Naoroji (2007). Recently, Rahmani (2012) has collated all latest confirmed records from India.

From Odisha, historically this lesser known raptor has been recorded from Sambalpur, Nayagarh and Khariar (Ball 1878). Dev (1986) considered it a local migrant to Similipal, though no recent record exists from there. The other places where it has been reported are **Bhitarkanika**, **Hirakud** reservoir (Nair *et al.* 2014) and **Mangalajodi** wetlands. The only place where it breeds in the state is possibly **Bhitarkanika** where Gopi and Pandav (2007) term it an uncommon resident.

Ecology: The Indian Spotted Eagle is mainly found in light wooded forest, forest clearings, cultivated areas and even in urban gardens. It is also found sometimes near water but is not as dependent on wetlands as the Greater Spotted Eagle *Clanga clanga*. Its food consists of birds, small mammals and amphibians. It nests on trees in open countryside. It occurs in low density, and difficulty in identifying the species compounds the problem of recording. The general ecology of this species was studied in detail at Keoladeo National Park (Prakash 1989). All existing knowledge on this species was compiled by Naoroji (2007).

Threats and conservation: Like all other raptors in India, it is also threatened by the destruction and disturbance of its habitat, the modification of forest/grassland mosaic across India and Indochina, and also through pesticide poisoning. Research is required to know the specific threats to this species and how to mitigate them. It is protected under the Indian Wildlife (Protection) Act, 1972, not specifically but as a member of family Accipitridae. It is listed in Schedule I of the Act. It is found in many well-known Protected Areas/IBAs such as Keoladeo, Kaziranga, Corbett, Ranthambore and Mudumalai Tiger Reserve (Naoroji 2007, Rahmani 2012).

RECOMMENDATIONS

It is necessary to conduct proper breeding surveys throughout the state particularly in areas such as Bhitarkanika as there have been regular sightings from there.

Pallas's Fish-eagle *Haliaeetus leucoryphus*
(Pallas 1771)

GETHIA RAO

IUCN and BirdLife International (2014) list Pallas's Fish-eagle in the Vulnerable category as this species has a small, declining population as a result of widespread loss, degradation, and disturbance of wetlands and breeding sites throughout its wide range.

Field Characters: A large (76–84 cm), dark brown eagle with pale golden brown head and neck, and blackish tail with a broad, white central band. The band is particularly conspicuous in flight. Juvenile is more uniformly dark, with all-dark tail, but in flight shows strongly patterned underwing, with whitish band across coverts and prominent, whitish primary flashes. Female is larger. Voice is a loud, guttural *kha-kha-kha-kha* or *gao-gao-gao-gao*, and sometimes high-pitched, excited yelping. Hoarse, guttural, continuous *kook-kook-kook* is the commonest call.

Distribution: Pallas's Fish-eagle has a wide range from central Asia, southern Russia, east Mongolia and China, northern India, Pakistan, Bhutan, Bangladesh, and Myanmar. In India, we have a small resident population which is augmented in winter by the arrival of migrant birds from temperate regions. The main breeding populations are believed to be in China, Mongolia and the Indian subcontinent. The population is likely to be <10,000 mature individuals (BirdLife International 2014).

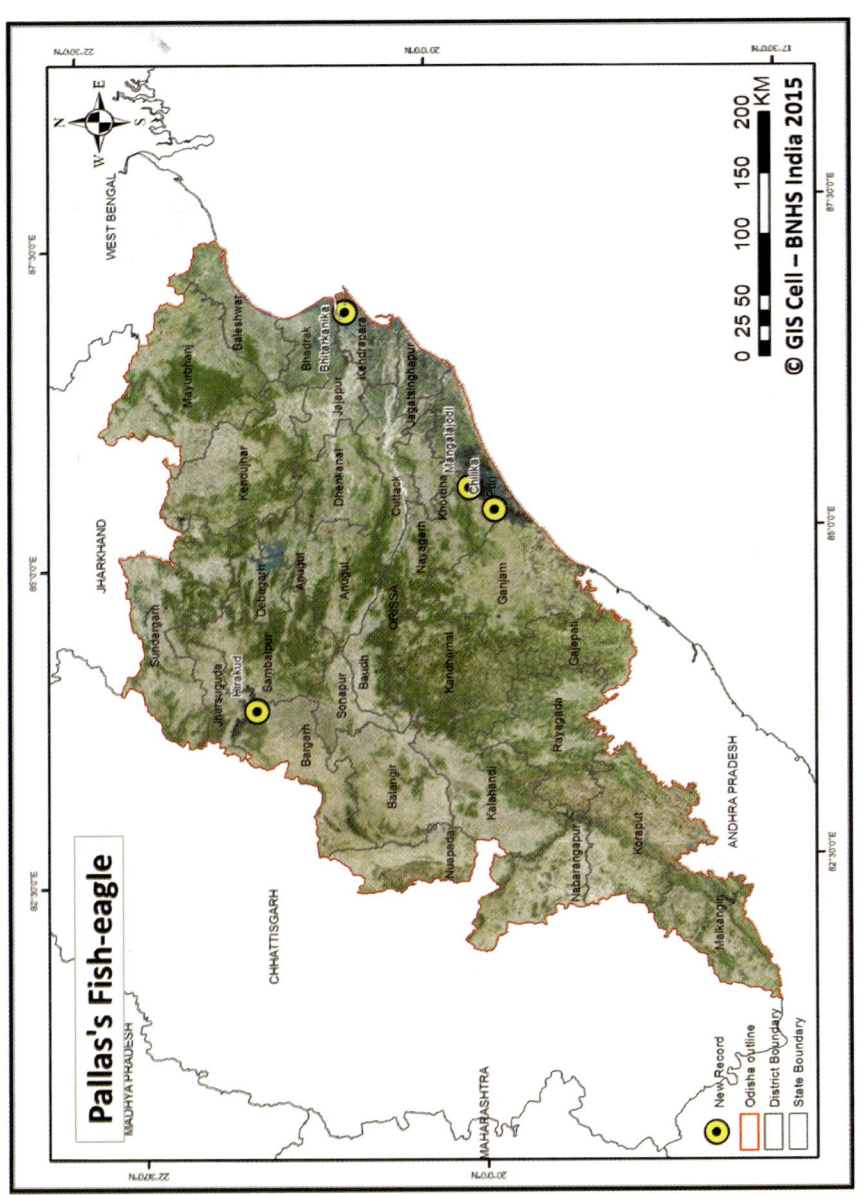

Pallas's Fish-eagle

In India, it is still reported from larger rivers and wetlands in the north and northeast (see Naoroji 2007 for recent records). Rahmani (2012) has given important records from India. Here we give records from the state.

In Odisha, this majestic bird of prey is a very rare winter visitor and is reported mainly from **Chilika** (Nalabana and Kalijai islands) (Balachandran *et al.* 2009), **Mangalajodi** wetlands (Dev 2013), **Bhitarkanika** (Gopi and Pandav 2007) and **Hirakud** reservoir (Nair *et al.* 2014).

Ecology: Pallas's Fish-eagle is invariably found near water, mainly large wetlands, rivers and *jheels*, from lowlands to 5,000 msl. It feeds mainly on fish, which are sometimes heavier than it can lift, and small waterfowl. It is well known for pirating prey from Osprey, Marsh Harrier, and Brahminy Kite, continuously harassing them till the prey is stolen.

In heronries, it feeds on chicks of cormorants, Oriental Darter, egrets, ibises and Asian Openbill, and is capable of killing birds as large as the Common Crane and Bar-headed Goose. In earlier literature it was mentioned that Pallas's Fish-eagle takes a heavy toll of young Bar-headed Geese in the lakes of Ladakh, but during five visits to these lakes from 2005 to 2008, no Pallas's Fish-eagle was seen. It generally nests on large trees near water. In India, the nesting season is from October to February. For details of its ecology and behaviour see Naoroji (2007).

Birds breeding in northern climes are migratory and leave the area by October, and first breeders return by end-March. In north India, both resident and migratory birds are seen in winter, when the resident birds breed while adults and immatures arrive from Mongolia, China, and Central Asia. After breeding, the resident birds move from the hot lowlands to cooler higher areas.

Threats: Pallas's Fish-eagle suffers from the same problems as almost all waterbirds (and being at the apex of the food pyramid, it is the first to disappear): habitat degradation through pollution, spread of Water Hyacinth *Eichhornia crassipes*, overfishing, felling of large trees near wetlands, and agriculture pesticides and industrial runoff to wetlands.

Conservation measures underway: It is listed in Schedule IV of the Indian Wildlife (Protection) Act, 1972, and also CITES Appendix II and CMS Appendix II. It occurs in many PAs/IBAs in India (Islam & Rahmani 2004).

RECOMMENDATIONS

1) Conduct surveys in the whole state to establish its status, distribution and threats.

2) Study its movement and dispersal through ringing/tagging and satellite telemetry.

3) Pesticide level in prey species should be monitored, and if high, remedial measures should be taken.

4) Control Water Hyacinth at important breeding/feeding sites.

Sarus Crane *Grus antigone*
(Linnaeus 1758)

ASAD R. RAHMANI

The justification for including Sarus Crane in the Vulnerable category is that it has suffered a rapid population decline, which is projected to continue as a result of widespread reductions in the extent and quality of its wetland habitats, poisoning, and pollutants (BirdLife International 2014).

FIELD CHARACTERS: Sarus Crane is the tallest flying bird in the world. It stands 152–156 cm in height. Adults are grey overall, with whiter mid-neck and tertials, mostly naked red head and upper neck, blackish primaries, mostly grey secondaries, and reddish legs that are bright during the breeding season and pale otherwise. Females are supposed to be slightly smaller, but sometimes this difference is imperceptible. Race *Grus antigone sharpii* is a more uniform, darker grey. Juvenile has feathered buffish head and upper neck, and duller plumage with brownish feather fringes. The bare red skin of the adult's head and neck is also brighter during the breeding season. This skin is rough and covered with papillae, and a narrow area around and behind the head is covered with black bristly feathers.

Distribution: The Sarus Crane has three disjunct populations—in the Indian subcontinent, Southeast Asia, and northern Australia. In India, it is found in many states. Historically, this species has been recorded in Sambalpur, north of the Mahanadi (Ball, 1878). There are no other records thereafter and it seems to have been locally extinct in Odisha.

Although it is a marginal species for the state and is probably extinct, considering India's global role in its protection, we are describing it in detail.

Ecology: The Sarus uses open wet and dry grasslands, agricultural fields, marshes and jheels for foraging, roosting, and nesting. Wetlands, even those which are very small and close to roads and human habitation, are the preferred habitat for constructing nests. For foraging, Sarus usually uses crop fields to a lesser extent, and prefers feeding in wetlands. It is omnivorous, feeding on a variety of roots and tubers as well as invertebrates and amphibians. Rahmani (2012) has described the latest researches on the Sarus Crane.

Threats: In India, Sarus is considered a sacred bird, so hunting is not the main problem; it is habitat destruction and habitat alteration which are taking their toll. Wetlands are under tremendous pressure from human use, drainage and conversion to agriculture, housing colonies and even construction of highways. A recent hazard has emerged in the form of poisoning. Collision with power lines may be a significant threat in parts of its range

Conservation measures underway: The Sarus Crane is listed in Schedule IV of the Wildlife (Protection) Act, 1972, and in CITES Appendix II and CMS Appendix II. Ecological, behavioural and conservation studies have been done in India and some are still continuing (Kaur & Choudhury 2002, Kaur 2008, Kaur *et al.* 2008, Sundar 2009).

RECOMMENDATIONS

BirdLife International (2001, 2014) has given many suggestions for all the range countries, and Rahmani (2012) has given India-specific recommendations based on inputs by Sarus experts. In Odisha, Sarus is probably extinct but an extensive survey is required.

Great Knot *Calidris tenuirostris*
(Horsfield, 1821)

JAN VAN DE KAM

BirdLife International (2014) has listed this species as Vulnerable owing to a rapid population decline caused by the reclamation of non-breeding stopover grounds, and under the assumption that proposed reclamation projects will cause additional decline in the future.

Field Characters: Among all the waders of *Calidris* genus wintering in India, the Great Knot is the largest (27 cm), with a comparatively long bill. It is light brownish grey above, boldly streaked with black. Lower back, rump and upper tail-coverts are dark brown scalloped with white, much more broadly on the last, making the feathers sometimes almost all white. Below, it has white foreneck and upper breast streaked or spotted with dark brown (Ali and Ripley 1987). Sexes are alike. This is the plumage in winter in India when it is seen. They are usually silent in winter, but occasionally make *prrt* sound.

Distribution: It has large breeding and wintering distribution. It breeds in northeast Siberia, Russia, and winters throughout the coastline of Southeast Asia, South Asia, Australia, and some birds reaching up to Saudi Arabia.

In India, it is a rare winter visitor, and earlier reported from Assam, Kolkata, Chennai, Andaman and Lakshadweep Islands (Ali and Ripley 1987).

In **Chilika Lake**, one individual was ringed at Parikud in December 2002, and a few were sighted in the 2004–05 season (Balachandran and Sathiyeselvam

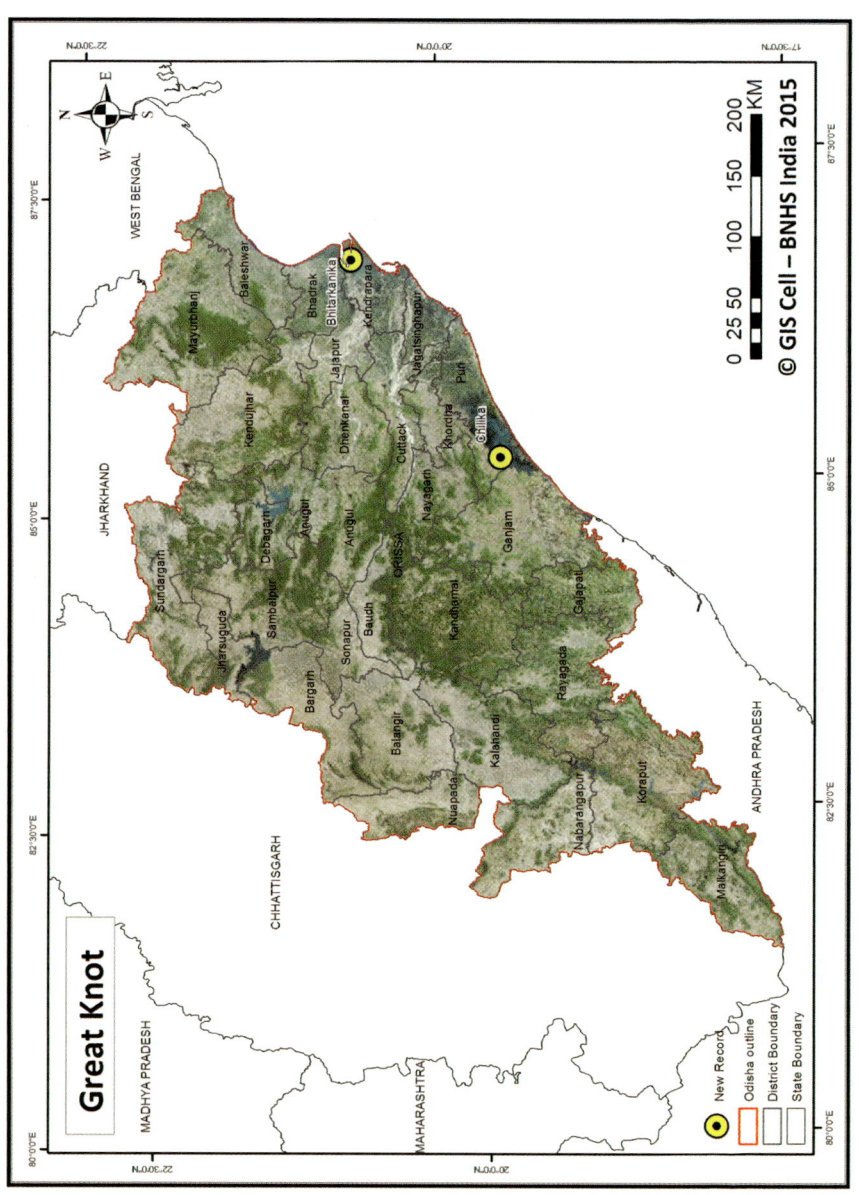

Great Knot

Legend:
- New Record
- Odisha outline
- District Boundary
- State Boundary

© GIS Cell – BNHS India 2015

0 25 50 100 150 200 KM

2007, Balachandran *et al.* 2009). A flock of 54 birds was seen by this team during the AWC-2005 carried out at **Bhitarkanika**.

Ecology: Since India is only a marginal country for this species, we are not describing its ecology in detail. It breeds in Siberia from May to June-July in open lichen-covered gravelly ground, with stunted bushes and herbs. The clutch size is four eggs. Chicks are mainly fed insects, but adults are seen feeding on small berries, bivalves, small gastropods, etc. During migration and in the winter areas, it is usually found in estuaries, coasts, sandy beaches, mud flats and mangroves. For more details of its ecology, behavior, breeding and migration, please see del Hoyo *et al.* (1996).

Threats: As it is an uncommon winter migrant to India, its major threats lie outside as described in detail by BirdLife International (2014). In India, it could be threatened by trapping of all types of waders by *Narikurvas* on the Tamil Nadu coast, development of ports in Odisha and Andhra Pradesh and general deterioration of coastal environment due to pollution, litter, fishing activities and increased human disturbance by beach tourism.

Conservation Measures taken: Like all other species of waders in India, it is also protected under the Indian Wildlife Protection Act, 1972. According to BirdLife International (2014) no specific conservation action is known for this species, although population trends are being monitored in Australia as part of the Monitoring Yellow Sea Migrants in the Australian project.

RECOMMENDATIONS

(a) Control poaching and trapping of waders through strict enforcement of the law.

(b) To provide better protection, identify important wintering areas particularly mudflats and sandflats, wave-dampened beaches, shallow water in sheltered sites and salt-flats amongst mangroves.

(c) Start shorebird monitoring programme through trained volunteers.

(d) Start large-scale ringing programme for all shorebirds to understand the movement of these birds.

Indian Skimmer *Rynchops albicollis*
Swainson 1838

MANOJ V. NAIR

BirdLife International (2001, 2014) justifies the listing of the Indian Skimmer as Vulnerable as its population is undergoing rapid decline due to widespread degradation and disturbance of lowland rivers and lakes which are the Skimmer's habitats.

Field Characters: A large tern-like bird, 40–43 cm, with a characteristic large orange bill with the lower mandible elongated and the bill highly compressed laterally. The lower mandible has a yellow tip. Adult is all black above, with white forehead and collar and white below. It has long pointed wings, projecting much beyond its tail. Small, bright red legs are characteristic features. In flight, it displays a white trailing-edge to wing, and short forked tail with blackish central feathers. Sexes are alike, though females are smaller. Non-breeders are duller and browner above. Juvenile has dusky orange bill with blackish tip, paler brownish-grey crown and nape with dark mottling; paler, more brownish-grey mantle and whitish to pale buff fringing scapulars and wing-coverts. Call is a nasal *kap* or *kip*, particularly in flight and when disturbed.

Distribution: The Indian Skimmer is found on larger rivers from Pakistan, through Nepal and India to Bangladesh and Myanmar. It was common in the 19th century in Myanmar, Laos, Cambodia, and Vietnam, but there are very few recent records from Myanmar and none from Laos, Cambodia or Vietnam

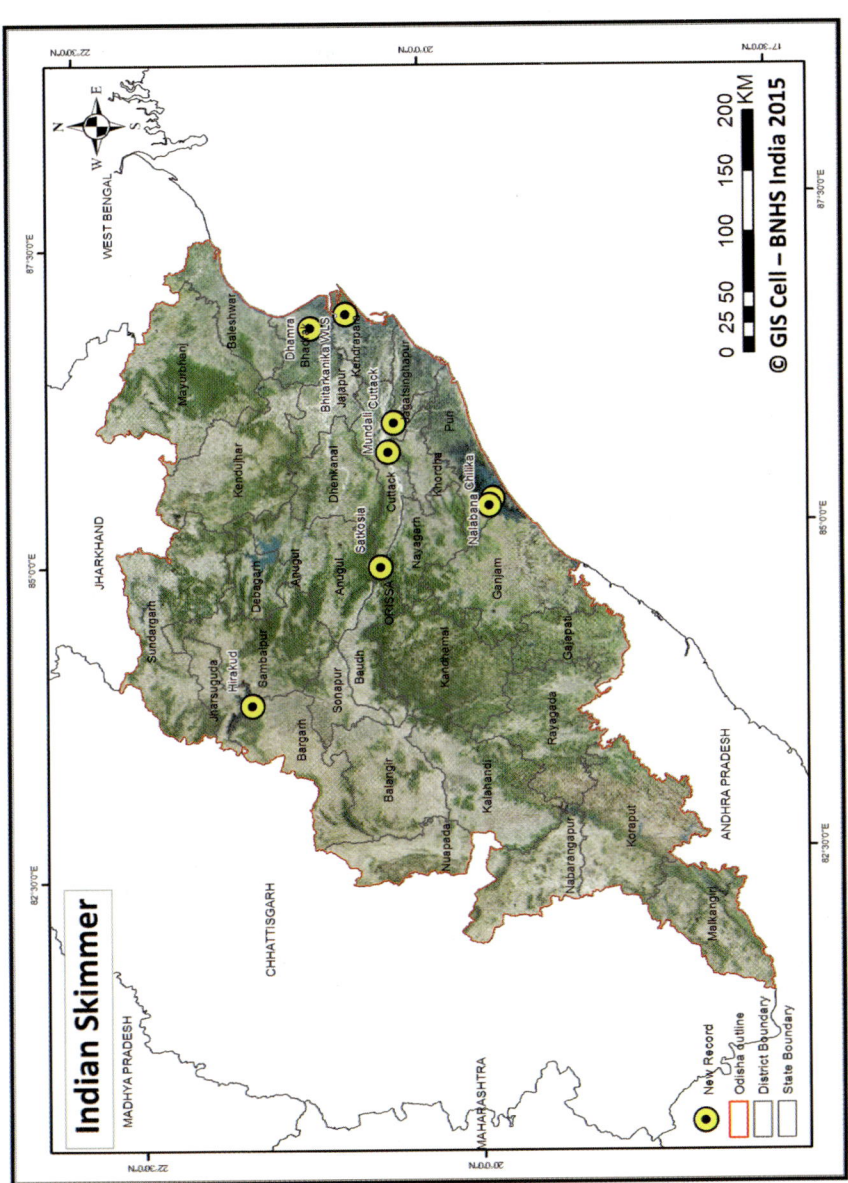

Indian Skimmer

© GIS Cell – BNHS India 2015

Though no nest of Indian Skimmer has been located in Odisha, they are frequently seen mating and congregating on sandy river islands of Mahanadi and other large rivers, indicating that they could be nesting in some remote islands

(BirdLife International 2014). It is uncommon in Pakistan and Nepal. In India also, it is becoming uncommon, although it is still seen on larger north Indian rivers.

Recent records from India have been collated by Rahmani (2012). In Odisha, this species has been recorded from **Bhitarkanika** Wildlife Sanctuary and National Park (Gopi and Pandav 2007), **Dhamra** area (Dutta 2007), **Nalabana** Bird Sanctuary and outer channel area of **Chilika Lake** (Balachandran et al. 2009), **Hirakud** reservoir (Nair *et al.* 2014), **Satkosia Gorge** Wildlife Sanctuary and banks of the Mahanadi at **Mundali** (Dev 2013). In Bhitarkanika, Praharajpur and Barunei estuary are key congregation areas and winter habitat for this species, with about 100 birds congregating there. Similarly, the shingle islands along the Mahanadi River bed in the gorge at Tikarpara inside **Satkosia Gorge** Sanctuary is also a stronghold.

Though it is thought to be a winter visitor to the state, year-round presence of some individuals and observations of mating pairs in Satkosia Gorge indicate likely breeding, possibly in the isolated sand banks downstream of Satkosia Gorge.

Ecology: It is one of the least-studied birds in India, with much of the information on its ecology and habits being anecdotal and descriptive. It occurs primarily on larger, sandy, slow-moving, lowland rivers, around lakes

Threatened Birds of Odisha

and adjacent marshes, and in the non-breeding season, estuaries and coasts. It breeds colonially on large, exposed sand-bars and islands. It may hunt singly, but mostly hunts in small flocks of 10–15 birds, sometimes more, much like a tern, skimming the water, the projecting tip of the lower mandible immersed in water at an acute angle; as soon as its prey is struck, the mandibles are closed. The prey, generally small fish, is gulped head first. The Skimmer feeds mainly on fish, but also takes small crustaceans and insect larvae (del Hoyo *et al.* 1996). It often feeds at dusk and through the night. It has a high, nasal, screaming call but is often silent.

It breeds on small sandy islands in larger rivers, mostly from April onwards. There is no attempt at nest-making; a scrape on the sand serves as a nest where 3–4 eggs are incubated, mostly by the female with some assistance by the male. However, the males live near the nesting colony and help to chase away small ground and aerial predators. Chicks are semi-precocial and start moving around within five to six days. They are perfectly camouflaged.

Threats: The Indian Skimmer is under multiple sources of pressure. Although it is legally protected under the Indian Wildlife (Protection) Act, 1972, its habitat of large rivers in northern and central India is under heavy anthropogenic pressures.

Conservation measures: The Indian Skimmer is protected under the Indian Wildlife (Protection) Act, 1972.

RECOMMENDATIONS

BirdLife International (2014) has given suggestions for the whole range of this species, while Rahmani (2012) has given recommendations for India. In Odisha there is a need to survey all the larger rivers during April–May (breeding season) to find out its distribution and status. As the bird moves a lot in the non-breeding season, there are chances of multiple counts of the same individual but during breeding season the bird is confined to a particular area.

Pale-capped Woodpigeon *Columba punicea*
Blyth 1842

PANCHAMI MANOO UKIL

This pigeon has a small population that is assumed to be declining owing to destruction of its evergreen forest habitat. It therefore qualifies as Vulnerable (BirdLife International 2014).

Field Characters: A large pigeon of 36–40 cm. Adult male has chestnut-brown upperparts, with a dark slaty rump and blackish brown tail, and lower parts vinaceous-chestnut. Crown and nape greyish white, hence its name. The entire plumage has a brilliant metallic green and amethyst sheen (Ali & Ripley 1987). It has a reddish cere, base of bill and eye patch. Female is somewhat smaller and duller, with greyish crown. Juvenile similar to female, but its head more or less the same colour as its body.

Distribution: The Pale-capped Pigeon is a forest bird and had a wide distribution in the past. Even now it is found in northern India, Bangladesh, Myanmar, Thailand, Laos, Cambodia and Vietnam.

In India, it is resident but very local from the plains to about 1,600 msl. We have historical records from Maharashtra, Bihar, Jharkhand, West Bengal, Andhra Pradesh, Assam, Nagaland, and Manipur (Ali & Ripley 1987). In Odisha it was earlier reported only from the Eastern Ghats (Mooney 1934; Jayakar 1967) but now it is reported from the coastal **Bhitarkanika** (Gopi and Pandav 2007) and **Chandaka** Sanctuary. Its main stronghold is the **Similipal** Tiger Reserve. There are several recent reports from **Ekamra Kanan** (bamboo scrub adjoining Chandaka

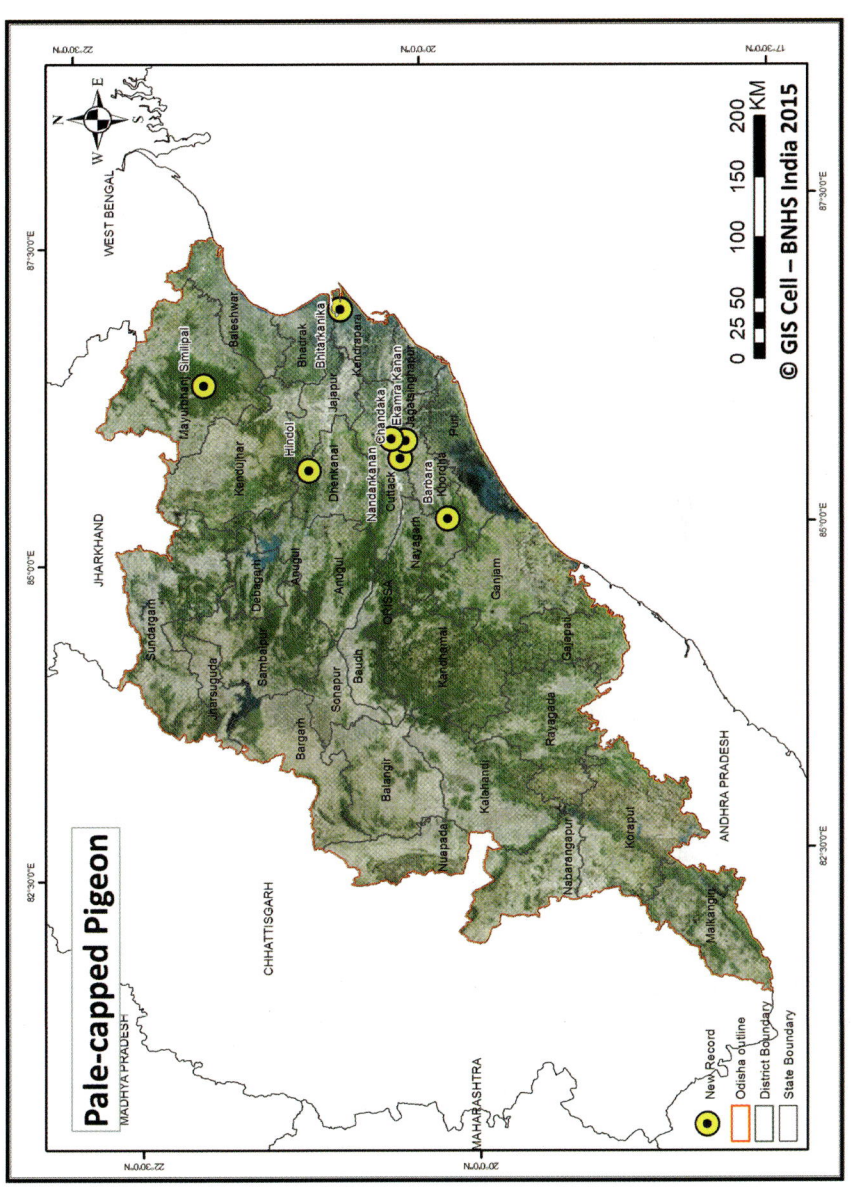

Pale-capped Pigeon

© GIS Cell – BNHS India 2015

0 25 50   100   150   200
KM

New Record
Odisha outline
District Boundary
State Boundary

Wildlife Sanctuary), **Barbara Reserve Forest**, **Nandankanan** Sanctuary and **Hindol Reserve Forest** near Dhenkanal.

Similipal Tiger Reserve seems to be the stronghold of the species, not only in Odisha but probably also in the country. Second author's observations from end of 2006 to 2009 and then in spurts till 2011 show that this species is a rather patchily-distributed resident within the 2,750-km² Similipal Tiger Reserve, in some localities even locally common. Among 19 ranges that constitute the Tiger Reserve, there are records only from five ranges (Pithabata, Chahala, Upper Barakamura, Jenabil and Kendumundi; encompassing *c.* 500–550 km²), almost all in Semi-evergreen and Dense Moist-deciduous Sal Forests.

Ecology: The Pale-capped Pigeon frequents a wide variety of habitats from the lowlands up to 1,600 msl, chiefly primary or secondary evergreen forest, but also open, deciduous dipterocarp forest, bamboo and agricultural fields, particularly in close proximity to forest (BirdLife International 2001, 2014). It usually keeps singly, occasionally in small groups, but large gatherings of 30 to 40 birds are found where food is abundant. BirdLife International (2014) mentions a roosting flock of 174 individuals at Don Mamuang, Thailand in 2002. It mainly feeds on fruits (figs especially) and berries on tall dense trees, but occasionally descends to the ground to pick up seeds and grains. It takes slow and short flights, disappearing into dense foliage at the approach of danger.

In Similipal they have been seen throughout the year except the peak monsoons. Group size varies from 3–5 but flocks of 10+ have also been seen. The highest was a scattered flock of 17 birds at a salt lick at Upper Barakamura, during winter. They are mostly seen in pairs during summer, but occasional flocks are noticed in salt-licks. Three instances were observed where birds have been seen collecting nesting material, all during summer months. A nest under construction was seen in June at Kairakocha, Chahala range at *c.* 15 m height, on a medium-sized tree which stood along a hill stream in a densely wooded narrow valley. The male was seen displaying intermittently and chasing the female which flew in short spurts from tree to tree, strutting in typical pigeon fashion, uttering *hoop-hoop-hoop-hoop* calls. Though largely a silent bird as far as pigeons go, slightly different vocalisations have also been noticed during other occasions. Interestingly, they have also been recorded on many occasions coming down to salt-licks and gobbling clods of salt-stained earth, often accompanied by Oriental Turtle Dove *Streptopelia orientalis*. During winter, they bask for long periods of time perched on exposed leafless tips of emergent forest trees.

Not much is known about their breeding behaviour but it could not be very different from other pigeons of their size and habitat. They nests from May to August, sometimes just before the heavy monsoon sets in. The nest is a collection of twigs, clumsily kept on trees or bushes that are generally not more

Simlipal Tiger Reserve is now perhaps the best place in India to see Pale-capped Pigeon *Columba punicea*. Sometimes they come down to salt lick as shown above

than 6 m high. Most pigeon species lay two eggs, but E.C. Stuart Baker says it is a "singleton". This needs verification. Both parents share incubation and chick rearing duties. It is resident and nomadic according to season and area, and in response to food availability.

Threats: Habitat loss and fragmentation are the most important threats in India. Hunting is the major threat in many parts of its range. Trade is also a threat in some areas, but not the major threat.

Conservation measures underway: It is a protected species under Schedule IV of the Indian Wildlife (Protection) Act, 1972. It is found in many Protected Areas and IBAs in India (and other countries). But as BirdLife International (2014) rightly states, their contribution to its conservation is not known, especially given its seasonal and nomadic movements. Indeed, site-based conservation strategies are unlikely to be successful, unless populations are able to follow seasonal patterns of fruit-ripening within secure protected sites (BirdLife International 2014).

RECOMMENDATIONS

(a) Conduct surveys in Odisha to know its current distribution and status.

(b) Start a project to study its ecology and behaviour, particularly with marked birds.

(c) Study its movement through satellite tracking.

(d) Enforce strict control on poaching in its whole range.

Bristled Grassbird *Chaetornis striata*
(Jerdon 1841)

RAHUL RAO

Like all grassland birds of the Indian subcontinent, the Bristled Grassbird is rapidly declining owing to loss and degradation of its grassland habitat, primarily through drainage and conversion to agriculture. It therefore qualifies as Vulnerable (BirdLife International 2014).

Field characters: A large (20 cm), chiefly brown warbler with thick streaks on upperparts, fine streaks on lower throat, and unmarked buffy underparts. It has a relatively short, thick bill and very pale supercilium. It has a heavy, broad rounded tail with whitish wash and pale uppertail with distinct heavy black central stripe. Male is 10% larger, with rufescent forecrown and dark bill in breeding season; female has browner fore-crown and paler bill (Rasmussen & Anderton 2005). Female appears to be paler than the male and her bill is not so solidly black (Grewal 1996).

Distribution: It is endemic to the Indian subcontinent: Pakistan, India, Nepal, and Bangladesh. Its wide distribution is deceptive as this grassland obligate species is restricted to undisturbed tall grasslands so there are not many records. Rahmani (2012) has compiled all recent records from India. Here we give only Odisha records.

In Odisha, this little known bird has been recorded historically from Sambalpur and Kalahandi (Ball 1877). Recently, records are from **Satkosia** Tiger Reserve (Islam and Rahmani 2004) and from the grasslands inside south Similipal. The

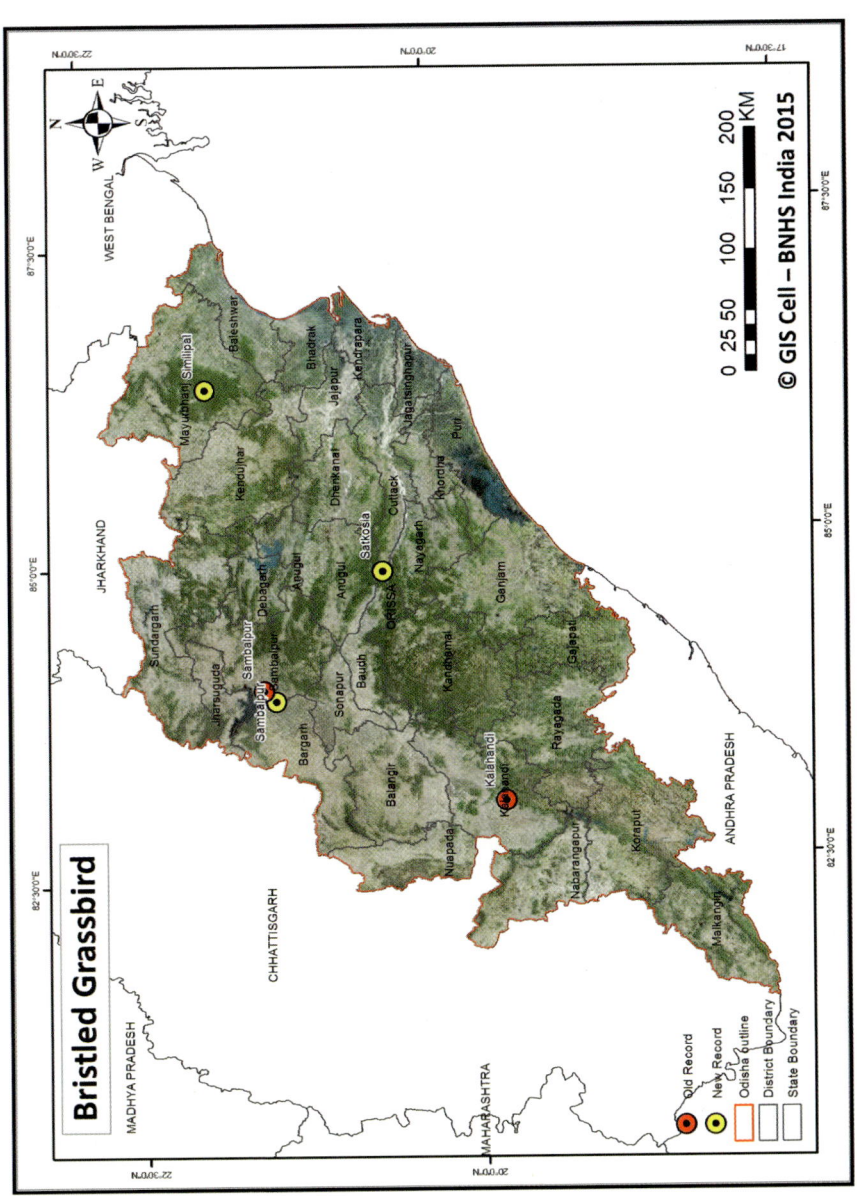

Bristled Grassbird

The Bristled Grassbird has been sighted in grasslands such as these in southern Similipal

second author saw it in January 2008 in **Similipal**. In all probability it is a scarce winter visitor to the state.

Ecology: The Bristled Grassbird lives in tall grasslands and reeds, with some shrubs, preferably near water, but sometimes in dry grasslands also. It lives singly or in pairs, is a very shy skulker, but during the breeding season, males become very vocal and conspicuous, and cannot be missed in the right habitat. The territorial male sings from an exposed perch on a tall grass stem, or a bush standing amongst the reeds, or during frequent sustained song flights. The nest is made in dense grass or shrub, a ball-shaped bundle of grass with side entrance, where the female lays 4–5 eggs and apparently incubates them alone.

Threats: Habitat destruction is the biggest threat to this species, as grasslands are totally neglected in India. Most of the wet grasslands have been converted to crop fields. Overgrazing, grass cutting, grassland burning and commercial plantations are other major threats. Burning of grassland during the breeding period of this species is a major management issue in certain areas.

Conservation measures underway: Although this species is not listed by name in the Indian Wildlife (Protection) Act, 1972, shooting and trapping of all wild bird species is prohibited under the Act. Thus it is also protected. It is recorded from some Protected Areas/IBAs.

RECOMMENDATIONS

BirdLife International (2014) has suggested measures for all the range countries. For India, Rahmani (2012) has suggested various measures. Although perhaps marginal to Odisha, detailed survey is required to know its distribution and special efforts should be made towards grassland protection wherever it is found.

Green Munia *Amandava formosa*
(Latham, 1790)

BHASMANG MEHTA

According to BirdLife International (2001, 2014) Green Munia is listed as Vulnerable because it has a rapidly declining population owing to widespread trapping for the cagebird trade, compounded by habitat loss and degradation through agricultural intensification.

Identification: It is a small (10 cm) munia with distinctive green-and-yellow colour with black-barred flanks and reddish bill. Female is duller with indistinctly barred flanks.

It cannot be confused with any other bird, particularly munias, of same size.

Distribution: The Green Munia is an endemic bird of India, known from southern Rajasthan, central Uttar Pradesh, southern Bihar and West Bengal (historically), south to southern Maharashtra, northern Andhra Pradesh and southern Odisha.

In Odisha, this species has been reported mostly from **Jeypore** (Whistler and Kinnear 1933) and **Koraput** (Majumdar 1988) in Koraput district. At present, the most promising site seems to be **Karlapat** Sanctuary, Kalahandi district where these birds were common in the Eastern part of the Sanctuary (Palei *et al*. 2011; Palei 2012). Other recent records are from **Sohela**, Bargarh district (second author *pers obs*.) and from outskirts of **Bolangir** town (January 2013, Partha Pratim Patra, *pers comm*. 2015) and 20 birds from **Kotagarh** Wildlife Sanctuary (S.K. Sajan and P. Moahapatra *pers .comm*. 2015).

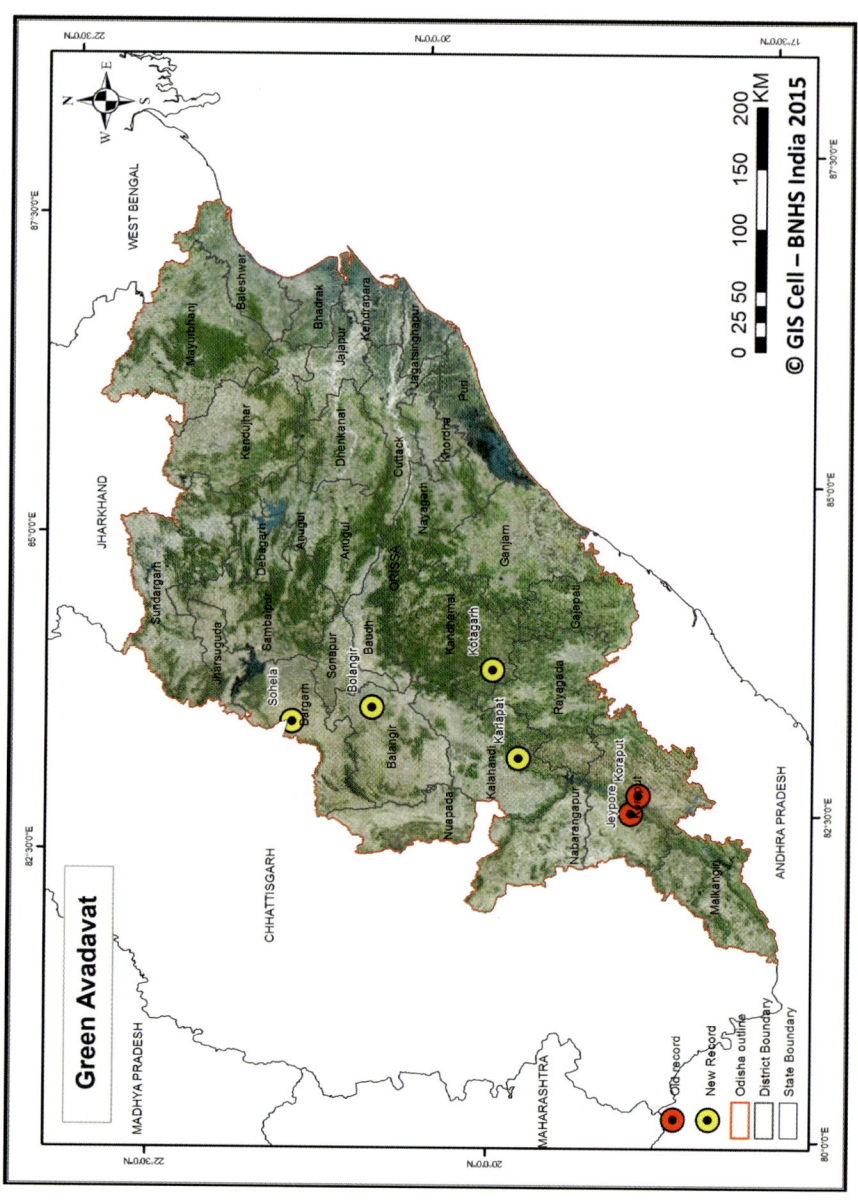

Green Avadavat

© GIS Cell – BNHS India 2015

The popularity of the species as a charismatic cagebird is one of the prime reasons for its decline (Ahmed, 1998). In Karlapat Wildlife Sanctuary, Palei (2012) lists habitat loss along with a lack of awareness about this species among stakeholders (local and forest officials) as major threats.

Ecology: The Green Munia resides in relatively dry areas, boulder-strewn scrub jungle, small patches of grasslands with low bushes, sometimes sugarcane fields, and open shrubby forest, often near water, generally in lowlands and foothills. Nesting starts just before monsoon sets in and may extend up to January. Nest is a globular structure, typical munia-fashion in a low thorny bush or attached to sugarcane leaf. The incubation chamber is lined with soft grass. The clutch size is 5 to 6, and incubation is probably done by both parents. It feeds on seeds and small insects, but chicks are mainly fed small soft insects. Gaston and Mackrell (1980) and Ali and Abdulali (1945) also found it feeding on seeds. Majumdar (1988) analysed the stomach contents of the Green Munia and found only seeds. Song is high-pitched warble, ending with prolonged trill. Calls include weak *seee* and *swee* notes.

Threats: Ahmad (1997, 1998) considers Green Munia trade as the major threat, leading to local extinction of several populations (Bhargava 1996).

Conservation measures underway: Although it is not listed by name in the Indian Wildlife Protection Act, shooting and trapping of all wild bird species is prohibited under the Act. All members of Estrildinae are included in Schedule IV of the Act. It is listed in CITES Appendix II. Studies on its trade have been conducted by TRAFFIC India from time to time highlighting the plight of this species (Ahmed 1997, 1998, 1999, 2008, 2009). Some field studies have also been done (Mehra *et al.*, 2005). It has been reported from very few Protected Areas /IBAs.

Conservation measures proposed: As it is an endemic species, India has to play major role in its conservation.

The following are the recommendations:

RECOMMENDATIONS

(a) Upgrade the species legal protective status to Schedule I of the Wildlife Protection Act (1972) and CITES Appendix I.

(b) Strict control on its illegal trade.

(c) Conduct widespread interviews with bird-trappers to identify locations of remaining populations, followed by extensive field surveys in suitable habitat to establish more clearly its current distribution and population status.

(d) Investigate its ecological requirements for better protection of its habitat, particularly in protected areas.

Ferruginous Duck *Aythya nyroca*
(Güldenstädt 1770)

SATISH PANDE

Based on the information gathered by BirdLife International (2014), IUCN has categorised the Ferruginous Duck as Near Threatened.

Field Characters: An overall dark chestnut diving duck, *c.* 41 cm, with a large oval white patch on the belly (clearly visible in flight), with conspicuous white eyes in male visible clearly at short distance. Female is like the male but duller, with brown eyes. Both sexes are slightly darker on the back. Juvenile similar to adult, but belly and undertail are grey-buff. In flight, a broad white wing-bar extends to outer primaries.

Distribution: The Ferruginous Duck or White-eyed Pochard is widely distributed in the Palaearctic region from western Europe to western Mongolia. In India, it is a common winter migrant mainly to the Northeast, with scattered records from northern and southern India (Ali & Ripley 1987, Grimmett *et al.* 1998). Rahmani & Islam (2008) and Rahmani (2012) have given historical and recent records from India. Here we mention only records from Odisha. It is recorded from **Chilika**, where it is mostly seen at Nalabana near Barkul and Tinimuhani. It is also recently reported from **Badjor Reservoir**, Mayurbhanj and **Rengali Reservoir** (A.K. Nayak *pers.comm.* 2015).

Ecology: In India, it can be seen in shallow ponds, pools, and marshes near vegetated shoreline, large marshes, wetlands and sometimes in rivers. Prefers

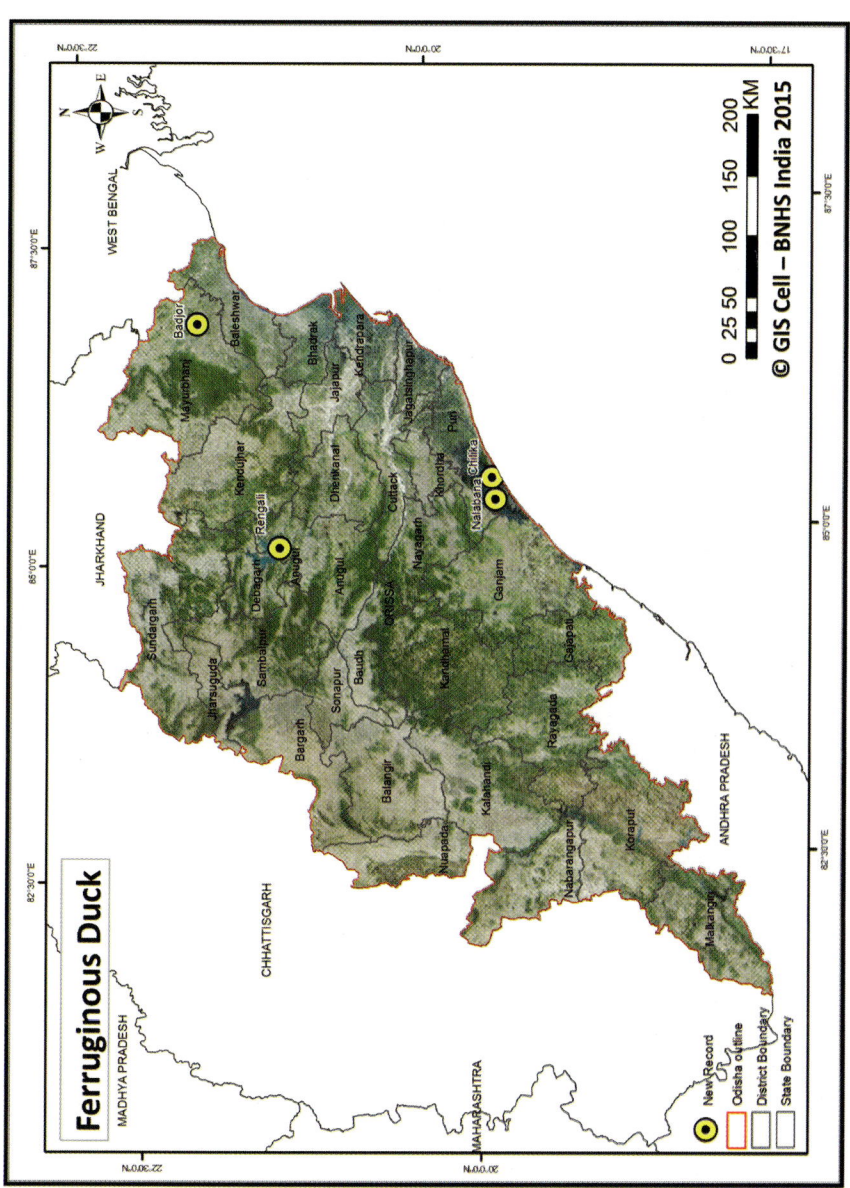

Ferruginous Duck

The vast Hirakud Reservoir is a good habitat for diving ducks such as pochards

shallower and more vegetated areas than other *Aythya* species and seldom sits out in open water. Feeds on seeds, roots, and the green parts of aquatic plants. It also feeds on insects, worms, molluscs, crustaceans, amphibians, and small fish. It often feeds at night, and will upend (dabble) for food as well as the more characteristic diving. In India, it was found breeding in some wetlands of Kashmir but we do not have recent confirmed records of breeding.

Threats: In India, it is mainly threatened by habitat destruction and modification, and by trapping and poisoning.

Conservation measures underway: It is protected under the Indian Wildlife (Protection) Act, 1972, which bans its hunting, trapping, trading and poaching. It is listed in Schedule IV of the Act.

RECOMMENDATIONS

1) Strict prevention of trapping and poisoning of waterfowl which unfortunately is quite common in some areas.
2) Development of National Wetland Conservation Act for protection of wetlands.
3) Better protection of non-protected wetland IBAs.
4) Regular monitoring of all waterfowl, particularly threatened species.

Falcated Duck *Marcea falcata*
Georgi 1775

DHRITIMAN MUKHERJEE

In India the Falcated Duck is a rare migratory species. IUCN and BirdLife International (2014) have listed it as Near Threatened owing to a rapid decline in its population in China and very high levels of hunting, although elsewhere it is more abundant than was once believed.

Field Characters: Ali & Ripley (1987) describe it as follows: Male [breeding] strikingly peculiar and beautiful, with metallic bronzy green head with a chestnut-purplish crown and a bushy mane-like nuchal crest which falls over the hindneck and rests on the back, giving the appearance of a thick neck. Throat and foreneck white, with a narrow green collar near base. Its body plumage is mainly grey, wavily pencilled with black, the marking becoming bolder and more crescentic on the breast. Speculum glossy black and green, bordered in front by a grey band (wing-coverts); inner secondaries very long, sickle-shaped (falcated, hence its name), velvety black, white and grey, covering hind part of body and tail. Uppertail-coverts black, overtopping tail. Female quite drab, with greyish head, dark spotting and scalloping on brown underparts, and greyish-white fringes to exposed tertials. It is between 48 and 54 cm, about the size of a Gadwall *Anas strepera*. The eclipse male is like the female, but darker on the back and head. In flight, both sexes show a pale grey underwing.

Distribution: The Falcated Duck breeds from southeast Siberia and Mongolia to the Kuril Island and northern Japan and China. Although the global population

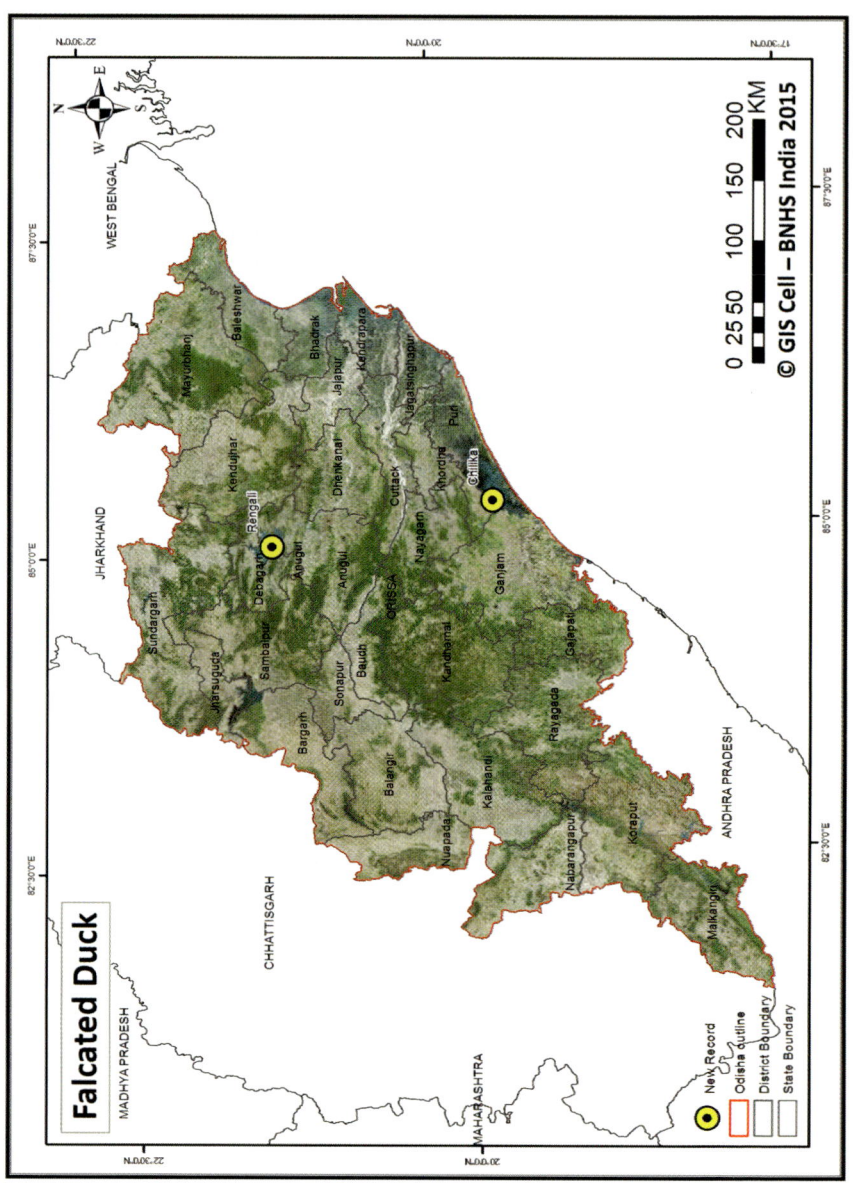

Falcated Duck

Threatened Birds of Odisha

was previously estimated to be 35,000 individuals, recent counts indicate that it is considerably higher, totalling perhaps as many as 89,000 (BirdLife International 2014). In India, the Falcated Duck is found mainly in the northern parts as an uncommon winter migrant. Rahmani & Islam (2008) and Rahmani (2012) have given detailed site records of India. This species is possibly a vagrant in Odisha and is known from two records—one from an old unsubstantiated record from **Chilika** (Anon. 1991) and the other recent one, a bird photographed in **Rengali Reservoir** (A.K. Nayak *pers comm.* 2015).

Ecology: In India, not much is reported about its ecology except that it is occurs singly or in pairs with other dabbling ducks on *jheel*s and shallow waterbodies. In its breeding areas, it is usually seen in pairs or small parties. According to del Hoyo *et al.* (1992), it breeds in freshwater lakes, rivers, ponds, lagoons, and often in wooded country, while in the winter it can be seen on the coast and in larger, shallow waterbodies, in rice fields and flooded meadows. It feeds on seeds including rice and other grains, grasses, and also molluscs and insects. It starts breeding in May–June in single pairs or loose groups, nesting on the ground in vegetation near water. It lays 6–9 eggs and incubates them for 24–26 days (del Hoyo *et al.* 1992). Like other species of *Anas* and *Mareca*, it is mainly vegetarian, and primarily feeds on emergent and submerged vegetation by dabbling and upending, but it also grazes on wet grasslands and crops. The male Falcated Duck has a clear low whistle, whereas the female has a gruff *quack*.

Threats: Degradation and drainage of its wetland habitat is the main threat in **India**, but elsewhere, BirdLife International (2014) found that hunting for food for subsistence and local markets is probably the major threat.

Conservation measures underway: Like all Anatidae species, it is protected under the Indian Wildlife (Protection) Act, 1972. It is listed in Schedule IV of the Act. It also occurs in some Protected Areas/IBAs.

RECOMMENDATIONS

As it is an uncommon winter visitor in Odisha, no specific recommendations can be made. In general, wetlands should be protected and hunting and poisoning of all waterfowl should be stopped at once.

Painted Stork *Mycteria leucocephala*
(Pennant 1769)

The Painted Stork has been classified as Near Threatened by BirdLife International (2014) because it is thought to be undergoing a moderately rapid population decline in Southeast Asia owing to hunting, drainage and pollution in its habitat.

Field Characters: A long-legged, long-necked, lanky bird, slightly less than a metre (93 cm) in height, the Painted Stork inhabits marshes and lakes. It has a long, heavy, yellow bill, slightly decurved at the tip, and an unfeathered waxy yellow face. Head, neck, breast and back are white, with closely barred belly band, and black-and-white wing-coverts. Inner secondaries which are rose pink and fall over the black tail give it the name Painted. Legs and feet are fleshy, sometimes nearly red, often appearing white due to their habit of defecating on their legs (urohydrosis) especially when in the nest. Sexes are alike, but female appears to be smaller. The downy young are mainly whitish with grey bill and blackish facial skin. The juveniles assume a brownish plumage and like most other storks reach breeding condition after two to three years.

Distribution: In India, the Painted Stork is found throughout the plains, rarely in the Brahmaputra Valley and is not recorded in the Andaman and Nicobar Islands. It is growing much more common in south India where many nesting colonies are protected by villagers and also in sanctuaries. Rahmani (2012) has

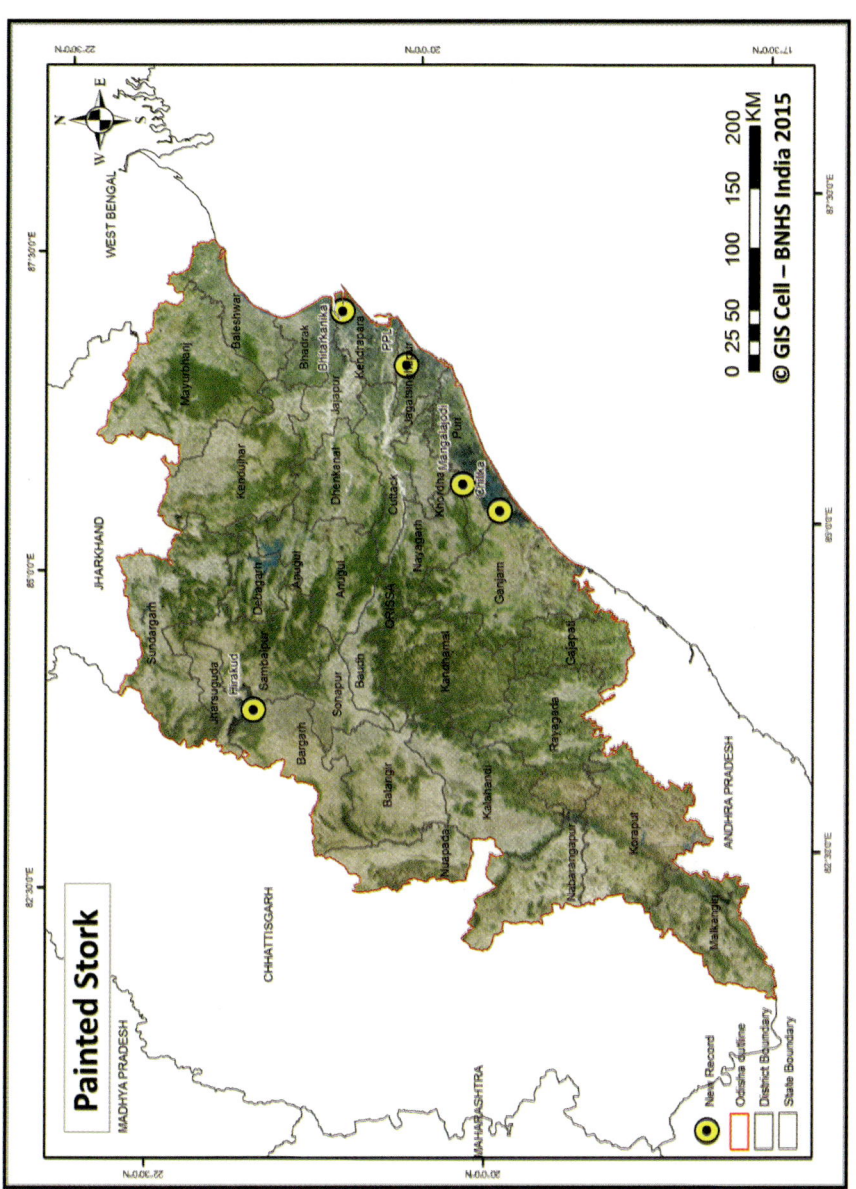

Painted Stork

collated all the important records from India. In Odisha, it is a rare resident in small numbers, its population possibly augmented in winters by migrating birds. It is mainly recorded from Nalabana in **Chilika** (fairly common summer migrant), **Mangalajodi** and **Bhitarkanika**. Balachandran *et al.* (2009) once recorded a total of *c.* 5,000 soon after the flooding at Nalabana in May 2002. Scattered reports exist from the **(PPL) Paradeep Phosphates Limited wetlands**, **Hirakud Reservoir** and in the paddy fields along NH–5. The only breeding record from the state is from **Bhitarkanika** where Pandav (1997) estimated about 70 individuals. Pandav reported that nesting takes place between December and February. He recorded 28 nests on tall trees of *Sonneratia apetala* and *Xylocarpus moluccensis* along the Bhitarkanika river during January 1993. Gopi and Pandav (2007) reported a small colony of eight pairs nesting in *Heriteria fomes* trees along Ganjaikhia creek in **Bhitarkanika** NP.

Ecology: The ecology of the Painted Stork has been well studied in India (for references see Rahmani 2012). It frequents freshwater marshes, lakes and reservoirs, flooded fields, rice paddies, freshwater swamp forest, river banks, intertidal mudflats and salt pans. It forages in flocks in shallow waters along rivers or lakes. It makes short-distance movements in some parts of its range in response to food and for breeding. Like other storks, it is often seen soaring on thermals. It breeds colonially in single-species or mixed heronries and if not molested, such heronries become traditional. The birds arrive just before the monsoon breaks and spend considerable time on the selected nesting trees, perhaps waiting for the right cue to start making nests of sticks and leaves. Mating frequently takes place on the nest or a nearby branch, and the female lays three or four, rarely five, eggs. Both parents incubate and rear the chick.

Threats: In India, though it is protected traditionally in many areas, poaching by tribal and amateur hunters and pesticide poisoning are major threats. Nest predation by mammalian and avian predators is the major threat in some colonies, aggravated by human interference.

Conservation measures underway: It is listed in Schedule IV of the Indian Wildlife (Protection) Act, 1972. Further, its nesting sites are traditionally protected, as a result of which its population is increasing in some areas. It also occurs in a number of Protected Areas/IBAs.

RECOMMENDATIONS

1) Conduct studies on the level of threat to this bird due to pesticide poisoning of its food.
2) Conduct state-wide surveys every two years to monitor its populations.
3) To study movement and dispersal, conduct satellite telemetry studies in major breeding areas.
4) Bring about strong legislation to protect all types of wetlands.

Black-necked Stork *Ephippiorhynchus asiaticus* (Latham 1790)

Based on information gathered by BirdLife International (2014), IUCN includes Black-necked Stork in the Near Threatened category as this species has undergone a moderately rapid overall population reduction, which is projected to continue. The population estimate varies between 10,000 and 20,000 in the whole world.

Field Characters: Characteristically large bird between 130 and 150 cm tall, with bright red legs, white body, extensive black on the wings and tail, and notably an iridescent black head and neck with large black bill. The young look like a washed-out version of the parents, with dull brown replacing glossy black parts, and dirty white replacing pure white. Genus *Ephippiorhynchus* is unique among storks in exhibiting sexual dimorphism in coloration: iris dark brown in male and yellow in female. Like most storks, the Black-necked Stork flies with its neck outstretched, not retracted like a heron. The wingspan measures up to 230 cm.

Distribution: The Black-necked Stork is found South and Southeast Asia, but nowhere is it common. In India, it is found all over the Indian plains in wetlands, shallow river beds and mangrove swamps. This large and imposing bird is a very rare winter visitor to **Chilika**. Balachandran *et al.* (2009) did not record it from 2001 to 2009 in Chilika. Therefore, its inclusion in the checklist of Chilika

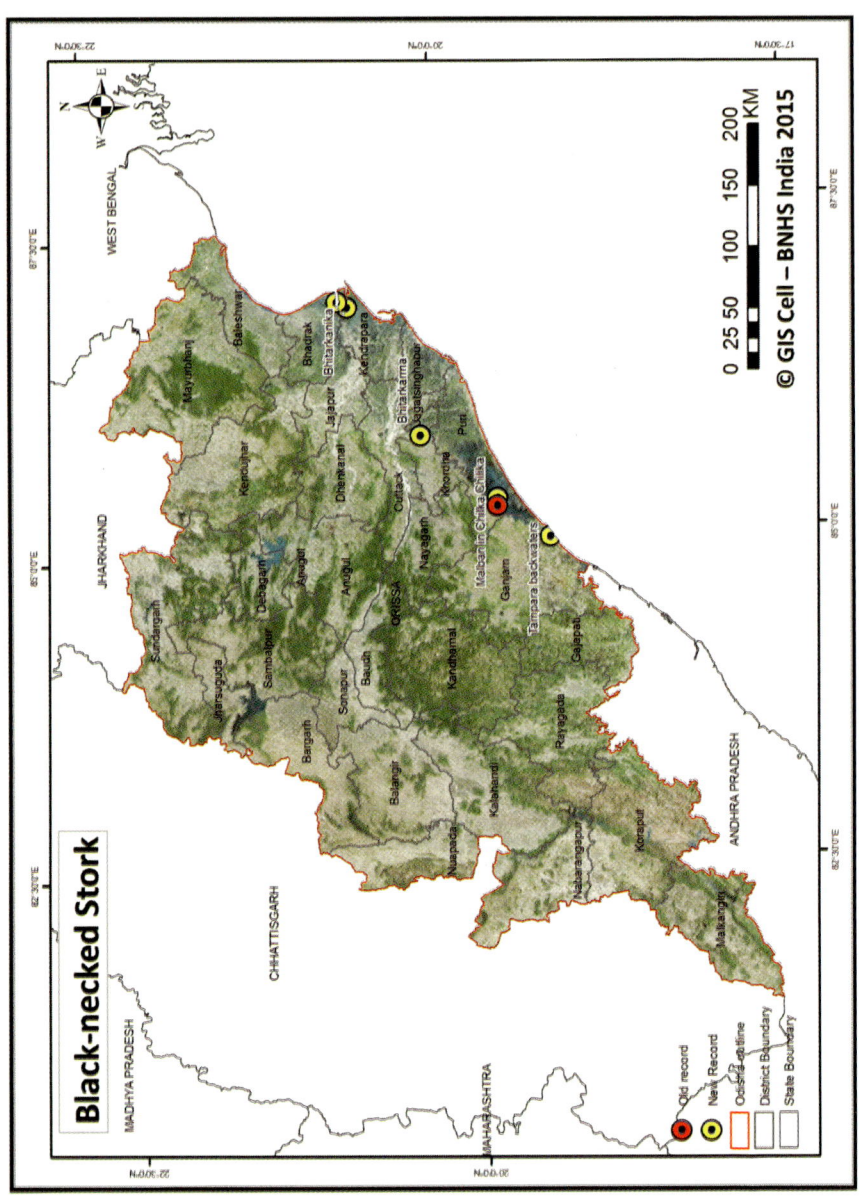

Black-necked Stork

Legend:
- Old record
- New Record
- Odisha outline
- District Boundary
- State Boundary

0 25 50 100 150 200 KM

© GIS Cell – BNHS India 2015

Threatened Birds of Odisha

is based on earlier records. However, it is still seen infrequently in **Bhitarkanika**. Though no confirmed breeding record exists from Odisha, observations of a male collecting nesting material (Pandav 1997) and presence of a juvenile (Gopi and Pandav 2007) indicate possible breeding in Bhitarkanika.

Ecology: Its ecology and breeding biology has been studied by Ishtiaq (1998), Maheswaran (1998) and Sundar (2003) in Uttar Pradesh. It is generally found in pairs, even outside the breeding season, and pairs maintain large feeding territories throughout the year. It has the characteristic stork habit of soaring and circling aloft in the heat of the day. It prefers large marshes and jheels, and margins of large rivers and brackish lagoons where it feeds on fish, frogs, snakes, small turtles, injured and unwary birds and any animal which it can swallow (Ishtiaq *et al.* 2010). The nest is built on large trees, mostly near water. If left undisturbed, the same tree is used year after year. Pairs spend considerable time on the nest, and mating also takes place there. The female lays two to four eggs, and both parents incubate and raise the chicks. Generally one to three chicks are raised, but in good habitats it is not uncommon to see four juveniles with parents in some years.

Threats: The main threats to the Black-necked Stork are destruction and degradation of its habitat and overfishing.

Conservation measures underway: It is listed in Schedule I of the Indian Wildlife (Protection) Act, 1972 and also included in CITES Appendix I. It occurs in a number of Protected Areas/IBAs.

RECOMMENDATIONS
1) Systematic surveys should be conducted periodically in the whole state.
2) Strict control on the use of harmful pesticides, particularly near wetlands.
3) Initiate an active advocacy programme to educate farmers on the importance of wetland birds and their protection.
4) Make Black-necked Stork an icon of healthy wetlands.

Black-headed Ibis *Threskiornis melanocephalus* (Latham 1790)

In India, the Black-headed Ibis is widespread and locally common in all the wetter parts of the country, less common in the east. Based on the assessment done by BirdLife International (2014), IUCN has listed the Black-headed Ibis in Near Threatened category as it is undergoing population decline in many countries due to hunting and disturbance at breeding colonies, and drainage of wetlands for agriculture.

Field Characters: A large, domestic hen-sized white bird, with black neck, naked black head, and long stout downcurved black bill. Legs and feet are also black. Adult breeding birds have white lower neck plumes, variable yellow wash to mantle and breast, and grey on scapulars and elongated tertials. Immature birds have white chin and neck, naked face, bare skin around the eyes, while the rest of the head and neck are feathered. Sexes are alike.

Distribution: The Black-headed Ibis, also called White Ibis, is widespread and is even extending its range in many parts of India (e.g., Thar Desert) due to the development of canal irrigation. It is resident, nomadic and local migratory, depending upon the availability of water. In Odisha, it is an uncommon resident and local migrant. It is a common winter visitor to **Nalabana** and other areas of Chilika. Other records are from **Satbhaya** wetlands, **(PPL) Paradeep Phosphates Limited wetlands**, **Mangalajodi** and **Hirakud Reservoir**.

Threatened Birds of Odisha

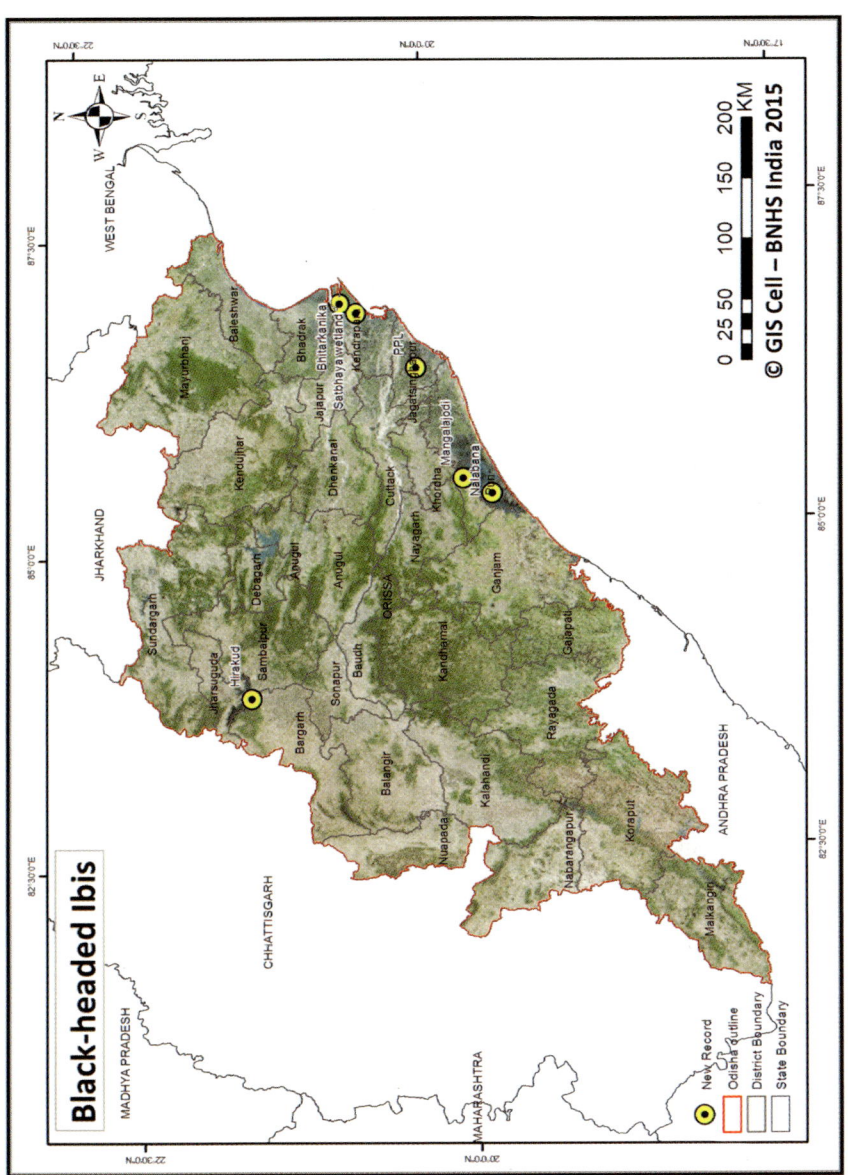

Black-headed Ibis

© GIS Cell – BNHS India 2015

New Record
Odisha outline
District Boundary
State Boundary

0 25 50 100 150 200 KM

They breed in Bagagahana heronry in **Bhitarkanika** where about 120–150 nests are found during August, and also in small numbers near Anthapalli–Karlajuri village near **Hirakud Reservoir** (Nair *et al*. 2014). They have a habit of congregating together with conspecifics to form sub-colonies within the overall heronry (Gopi and Pandav 2007).

Ecology: The Black-headed Ibis is found in all sorts of wet areas, from paddy fields, freshwater marshes, lakes, rivers, flooded grasslands to tidal creeks, mudflats, brackish marshes and coastal lagoons, from lowlands to 950 msl. It is gregarious, mixing easily with other waders such as storks, egrets, spoonbill and other small waders. It is never found far from water. It feeds almost entirely on animal matter, fish, frogs, aquatic insects, crustaceans and worms, the last two generally probed out from squelchy mud by its downcurved bill.

It nests colonially with other heronry species during the monsoon in partially submerged thorny trees to avoid ground predators. A platform nest is made where two to four eggs are laid. Incubation and chick-rearing are shared by both parents. Where unmolested, it nests on trees growing even in crowded villages, sometimes away from water, with other colonial nesters such as Painted Stork, Grey Pelican, and egrets.

Threats: It suffers from the threats common to all wild birds dependent on natural wetlands in South and Southeast Asia: drainage, disturbance, pollution, conversion of habitats to agriculture, hunting, and collection of eggs and nestlings from colonies. A combination of these factors has probably caused its decline in some countries.

Conservation measures underway: It is listed in Schedule IV of the Indian Wildlife (Protection) Act, 1972 so its hunting in India is totally prohibited. It is found in many Protected Areas/IBAs and also gets protection due to religious and traditional practices in many areas (e.g., temple tanks).

RECOMMENDATIONS

1) Strict enforcement of the law at the grassroots level to prevent trapping and poaching of this species, particularly during the breeding season.

2) Conduct surveys to identify and protect important breeding colonies.

3) Study the impact of pesticides on its food chain.

4) Conduct ringing, colour banding and satellite tracking studies to determine its movements.

Spot-billed Pelican *Pelecanus philippensis*
Gmelin 1789

VINAYAK YARDI

In 2001, BirdLife International had listed the Spot-billed Pelican as Vulnerable as it had declined at a moderately rapid rate owing to a number of threats. However, increased protection, mainly in India, has since enabled recovery in its numbers, and the status of the species was downlisted from Vulnerable to Near Threatened in 2007.

Field Characters: The Spot-billed Pelican, though it is the smallest pelican in India, is still a large bird (length *c.* 140–152 cm). It is mainly drab white with spotted bill and pouch, and dusky, curly feathers on hind crown and hind neck. The large bill is pinkish with spots, which appear only after a year. The full adult breeding plumage appears in the third year. In flight, primaries are dusky and secondaries dark from below. It is easily confused with the two other pelicans found in India: Dalmatian Pelican *P. crispus* is larger, and a brighter white with orange pouch and bushy, curly crest; the juvenile Great White Pelican *P. onocrotalus* is larger with darker head, neck and upperparts, paler lores and blackish flight feathers. At a distance, it is difficult to differentiate from other pelicans in the region although it is smaller, but at close range the spots on the upper mandible, the lack of bright colours and the greyer plumage are distinctive.

Distribution: The Spot-billed Pelican is a resident and local migrant in well-

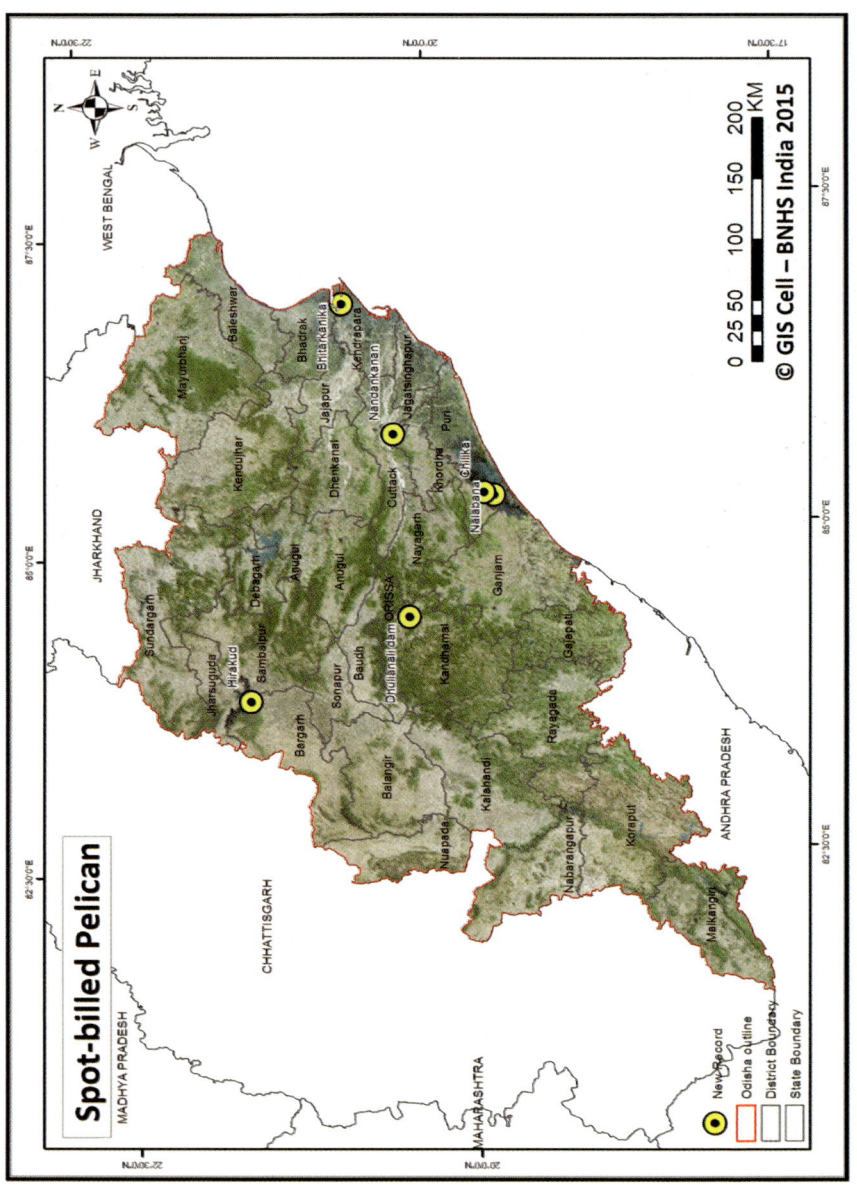

Spot-billed Pelican

Threatened Birds of Odisha

© GIS Cell – BNHS India 2015

watered tracts of South and Southeast Asia. In India, it mainly breeds in the south and scatter colonies are found in the Brahmaputra valley, but it can be seen in the non-breeding season in large wetlands in other parts.

This species is a local migrant to Odisha, primarily to **Chilika**. Dev (2013) states that it is a summer migrant to the lake after it breeds in Telineelapuram village in northern Andhra Pradesh, bordering Paralakhamundi in Odisha. In Chilika, its most favoured habitat is near **Nalabana**, where it is seen throughout the year except November in numbers ranging from 200 to 400; other spots in the lake where it is occasionally seen are Kansari, Kalapuraghat, Tinimuhani, Parikud, Palur Canal and Gurubai (Balachandran *et al.* 2009). Other specific records are from Kanjia lake in **Nandankanan** Sanctuary and **Hirakud Reservoir**. It is a monsoon migrant to **Bhitarkanika**, the maximum number sighted being 25 (Nayak 2003).

Ecology: The Spot-billed Pelican inhabits a variety of deep and shallow wetlands, both man-made and natural, freshwater and saline, open and forested. It forages and flies in small flocks and breeds colonially in tall trees. The nests are usually built alongside those of other colonial waterbirds, particularly egrets, cormorants, and Painted Stork. Its main food is fish, but it also catches frogs, aquatic snakes, and insects. Its breeding behaviour and ecology have been studied in great detail (Nagulu 1983, Manakadan & Kannan 2003).

Threats: In India, hunting is not the main threat as the species is protected by law and also by local sentiment. However, its wetland habitat is under tremendous human pressure, particularly from the fishing community. Fishing is intense in almost all wetlands. Drainage of natural wetlands for agriculture is another problem, which will be further aggravated by climate change in future.

Conservation measures underway: The Spot-billed Pelican is protected by Schedule IV of the Indian Wildlife (Protection) Act, 1972, and its hunting and shooting is strictly prohibited. Even disturbance to its nesting sites is prohibited under the law. Although it nests and forages in some Protected Areas/IBAs, most of the nesting colonies are protected by local community initiatives (Manu & Jolly 2000).

RECOMMENDATIONS
1) Conduct survey to know its status in the state.
2) Intensive patrolling of sites known to have poaching pressure; establishment of a rehabilitation programme for traditional hunting communities.
3) Ban on fishing practices and gear that are non-sustainable and destructive to fish populations.

Oriental Darter *Anhinga melanogaster*
Pennant 1769

Based on the assessment done by BirdLife International (2014), the IUCN places this species in the Near Threatened category because of a moderately rapid decline in its population in some countries owing to pollution, drainage, hunting, and collection of eggs and nestlings.

Field Characters: A sleek water bird, mainly black in adult stage like the cormorants but with longer, more slender snake-like neck, narrow head and long, straight, pointed bill. Tail is long, stiff and fan-shaped when spread. Head and neck are velvety chocolate-brown with white chin, throat and a narrow white line from below eye halfway down each side of the neck. Back and wings have longitudinal silvery-grey streaks. Legs and webbed feet are black, lower mandible flesh-coloured. Sexes are alike. Young ones have white down which persists on some parts till almost fledged. Immature birds are dark brown above, with paler neck and head, and below dark brown, almost black. Leg and feet are pale. The mantle is also dull, streaked with rufous and silvery grey.

Distribution: The Oriental Darter or Snakebird is widespread in suitable wetlands in South and Southeast Asia. In India it is found from coastal wetlands to about *c.* 300 m in the Himalaya. Its only requirement is clear, deep, unpolluted water with plenty of fish. It is also found in jheels with deep pools of 1–2 m, larger rivers and man-made reservoirs. Rahmani (2012) has recently given important site records of India.

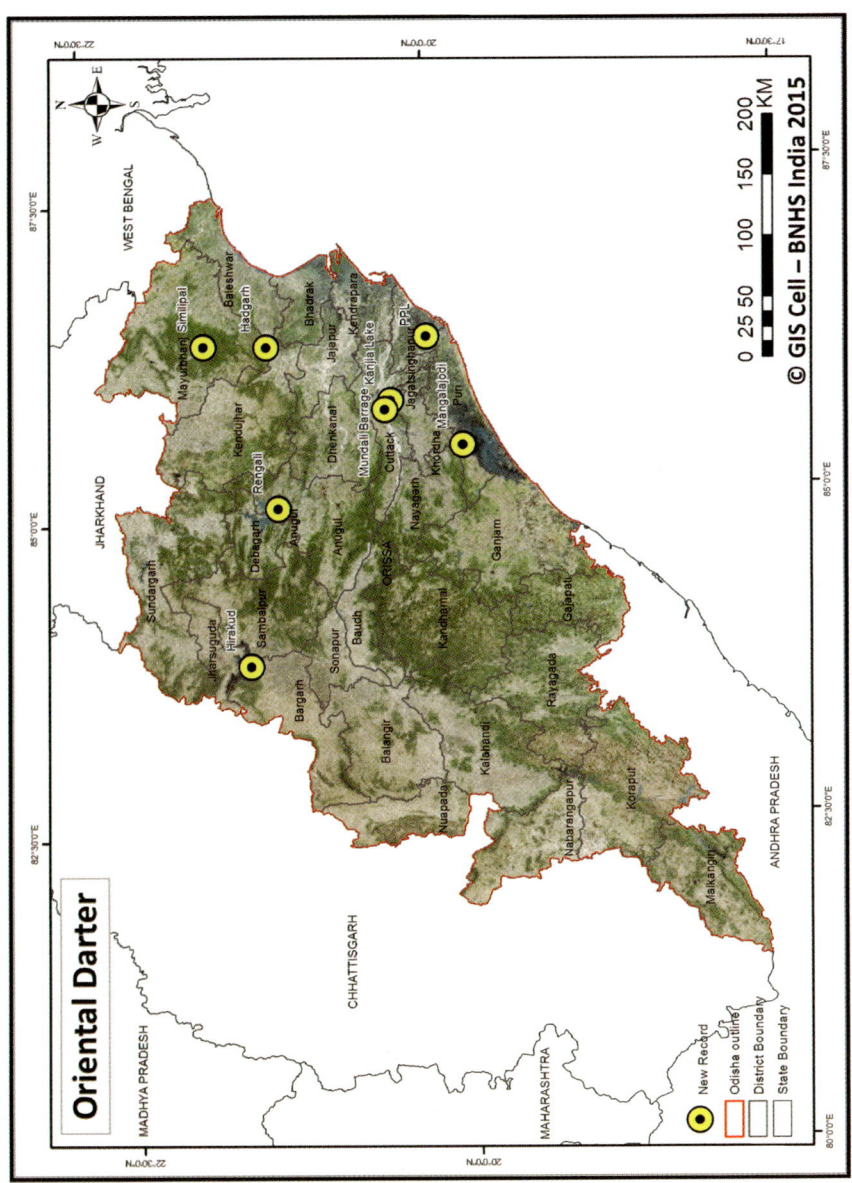

Oriental Darter

© GIS Cell – BNHS India 2015

0 25 50 100 150 200 KM

New Record
Odisha outline
District Boundary
State Boundary

Though widespread in Odisha, it is nowhere common. It has been recorded specifically from **Similipal, Kanjia Lake** in Nandankanan Sanctuary, **Mundali Barrage, Mangalajodi, (PPL) Paradeep Phosphates Limited wetlands, Hirakud Reservoir, Rengali Reservoir** and **Hadgarh Sanctuary**. It is an occasional local migrant to **Chilika**. Balachandran *et al.* (2009) recorded thrice, each from Mangalajodi, Kaluparaghat and Bhusandpur. The main breeding stronghold is the Bagagahana heronry in **Bhitarkanika**. While Pandav (1997) reported 192 nests during 1993-95, Gopi and Pandav (2007) reported 89 nests in August 2006 and opined that the number of breeding pairs have shown a slight decline over the years. Breeding has also been reported from **Similipal** Biosphere Reserve (Nayak and Naik 2014).

Ecology: It generally occurs singly or in small discrete groups, each one hunting fish independently. In good hunting grounds, up to 100 are seen, solitarily or in small groups. It is an expert diver and feeds almost exclusively on fish caught by its stiletto-shaped bill. It often swims with only the neck above water: the long neck and pointed bill give it the appearance of a snake, hence its popular name Snake Bird. It nests colonially with egrets, storks and herons on thorny trees, generally half-submerged or near water. It makes a platform nest, sometimes very close to other nests, and lays 3–6 eggs which become soiled as the incubation progresses. Chicks are blind and naked but soon develop white down feathers which may persist even when almost fledged.

Threats: Main threat to this and all piscivorous species is from excessive fishing all over its range. Pollution and spread of invasive species such as Water Hyacinth *Eichhornea crassipes* and *Ipomea carnea* are other problems.

Conservation measures underway: In India, it is listed in Schedule IV of the Wildlife (Protection) Act, 1972 and its hunting and disturbance are totally prohibited. Its trade is also banned. It occurs in a number of Protected Areas/IBAs.

RECOMMENDATIONS

(a) Proper survey to determine its actual status in the state.

(b) Study on its ecology and habitat requirements.

(c) Regular monitoring (every 2–3 years) of major nesting sites to know the population trend.

(d) Involvement of local people for protection of its nesting sites, and if necessary augmentation of fish resources in some village ponds to improve its breeding success.

(e) Strict prohibition on fishing with very small mesh-size nets (zero net fishing).

(f) Strong directive from the Forest Department and its flying squads to stop and nab poachers hunting birds in heronries.

Threatened Birds of Odisha

Great Thick-knee *Esacus recurvirostris*

BHASMANG MEHTA

BirdLife International (2014) has uplisted this species to Near Threatened on the basis that it is expected to undergo a moderately rapid population decline over the next three generations owing to human pressures on riverine ecosystems and the construction of dams. It has already undergone precipitous declines in Southeast Asia but its status currently appears more secure in India.

Field Character: It is a large terrestrial wader of 49 to 55 cm, overall pale and unstreaked with huge, slightly recurved bill (7 cm), with characteristic head marking and large eyes (lores white). Legs are page yellow. In flight large wings show black and white markings.

Distribution: Great Thick-knee is widespread in South Asia and Southeast Asia but nowhere common. It is found on gravel beds along rivers and sometimes large lakes and reservoirs. It is a shy bird, hence has disappeared from intensively used riversides. It is a rare resident in Odisha and has been reported from **Athagarh** and **Mundali** along the Mahanadi river, and the islands of the southern sector of **Chilika** Lake such as Samala, Honey Moon and Breakfast. The resident population possibly gets augmented by migrant birds from north India during winter. It is also encountered along undisturbed sea coasts such as **Gahirmatha** and **Konark**. Possible breeding sites are along the undisturbed sand and shingle

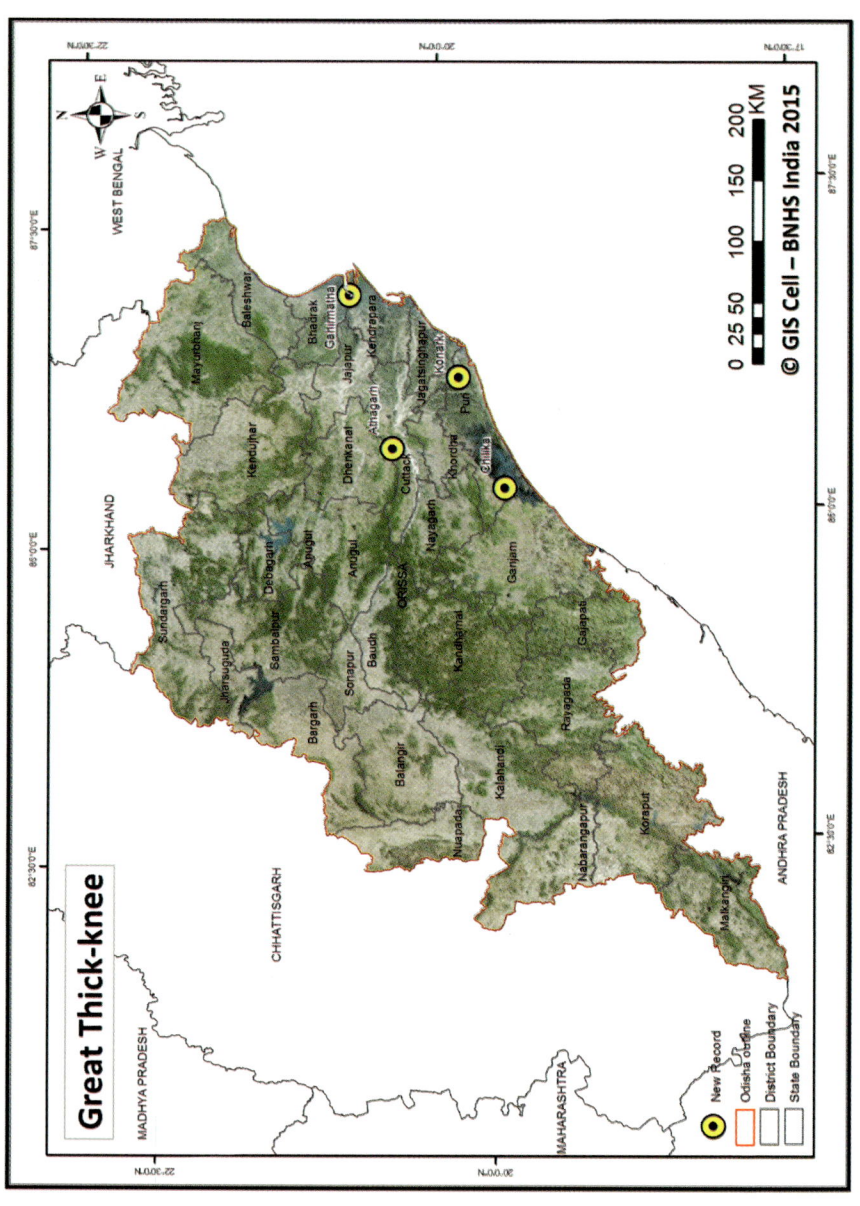

Great Thick-knee

Threatened Birds of Odisha

The barrage at Mundali over the River Mahanadi is a good habitat for the River Tern and Great Thick-knee

beaches along the lower course of **Mahanadi**, downstream of **Satkosia Gorge**, along **Athagarh** up till **Mundali**.

Ecology: It favours riverbed shingle and rocks, stony banks and mud around large lakes, but sometimes visits nearby grassy flats and also occurs infrequently on coastal beaches and estuaries. It is largely sedentary, but undergoes local movements forced by rising water levels (del Hoyo *et al.* 1996).

Threats: All waterbodies, rivers and lakes are intensively used by human beings in India. So this species faces all types of threats such as predation by domestic and free-ranging dogs, trampling of eggs and nestlings by livestock and sudden release of water from dams during the breeding season, drowning eggs and chicks.

Conservation actions: It is protected under the Indian Wildlife (Protection) Act, 1972. So its hunting and trade is banned.

RECOMMENDATIONS

(a) Survey throughout the state to know its status and major breeding areas.

(b) Quantify the severity and impact of threats across its range.

(c) Based on the results of studies, protect important breeding areas along the rivers.

River Lapwing *Vanellus duvaucelli*
(Lesson 1826)

MANOJ V. NAIR

In 2013, BirdLife International uplisted River Lapwing to Near Threatened as it is expected to undergo a moderately rapid population decline over the next three generations owing to human pressures on riverine ecosystems and the construction of dams.

Field Characters: The River Lapwing is 29–32 cm long. It has a black crest, crown, face, bill, centre of throat and legs, and grey-white neck sides and nape. The underparts are white with a black belly patch, and it has a grey-brown breast band. The back is brown, rump white and the tail black. In flight, the black primaries, white underwings and upperwing secondaries, and brown upperwing-coverts are conspicuous. The call of the River Lapwing is a sharp *did-did-do-weet*, reminiscent of the call of the Red-wattled Lapwing, yet distinctive.

Distribution: The River Lapwing is resident throughout the large river systems of north, northeast and central India, but rare in south. This riverine species is a widespread resident in the state in all large rivers with sand banks, especially the Mahanadi. Specific records are from **Salebhatta**, **Sambalpur**, **Hirakud**, **Boudh**, **Vedvyas**, **Satkosia Gorge**, **Mundali**, **Chilika** and **Chandaka**. Evidences of breeding have been obtained from Mundali and Satkosia.

Ecology: Normally keeps singly or in pairs. In general, the ecology is very similar to that of other lapwings. The coloration is remarkably obliterative in its

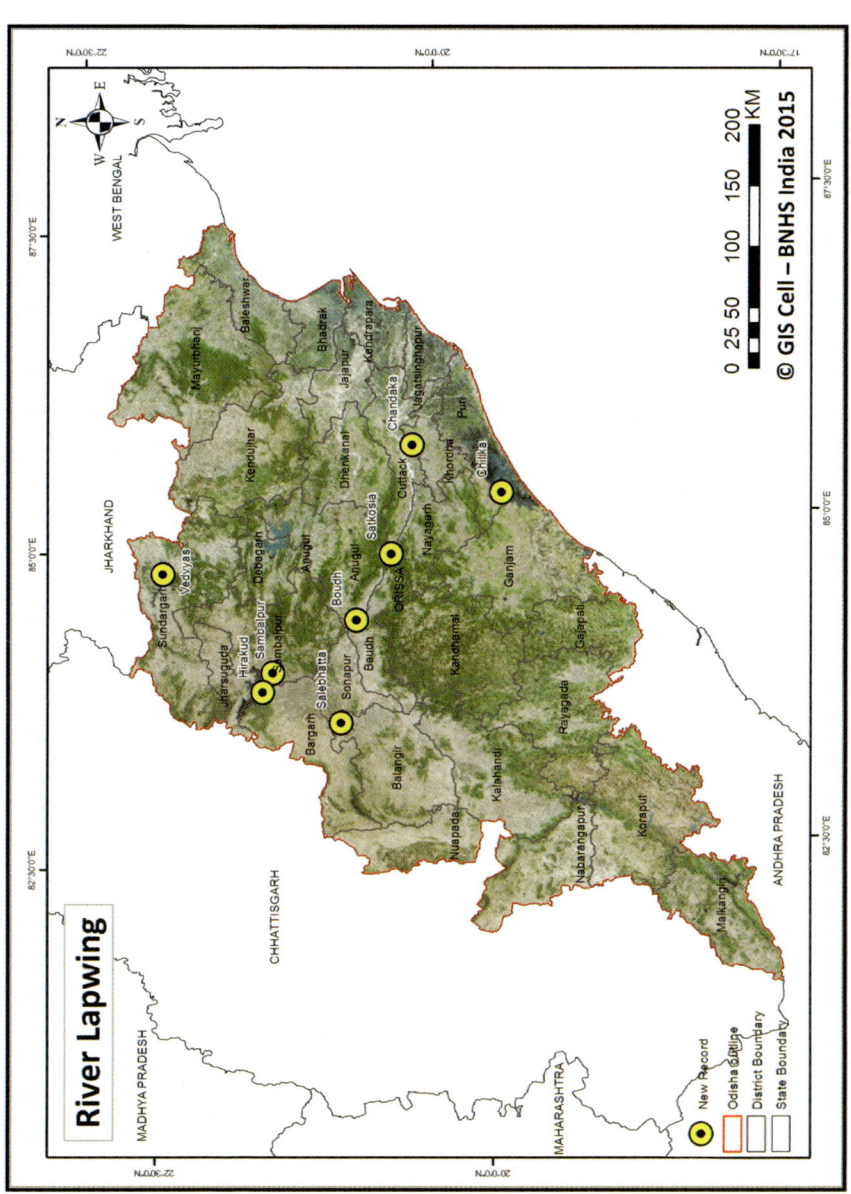

River Lapwing

© GIS Cell – BNHS India 2015

0 25 50 100 150 200 KM

New Record
Odisha Village
District Boundary
State Boundary

Undisturbed sandbanks such as these inside Satkosia Gorge Sanctuary provide ideal nesting habitat for the River Lapwing

habitat of dry river sand and shingle. It feeds on insects, worms, and crustaceans. It breeds from March to June; the nest is a shallow scrape on exposed sand or shingle. Generally four eggs are laid (Ali & Ripley 1987).

Threats: Disturbance to breeding birds by humans, dogs, cats and crows is the biggest danger to this and other species of large Indian rivers, as the ecology of the rivers is under great pressure. Construction of dams and reservoirs, sudden release of water, depletion and diversion of water exposing the nests to ground predators, increasing watermelon cultivation on sandy river islands and consequently constant human presence, all these pressures may be working against the species. These threats need to be quantified in its whole range of distribution and effective site-specific measures need to be taken. River Lapwing is occasionally seen in bird markets when it is caught in the clap-traps laid for other waterbirds. Organised collection of sand for commercial trade and associated transport is a disturbance in some pockets for breeding birds.

RECOMMENDATIONS

1) Proper baseline survey to know its status and distribution in the state.

2) Protection of small river islands and sand spits in larger rivers where this bird breeds.

3) Ringing and satellite tracking studies to monitor its movement and dispersal.

Eurasian Curlew *Numenius arquata*
(Linnaeus 1758)

BHASMANG MEHTA

BirdLife International (2014) considers it Near Threatened despite the fact that it remains common in many parts of its range. Its decline has been recorded in several key populations and overall a moderately rapid global decline is estimated.

Field Characters: A large (55–58 cm) pale sandy brown wader with long downcurved bill. It has mottled or scalloped brown plumage with whiter belly and undertail, and fine short black streaks on the underside. In flight it shows pointed whitish rump and barred tail as well as mottled whitish underwings. In flight, outer primaries are dark in contrast to whitish underwings. Flight is slow and gull-like. Sexes are alike. Juveniles are somewhat darker with finer black streaks on breast and very few on the abdomen.

Distribution: The Eurasian Curlew breeds across the northern hemisphere and winters around the coasts of northwest Europe, the Mediterranean, Africa, the Middle East, the Indian Subcontinent, Southeast Asia and East Asia. In India it is a winter migrant to the entire country, particularly coastal areas, but also on large jheels and rivers. It arrives by end August or early September and is generally gone by end April, but sometimes is seen up to May and June.

This large distinctive wader is a winter visitor to the coastal areas of the State. It is regularly seen in small numbers in **Chilika** in all zones of the lake and

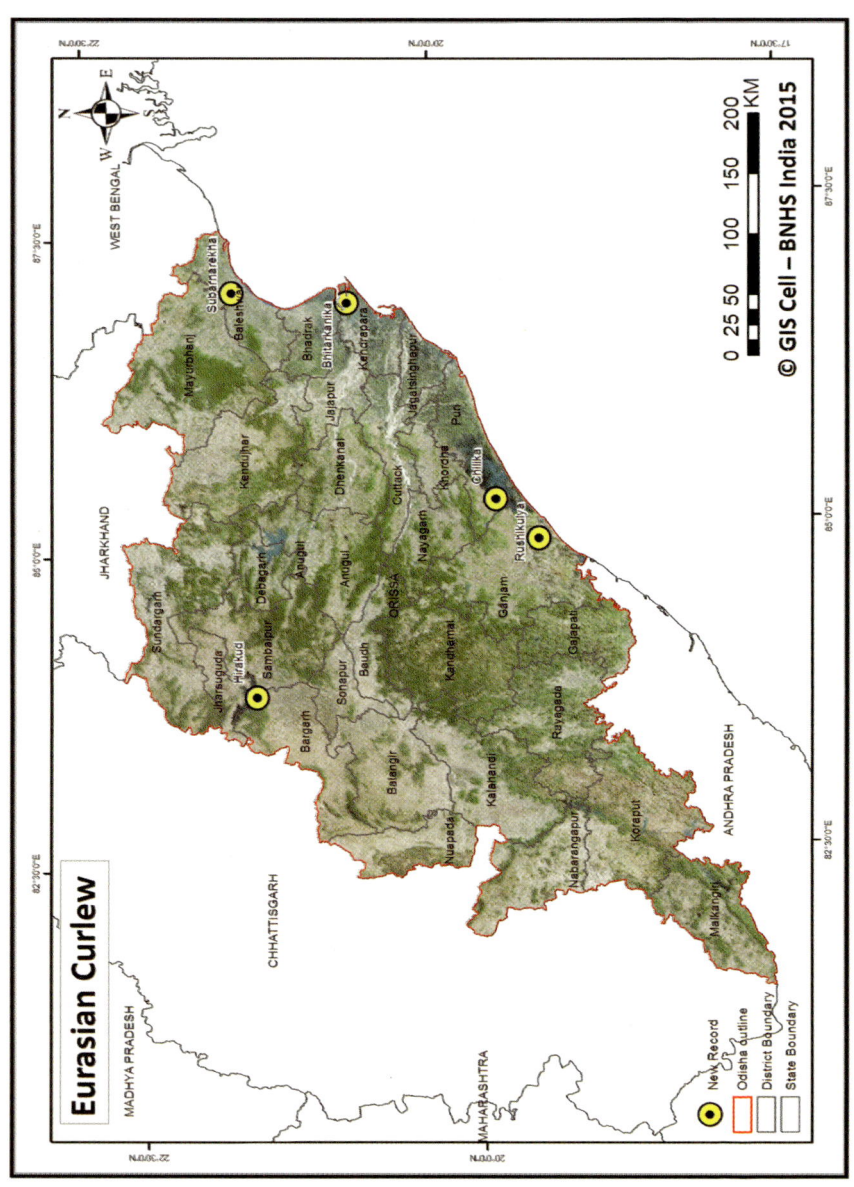

Eurasian Curlew

© GIS Cell – BNHS India 2015

Threatened Birds of Odisha

sometimes in hundreds in **Nalabana** and **Parikud**. A few individuals, probably non-breeding young birds, stay up to mid-May (Balachandran *et al.* 2009). Its other main wintering ground in the state is **Bhitarkanika** where it can be commonly sighted. Other specific records are from the **Rushikulya** river mouth, **Subarnarekha** river mouth and **Hirakud Reservoir**.

Ecology: The Eurasian Curlew is found singly or in small scattered flocks on coastal swamps, intertidal zones, beaches, edges of large rivers, jheels and reservoirs, often in the company of assorted waders and egrets. It feeds on annelid worms, aquatic insects and larvae, crustaceans, molluscs, spiders, berries and seeds. It is also found feeding in damp grassland, sometimes far away from the coast. Small fish, amphibians, young lizards, young birds and small rodents have been recorded in its diet (del Hoyo *et al.* 1996). Males are more likely to feed in inland grasslands than females. Some birds become territorial on wintering grounds, others feed gregariously (del Hoyo *et al.* 1996). The Eurasian Curlew does not breed in India, but in the temperate region it has been found breeding on upland moors, peat bogs, swampy or dry heaths, fens, open grassy or boggy areas in forests, damp grasslands, meadows, dune valleys and coastal marshlands (del Hoyo *et al.* 1996).

Threats: The main threat is conversion of wetlands in agricultural fields, pollution and trapping. Extensive trapping of all waders, including Eurasian Curlew, takes place in Bihar, Uttar Pradesh, Tamil Nadu, Andhra Pradesh, and certain parts of Gujarat (Ahmed 2002). The birds are sold directly to roadside hotels (*dhabas*) and sometimes brazenly advertised on the menu in some states!

Conservation measures underway: Like all waders, resident or migrant, it is protected under the Indian Wildlife (Protection) Act, 1972. It is listed in Schedule IV of the Act. This curlew occurs in many Protected Areas and IBAs in India, and throughout its range, features in several national monitoring schemes.

RECOMMENDATIONS

1) Protection of wetlands and periodic census to monitor its population.

2) Strict control on trapping and shooting.

3) Regular monitoring of Eurasian Curlew population through IBCN and AWC network.

Black-tailed Godwit *Limosa limosa*
(Linnaeus 1758)

Although Black-tailed Godwit is widespread and has a large global population, its numbers have declined rapidly in parts of its range owing to changes in agricultural practices. In 2006, BirdLife International (2014) classified this species as Near Threatened due to an estimated decline in the numbers of around 25% during the preceding 15 years.

Field Characters: One of the large waders (40–44 cm) found in India, with a distinctive long bill on a relatively small head, long neck, and long legs. In winter, the colour of its forebody is a pale grey-brown, which becomes a dull pink-chestnut by March-end or April when the birds migrate to their breeding areas. In flight it has a striking white wingbar and rump, and black tail. The female is *c*. 5% larger than the male. The difference between the two subspecies (or species according to Rasmussen & Anderton 2012) is in size, *Limosa l. melanuroides* (Eastern Black-tailed Godwit) is slightly smaller, darker, and has a shorter bill than *Limosa l. limosa* (Western Black-tailed Godwit). For finer differentiation in field characters of the two races, see Rasmussen & Anderton (2012).

Distribution: The Black-tailed Godwit is a fairly common winter migrant to the entire subcontinent. Outside India, it has a large discontinuous breeding range extending from Iceland to the Russian Far East, with wintering populations in Europe, Africa, the Middle East, and Australasia (del Hoyo *et al*. 1996, BirdLife International 2001).

Threatened Birds of Odisha

Although BirdLife International (2014) considers Black-tailed Godwit *Limosa limosa* as Near Threatened based on global assessment, in India, particularly in Odisha, it is very common in winter with enormous flocks seen in Mangalajodi area

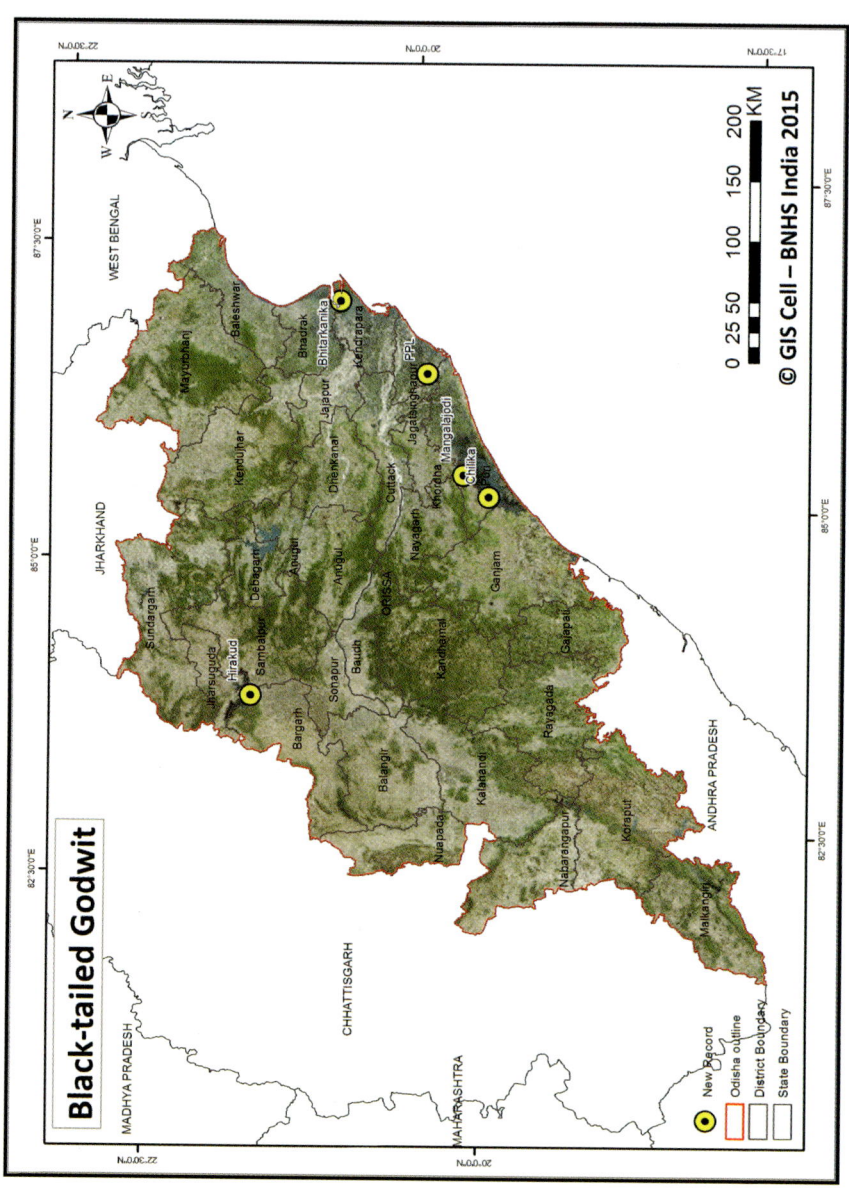

Black-tailed Godwit

© GIS Cell – BNHS India 2015

0 25 50 100 150 200 KM

New Record
Odisha outline
District Boundary
State Boundary

Threatened Birds of Odisha

A regular winter visitor to Odisha, its stronghold in the State is the **Chilika lake** and its adjoining wetlands. The most favoured site is the marshlands at **Mangalajodi** where several thousand can be seen in winter. Over-summering of few individuals in breeding plumage has also been observed. Also frequents paddyfields adjacent to Mangalajodi, Parikud and Satapada during harvesting season. Balachandran *et al.* (2009) report both the subspecies viz. *L.l.melanuroides* and *L.l.limosa* in Chilika, and opine that the former is more common. It is also reported from (**PPL) Paradeep Phosphates Limited wetlands**, **Hirakud Reservoir** and **Bhitarkanika**.

Ecology: It is a winter migrant in India, with the first birds arriving by the last week of August or early September, and becoming well dispersed all over India by late November and December. The majority depart, some in full breeding plumage, by end April, but some linger on till May and even June. Very gregarious, sometimes seen in tens of thousands (e.g., in Chilika) foraging on soft mud and ooze for small invertebrates. It is sometimes seen solitarily or in small parties of 5–10 individuals on roadside puddles or village ponds. It feeds on tiny molluscs, crustaceans, worms, and seeds of grass and marsh plants. It is very silent in winter, except for a low trisyllabic *wit-wit-wit* or *quick-quick-quick* uttered when taking off from the ground (Ali & Ripley 1987). During the breeding season, it gives high-pitched, nasal, rather strident calls, most common of which is a *weeka-weeka-weeka* (BirdLife International 2014).

Threats: In the breeding areas, loss of nesting habitat owing to wetland drainage and agricultural intensification, hunting (France) and poaching are the major threats (BirdLife International 2014). In its winter quarters, the same factors operate to a different degree. Trapping of waders, including Black-tailed Godwit is a huge problem in certain parts of India. Drainage of wetlands, afforestation of shallow wetlands and mudflats, poaching and pollution are the major threats. Climate change is likely to play a major role in further decline of this species.

Conservation measures underway: Like all waders, it is protected under the Indian Wildlife (Protection) Act, 1972. It is listed in Schedule IV of the Act. It occurs in large number of IBAs/Protected Areas.

RECOMMENDATIONS

1) Impose strict ban on trapping and shooting of all waders in areas where large numbers of godwits are reported during winter.
2) Develop policies to protect wetlands, estuaries, and mudflats by promulgating a Wetland (Conservation) Act.
3) Develop a Bird Monitoring Scheme involving forest officials, NGOs, universities and members of civil society to create awareness about the status of Black-tailed Godwit.
4) Prevent afforestation of wetlands, mudflats and swamps which are the wintering grounds of the Black-tailed Godwit and numerous other waders.

Asian Dowitcher *Limnodromus semipalmatus*
(Blyth, 1848)

SMITH SUTIBUT

BirdLife International (2014) considers this species as Near Threatened because, although it is quite widespread, it has a moderately small population overall and this is thought to be in decline, owing primarily to destruction of its wintering grounds. An even more rapid population decline may take place in the future owing to climate change.

Field Characters: It is a comparatively large stocky wader with long black legs, long blackish bill with a thick base and blunt tip, dark bars on flanks and on white rump, and unmarked central belly. In winter, when we see this bird in India, it is largely grey with broad dark streaks above and pointed, uniformly dusky tertials with narrow pale edges, and whitish below with heavy streaks on head and neck and fine stipples and streaks on throat and breast. Sexes are alike. In the breeding season, this drab looking male transforms into a conspicuous bird with head, neck, breast and belly becoming a bright rufous, and upper parts get black-and-rufous streaks. Breeding female is somewhat duller than the male (Rasmussen & Anderton 2005).

It closely resembles the Bar-tailed Godwit *Limosa lapponica*, but it has a straight, all-black bill, contra slightly upcurved, reddish bill with black tip. It also has a distinctive "sewing machine" feeding action and the yelping call is also different from the more widespread Bar-tailed Godwit.

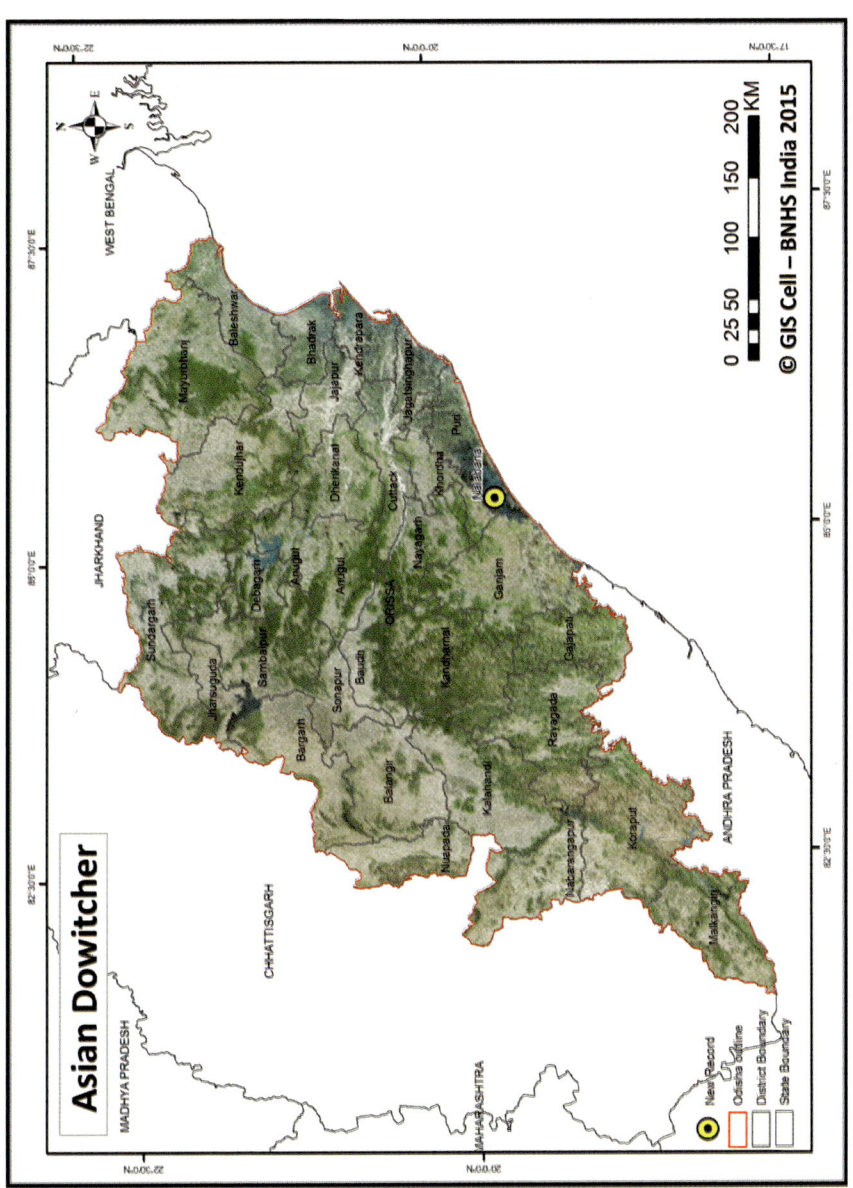

Asian Dowitcher

Distribution: In India, the Asian Dowitcher is fully migratory, seen from November to March, mainly on the east coast (West Bengal, Orissa, Andhra and Tamil Nadu). During an eight-year study by S. Balachandran and his team of the BNHS in **Chilika Lake**, 11 birds were ringed in the 2003–04 winter season (Balachandran *et al*. 2009). It was recorded only at **Nalabana** Sanctuary area of **Chilika Lake**. There is no other recent report.

Ecology: It mainly eats insect larvae, molluscs, crustaceans and polychaetes, and some plant material. It is gregarious and is seen with flocks of single species or mixed species of up to few thousand birds (e.g. Mangalajodi). On migration, the Asian Dowitchers move in small flocks and keep in close groups when on the ground (Johnsgard 1981).

Threats: According to BirdLife International (2014), the Asian Dowitcher may be particularly vulnerable to habitat loss, hunting, pollution and other pressures on both the breeding and wintering grounds, and also to the effects of climate change on its breeding grounds.

Conservation measures underway: Like all wild birds in India, it is protected under the Wildlife Protection Act, 1972. It is listed in Schedule IV of the Act. It is also listed in CMS Appendix II.

RECOMMENDATIONS

(a) Regularly monitor the population at important sites on both the breeding and wintering grounds.

(b) Its status should be monitored in Chilika Lake where perhaps the largest wintering population of India may be present.

(c) A study on the wintering ecology and distribution should be started in India.

(d) Banding and satellite tracking studies should be started to know its migratory pattern and important wintering areas.

(e) The mudflats of the state should be protected

River Tern *Sterna aurantia*
Gray 1831

BHASMANG MEHTA

The River Tern has been uplisted to Near Threatened category because increasing human disturbance and dam construction projects are expected to drive a moderately rapid decline in its population over the next three generations (BirdLife International 2014).

Field Characters: This is a medium-sized tern, 38–43 cm long, with dark grey upperparts, white underparts, a forked tail with long flexible streamers and long pointed wings. The bill is yellowish with black tip, the legs red, and it has a black cap in breeding plumage. Sexes are similar, but juveniles have a brown head, brown-marked grey upperparts, grey breast sides and white underparts.

Distribution: The River Tern is a common widespread resident in most of north and peninsular India. It breeds in summer on small islands formed in the backwaters of wetlands by the drying up of these water bodies.

It is a widespread resident in the state, but is common only in a few localities. **Chilika** Lake is its main stronghold, where it is found in all sectors. **Nalabana Island** is one of the largest known breeding colonies of this species throughout its global range. A record number of 540 nests were located in 2003 by the BNHS team (Balachandran *et al.* 2009). Other specific records are from **Satkosia Gorge**, **Hirakud Reservoir**, **PPL Paradeep Phosphates Limited wetlands**, **Ansupa Lake**, **Naraj**, **Mundali** and **Mangalajodi**.

It has been recorded laying eggs on rocky surfaces along the **Budhabalanga**, **Khairi** and **Deo** rivers in Mayurbhanj (Nayak and Naik 2014). Breeding is seen

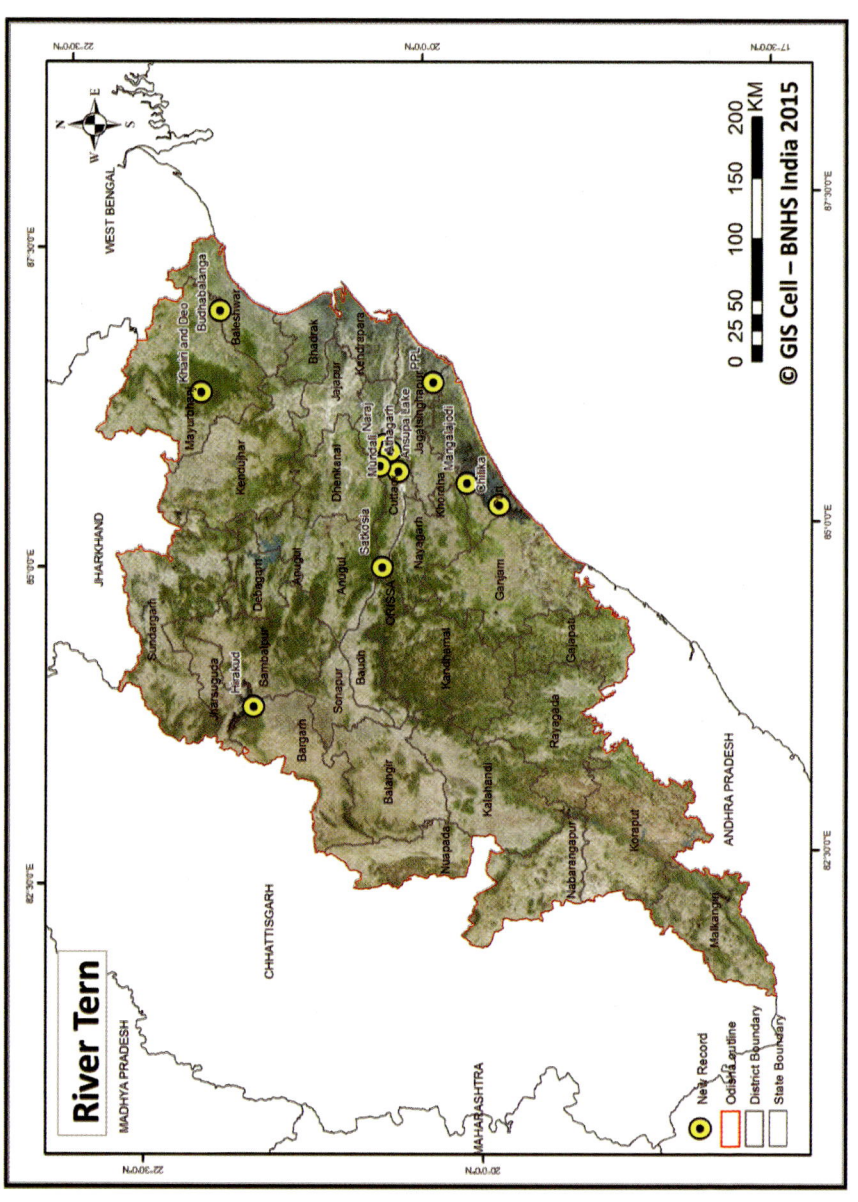

River Tern

Threatened Birds of Odisha

© GIS Cell – BNHS India 2015

Chilika Lake is one of the breeding strongholds of River Tern

downstream of Satkosia Gorge. Possibly also breeds in isolated islands along the Mahanadi in **Athagarh**, **Mundali** and also in the islands in **Hirakud** Reservoir.

Ecology: This species inhabits rivers and freshwater lakes, also occurring sometime on estuaries. It feeds predominantly on insects and small fish. It breeds from early March to early May and breeding occurs mainly in colonies in less accessible areas such as islands and sandbanks in rivers (del Hoyo *et al*. 1996). It nests in a scrape on the ground, often on bare rock or sand, and lays three greenish grey to buff eggs, which are blotched and streaked with brown.

Threats: Nesting areas are vulnerable to flooding, predation, and other disturbances (del Hoyo *et al*. 1996). The multitude of dam construction projects completed, underway, or planned may also threaten the species through changes in the flow regime and flooding of nest sites.

RECOMMENDATIONS

(a) As Odisha is very important for the survival of this species, a thorough survey of all the rivers of thes state should be conducted by the Forest Departments, ornithologists and NGOs.

(b) Based on the survey results, important nesting colonies should be given protection, particularly during the breeding season for theft of eggs, trampling by livestock and predation by free-ranging dogs.

(c) A long-term monitoring programme should be started in the State by the Forest Department with the help of conservation NGOs.

(d) Detailed ecological and behavioural studies may be conducted in Nalabana Island using modern technique of telemetry.

Cinereous Vulture *Aegypius monachus*
(Linnaeus 1766)

BHASMANG MEHTA

The Cinereous Vulture has a moderately small population which appears to be suffering an ongoing decline in its Asiatic strongholds, despite the fact that in parts of Europe its numbers are now increasing. Consequently, it qualifies as Near Threatened (BirdLife International 2014).

Field Characters: A huge, mostly black or dark-brown vulture between 98 and 107 cm, with broad wings and short, often slightly wedge-shaped tail. Adult is dark brown while juveniles are blackish, with dark crown, ruff and upper breast, contrasting with the paler adult. An almost naked head, with massive bill and crown, lores, and cheeks covered with black fur-like feathers and down. Sexes are alike but the female is larger (2–4%) and heavier (*c*. 7%) than the male. The Cinereous Vulture is one of the largest vultures found in India. In its wide distribution range, size increases from west to east, with the Mongolian and Chinese birds larger than the European birds (Ferguson-Lees & Christie 2001).

It has the typical unfeathered bald vulture head (actually covered in fine down) and dark markings around the eye, giving it a menacing skull-like appearance. The beak is brown, with a blue-grey cere, while legs and feet are grey.

Distribution: The Cinereous Vulture has a large range from southern Europe, North Morocco, Algeria, Sudan, the Middle East, Central Asia to Mongolia and east China. It has a small reintroduced population in France. It is resident except

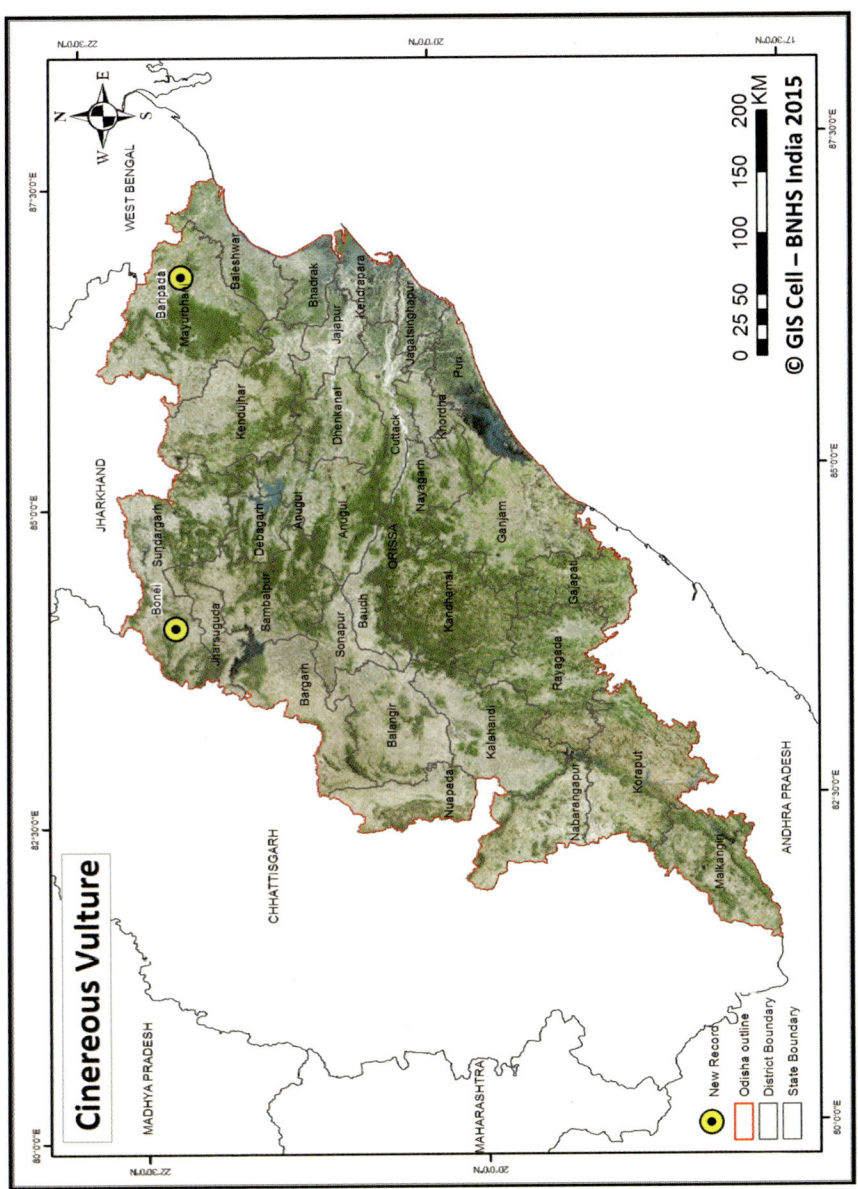

Cinereous Vulture

in those parts of its range where hard winters cause limited movement. In India, it is a winter visitor, mainly in the Thar Desert and other dry biotopes but occasional birds, particularly juveniles, are found in other parts of India.

In Odisha, this huge vulture is possibly a vagrant. There are two records from the state, both being rescued birds. The first was from Bhalupani village of **Bonei**, Sundergarh district in 2008 (Mishra *et al.* 2008; Nath *et al.* 2011). The second, more recent one is that of a juvenile individual from Kaliasole beat in Deuli Range of **Baripada** Forest Division on December 17, 2014 (Naik 2015). Both these birds still survive in a large aviary in Nandankanan Zoological Park.

Ecology: In India, Cinereous Vulture is seen singly or in twos or threes in dry biotopes and open countryside. In its breeding areas, it is found in forested hills, as also alpine grasslands and steppes. It feeds mainly on large mammal carcasses. It dominates the jostling rabble of other vultures at carcasses, and can be quite aggressive. It is equipped to tear open tough carcass skins using its powerful bill.

Threats: BirdLife International (2014) has listed two major threats to the Cinereous Vulture: direct mortality caused by humans (either accidentally or deliberately) and decreasing availability of food. Due to its large size and longevity, it is also caught for zoos (Roberts 1991) and in China it is trapped or shot for feathers. In India, hunting is probably not a threat as this bird is left alone, and lack of food is also not a problem, particularly in the arid Thar Desert where the bulk of winter birds are found. However, diclofenac poisoning through livestock carcasses could be a major threat, though it is still not confirmed for this species.

Conservation measures underway: It is protected under the Indian Wildlife (Protection) Act, 1972. It is listed in Schedule IV of the Act.

RECOMMENDATIONS

1) In India, mostly juvenile birds are recorded wintering. Juveniles of the species are known to wander long distances. Every winter a number of starving and dehydrated individuals are rescued. The birds recover within a few days if food and water is provided. There is a need to create awareness about the species, and people should be encouraged to send sick and injured birds to rescue centres. A lot of juveniles could be saved by providing water and care for a few days.

2) Thorough post-mortem examination should be carried out on any dead bird found and the tissue should be checked for the presence of diclofenac.

3) Regular surveys should be carried out throughout its known wintering range to determine its wintering population trends.

Pallid Harrier *Circus macrourus*
(Gmelin 1770)

YOGENDRA SHAH

Based on the steep population decline in Europe, BirdLife International (2014) has placed Pallid Harrier in the Near Threatened category of IUCN.

Field Characters: A slender, lightly built, small (46–51 cm) grey and white harrier of grasslands, savannahs and crop fields. Adult male almost white below, and has white wings with black wing tips. While sitting, the folded wings just reach the tail tip. Interestingly, its tail is not as long as other closely related harriers. Immature male may have rusty breast-band and juvenile facial markings. Female is umber brown, with distinctive underwing pattern. For details of sex and age-related plumages, see Naoroji (2007).

Distribution: The Pallid or Pale Harrier breeds in eastern Europe, southern Russia and Central Asia (including Turkey). In winter, it is found in the Indian subcontinent, the Middle East, eastern China, and mainly sub-Saharan Africa. It starts arriving in India by late August (mainly on passage through the Himalaya) and spreads out in the Subcontinent by October. In Odisha, it is a rare winter visitor. Scattered records exist from the dry grassy patches adjoining cultivated lands of **Mangalajodi**, near **Sohela**, near **Deongarh** WLS and **Similipal** Tiger Reserve.

Ecology: In winter, it is found in open countryside, singly or in small groups, systematically skirting the ground for prey (largely small birds). It is

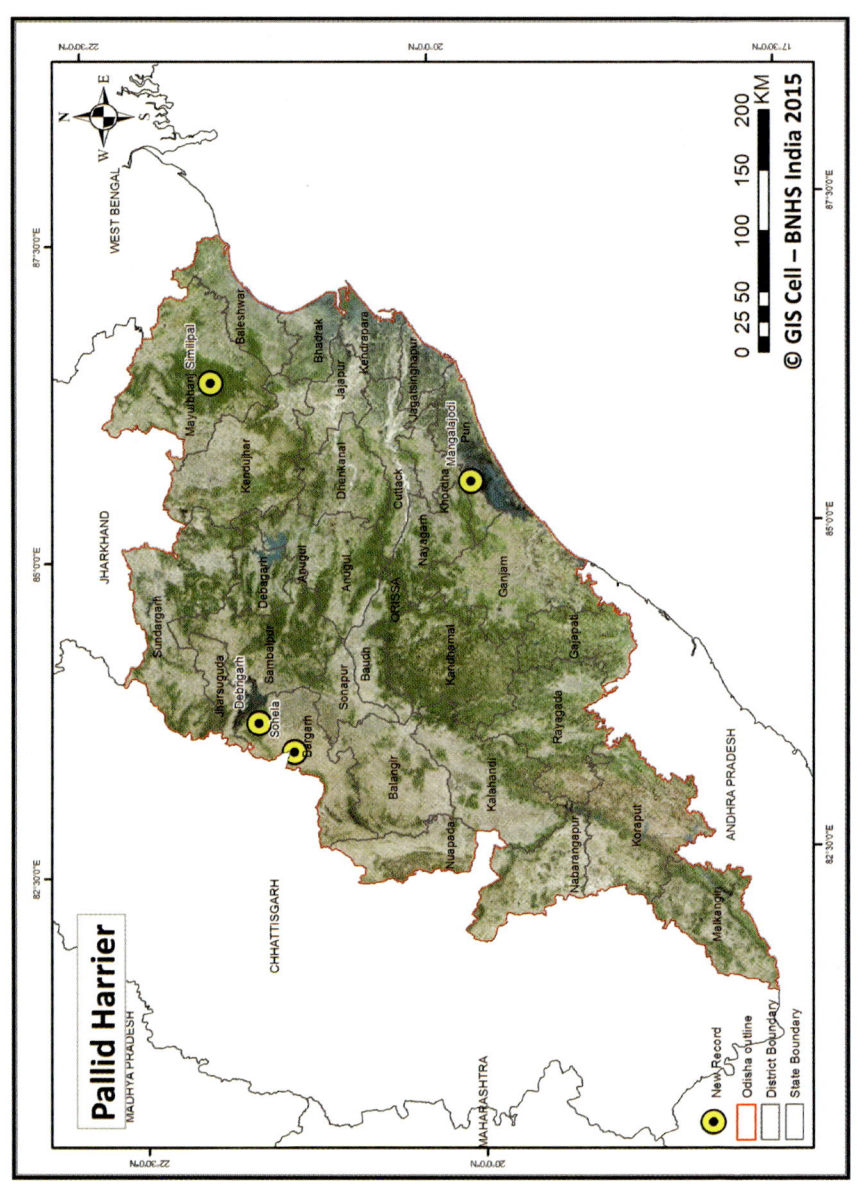

Pallid Harrier

Threatened Birds of Odisha

usually silent in winter, but occasionally heard calling *keck-keck-keck-keck* at dusk, before finally settling to roost (Naoroji 2007). It roosts on the ground with other harriers. It does not breed in India but in its breeding areas in the temperate regions, it prefers wet grasslands close to small rivers and lakes, marshlands, semi-desert, steppe and forested steppe, and sometimes even in boreal forest and forested tundra zones, from sea level to 1,200 msl. Clutch size is four or five, and incubation lasts up to 30 days. The female alone incubates, with the male bringing food to her during incubation and early brooding.

Threats: The main threat to Pallid Harrier in the breeding areas is the destruction and degradation of grasslands through conversion of arable land to agriculture, burning of vegetation, intensive grazing of wet pastures, and clearance of shrubs and tall weeds. Destruction of grasslands and extensive use of pesticides and rodenticides are the major threats in its wintering grounds. Like other harriers, it is vulnerable to the effect of pesticides building up in prey.

Conservation measures underway: Like all raptors, it is protected under the Indian Wildlife (Protection) Act, 1972. It is listed in Schedule I of the Act. Its hunting and trapping are strictly prohibited. It is listed in Appendix II of CITES, Annexure II of the Bonn and Berne Conventions and in Annexure I of the EU Birds Directive.

RECOMMENDATIONS

As it is marginal to Odisha, our first priority would be to conduct a proper survey to find out its exact status in the state. These surveys should also result in identification of important grasslands where this bird winters. A telemetry-based study would also give good scientific results on its habitat use.

Grey-headed Fish-eagle *Ichthyophaga ichthyaetus* (Horsfield 1821)

ASAD R. RAHMANI

BirdLife International (2014) considers it Near Threatened as this species is thought to be undergoing a moderately rapid population reduction owing to habitat degradation, pollution and overfishing.

Field Characters: A medium-sized raptor *c.* 69 to 74 cm, with grey head, neck, nape and breast merging with the paler brown of the mid-belly. Abdomen, flanks and tail are white. Upperparts are brown, darker on the wings, turning to blackish on the quill tips. Terminal tail band is dark brown, and particularly visible in flight. Sexes are alike. Juvenile is streaked overall, except on belly and vent, with white underwings and lightly barred flight feathers and tail.

Distribution: The Grey-headed Fish-eagle has a discontinuous distribution in South and Southeast Asia, perhaps due to its specialised habitat requirement of comparatively sluggish rivers and streams flowing through undisturbed forests. It is a resident in the north and northeast Indian plains, the Narmada river system, and the Western Ghats. A small population survives in the Gir forests of Gujarat.

In Odisha this species is probably a rare resident, though no photographic record has ever been obtained. The only site where it has been recorded is Similipal Tiger Reserve, where it was first reported by Dev (1986). The second author (MVN) during his stint in **Similipal** between 2006 and 2009 did not have a confirmed sighting of this bird there despite actively searching in likely habitats. However, Nayak and Naik (2014) state that in Similipal 'individuals can be seen very frequently along the West Deo river in Barhakamuda Range especially near Patbil and Kandadhanu. Also a good population breeds in the Pithabata Range

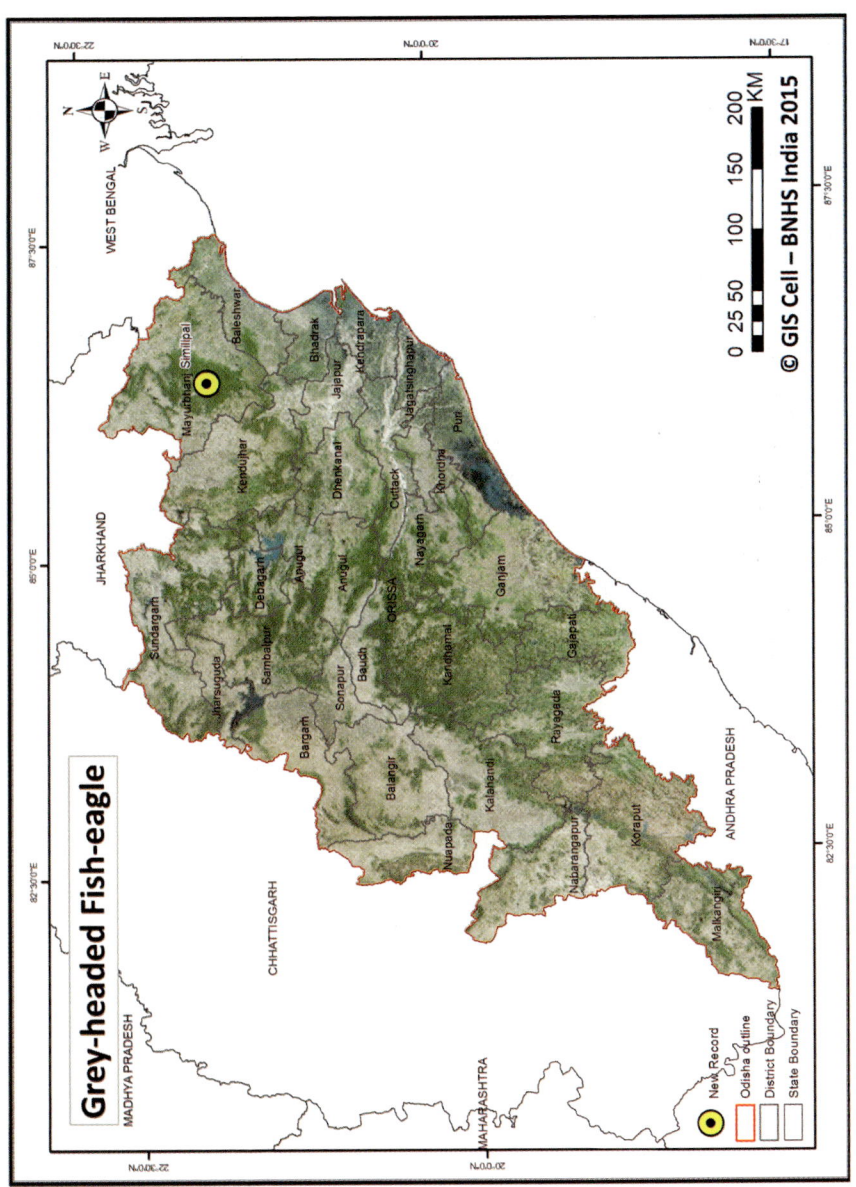

Grey-headed Fish-eagle

Legend:
- New Record
- Odisha outline
- District Boundary
- State Boundary

© GIS Cell – BNHS India 2015

0 25 50 100 150 200 KM

Grey-headed Fish-eagle prefers slow meandering forest rivers from which it can catch fish. Many such rivers are over-fished, polluted or dammed

along Palpala river. Except for these records, there are no recent sightings by any birdwatcher in the state.

Ecology: The Grey-headed Fish-eagle is found near slow-moving rivers and streams, lakes, reservoirs, and tidal lagoons in wooded country, usually in lowlands but ascending locally to 1,525 m (BirdLife International 2014). It feeds exclusively on fish, sometimes very large ones, but during the breeding season it pursues birds and small mammals also. It also consumes dead fish (del Hoyo *et al*. 1994). It is highly territorial and makes a large nest with sticks on a tall tree. It breeds during winter from November to January in north India but even up to April in southern India. Studies on sharing of nest duties, nest-building and incubation period are yet to be undertaken (Naoroji 2007).

Threats: The most pertinent threats are the loss of undisturbed wetlands, overfishing, siltation, pollution, and general persecution. All the threats that apply to Indian wetland birds (drainage, pollution, overfishing, disturbance) affect this species also.

Conservation measures underway: Like all birds of prey, the Grey-headed Fish-eagle is listed in Schedule I of the Indian Wildlife (Protection) Act.

RECOMMENDATIONS

As it is marginal to Odisha with very few records the first step is to survey the forested streams to locate this species.

Red-headed Falcon *Falco chicquera*

CLEMENT FRANCIS

According BirdLife International (2014) Red-headed Falcon is suspected to be undergoing a moderately rapid population decline over three generations owing to the effects of ongoing habitat degradation. It is therefore classified as Near Threatened.

Field Character: It is a small falcon, varying from 30 cm to 36 cm, with a characteristic chestnut crown and neck, white throat, and plain, pale blue-grey upper side and tail with a black sub terminal band and white tip. Underparts are white with fine black barring.

Distribution: Red-headed Falcon, earlier known as Red-headed Merlin, is widespread but nowhere common in India, Pakistan, Nepal and parts of Bangladesh. It is vagrant in Sri Lanka. The African race *ruficollis* is sometimes considered as a different species (Rasmussen and Anderton 2012). In Odisha, it is possibly a rare winter migrant, though resident populations could possibly exist in parts of western Odisha. Recent records are from **Bhitarkanika**, **Parikud**, **Chilika**, **Dhauli**, outskirts of **Bhubaneswar**, **Ansupa Lake**, **Debrigarh** Wildlife Sanctuary and **Sunabeda**.

Ecology: It is a falcon found in open countryside, grasslands, and outside villages and small towns where it feeds on small birds. Pairs can be seen hunting in the morning and sometimes very late evening. It nests on tall trees, often on old abandoned nests of House Crow. Nesting period is long from January to May.

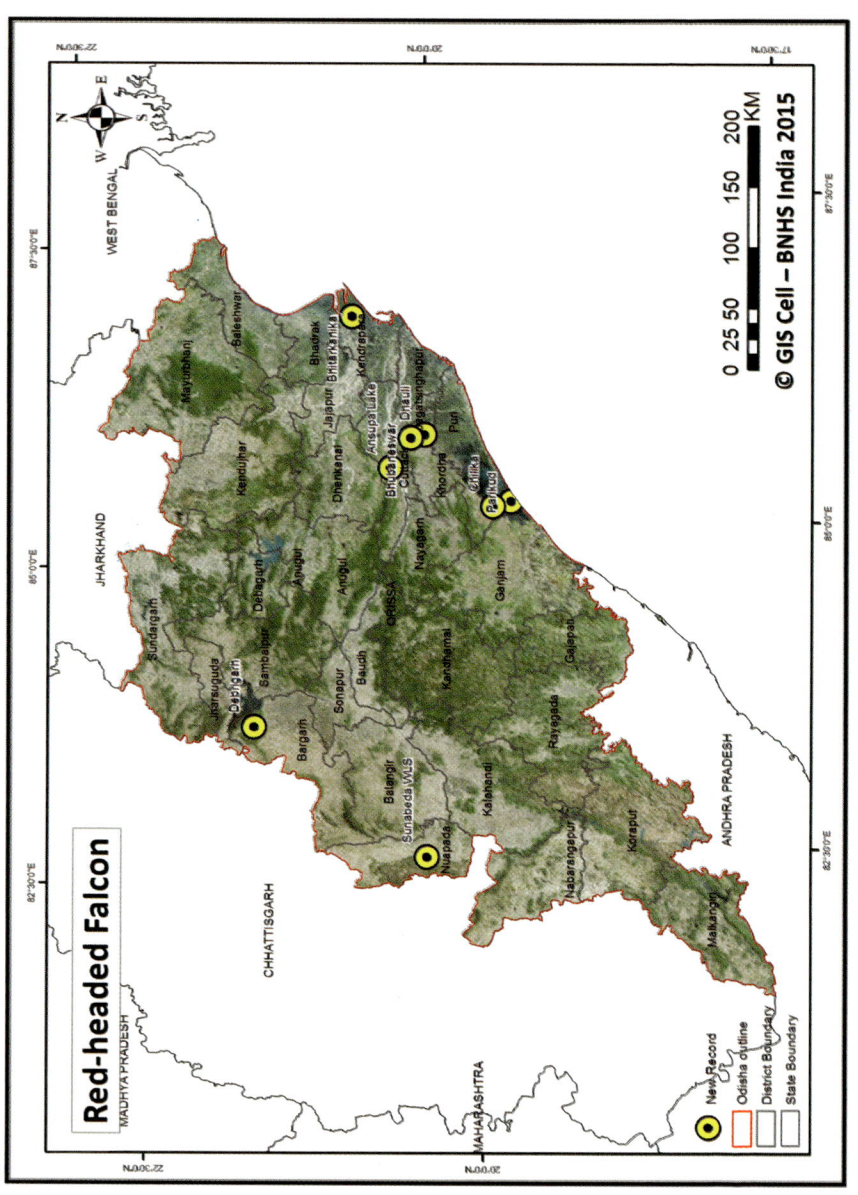

Red-headed Falcon

© GIS Cell – BNHS India 2015

Threatened Birds of Odisha

Red-headed Falcon, which is quite rare in Odisha, usually hunts in pairs. It mainly feeds on small birds and large insects which it catches in flight in dry open habitats

Outside the nesting season, it leads a nomadic life and can be found anywhere in suitable biotopes.

Threats: Industrialisation, urbanisation and extensive use of pesticides could be the major reasons for its rapid decline. It was naturally sparsely distributed, so its disappearance from many areas has not caught the attention of conservationists. It could be much rarer than we suspect.

Conservation Action: Like all raptors, it is protected under the Indian Wildlife (Protection) Act, 1972. Its trade is totally banned.

RECOMMENDATIONS

1) Regular surveys to monitor population trends.
2) Conduct further research into the effects of changes in urban areas, agricultural land and land management.
3) Prevent capture for trade through law enforcement, prosecution and awareness campaigns.

Laggar Falcon *Falco jugger*
Gray 1834

Despite its wide distribution in the Indian subcontinent, it is a poorly-known species. It is supposed to be undergoing a moderately rapid population decline owing to both pesticide use and incidental capture by trappers targeting the Saker Falcon *Falco cherrug cherrug* (BirdLife International 2014), hence it is listed as Near Threatened. If more accurate surveys prove that it is under greater threat, it may be uplisted to Vulnerable.

Field Characters: A large falcon (43–46 cm) with a white forehead and narrow supercilium above a black eyeline, and a long, narrow moustachial stripe running down in front of and below the eyes. The crown is pale rufous with variable black streaks. Below it is white from chin to belly, with longitudinal light brown drops, in some individuals very faint on breast and belly, darker on flanks and thighs. Sexes are alike, but female is larger. Juvenile is darker brown above with dark head and a broader moustache, and very heavily marked, almost uniformly dark, on breast, belly, and thighs. Immatures are even more heavily marked. In adults, legs and feet are yellow, with black claws, while juveniles have pale grey or greenish grey claws.

Distribution: The Laggar Falcon is widely distributed in the Indian subcontinent, except in Sri Lanka. It is probably a very rare winter visitor to Odisha. The only place where it has been reported is from **Similipal** Tiger Reserve.

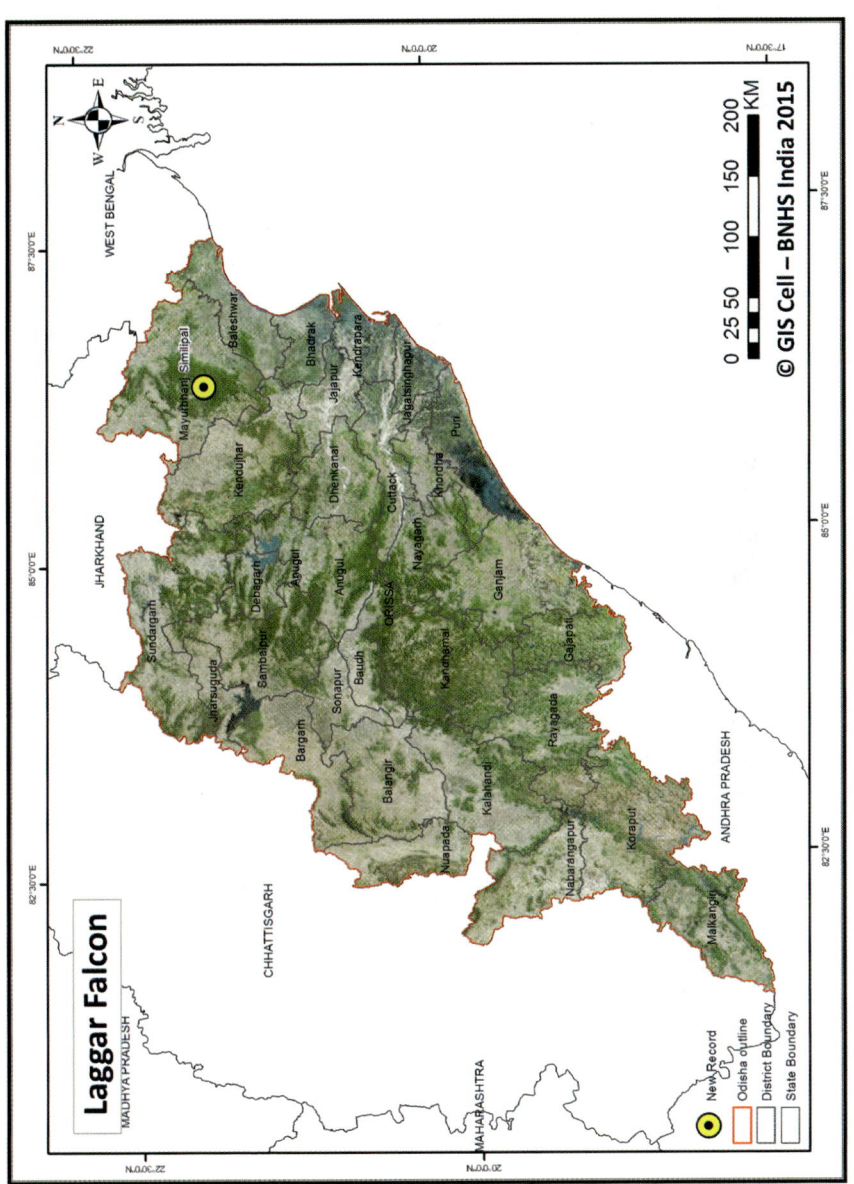

Laggar Falcon

Laggar Falcon lives in drier biotope and hunts small birds, reptiles and snakes by wait-and-watch method

Ecology: In India, it is partial to drier biotopes, from sea level to 1,000 msl. It is usually seen perched on poles or on top of large bushes, generally solitary, but sometimes in pairs (in the breeding season). It preys on small birds, flying insects (locusts), Spiny-tailed Lizard *Uromastix hardwickii*, and other reptiles. It does not build a nest but pirates or uses old nests of crows, kites, and even vultures. Usually three or four eggs are laid, and incubated mostly by the female, but both sexes feed the chicks. For details of behaviour and ecology, see Naoroji (2007).

Threats: Laggar Falcon is mainly threatened by increasing urbanisation, industrialisation, and expansion of agriculture in desert areas, particularly in the Indian Thar Desert. Many traditional nesting sites have been abandoned due to increase in human population, disturbance and traffic noise (Naoroji 2007).

Conservation measures underway: Like all birds of prey, it is legally protected and listed in Schedule I of the Indian Wildlife (Protection) Act, 1972. It is found in some Protected Areas/IBAs of India (Islam & Rahmani 2004).

RECOMMENDATIONS

As it is marginal to Odisha with a confirmed record only from Similipal Tiger Reserve, a proper survey of the state is required because it is likely to be present in many more areas, particularly dry biotopes.

Brown-winged Kingfisher *Pelargopsis amauroptera* (Pearson, 1841)

DHRITIMAN MUKHERJEE

Despite this species' large range, its total population size is likely to be moderately small as a result of the restricted nature of its preferred mangrove habitats. It is likely to be in decline as a result of habitat destruction, and is therefore considered Near Threatened by BirdLife International (2014).

Field Characters: A large (36 cm) salt-water kingfisher with massive red bill, and over-all brownish-yellow (head, neck, throat and belly) and dark brown (mantle, wings and tail). Back and mantle are bright pale blue, particularly conspicuous in flight. Chin is whitish. Legs and feet are red. Eyelids are also red. Sexes are alike.

Distribution: It has a linear distribution in mangrove, creeks and tidal rivers from northern Odisha, West Bengal, Bangladesh, Myanmar, peninsular Thailand to peninsular Malaysia.

In Odisha, this mangrove specialist kingfisher occurs only in **Bhitarkanika** National Park. Here, it frequents the edges of the main river as also the creeks inside the mangrove forests.

Ecology: It is a bird of mangroves, creeks and rivers where it debouches into the sea—an exclusively coastal species. It is found singly or in pairs. Its main food is small crustaceans and fish (del Hoyo *et al*. 2001). Not much is known about it nesting behavior but may not be very different from other similar kingfishers.

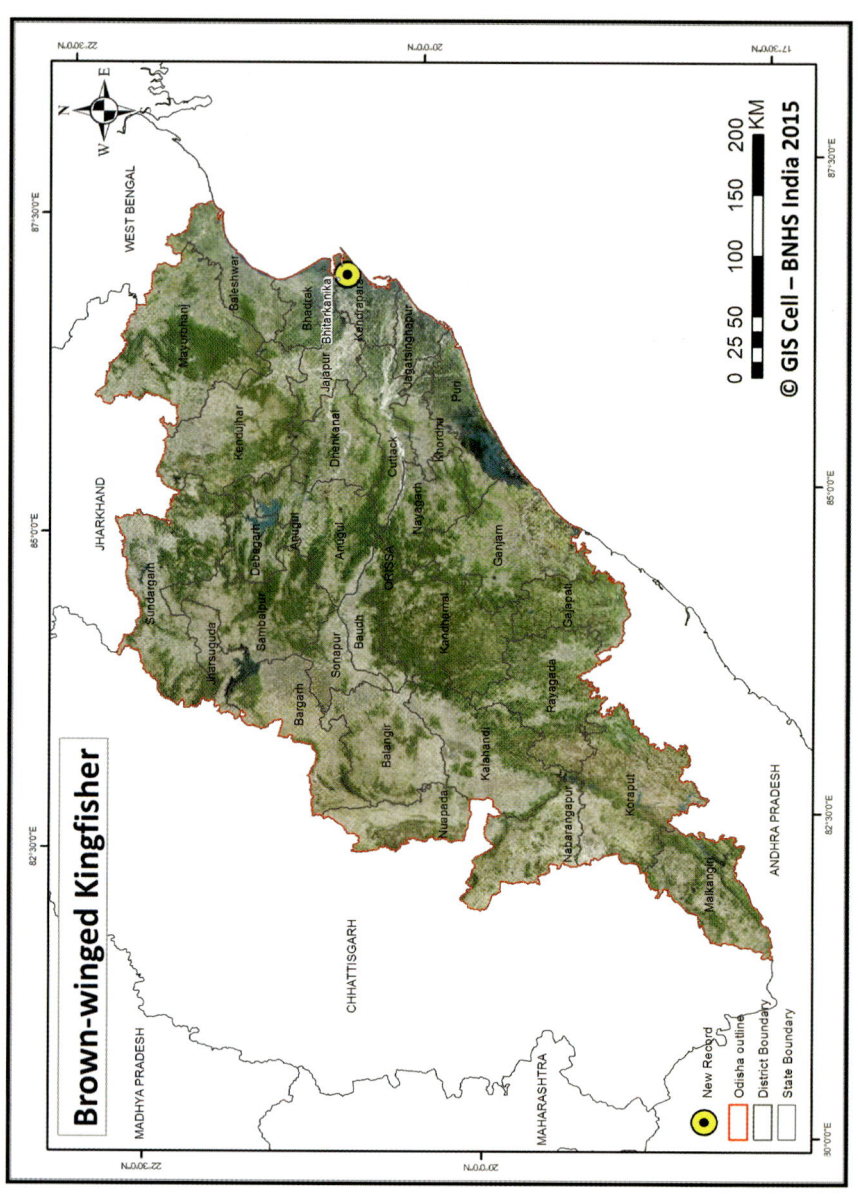

Brown-winged Kingfisher

Legend:
- New Record
- Odisha outline
- District Boundary
- State Boundary

© GIS Cell – BNHS India 2015

0 25 50 100 150 200 KM

Threatened Birds of Odisha

DHRITIMAN MUKHERJEE

In Odisha, this mangrove specialist kingfisher occurs only in Bhitarkanika National Park

It is very noisy and the call is loud and raucous *chak-chak-chak-chak*, and also short, descending sequence of whistles, *tree, treew, treew*.

Threats: Although it has a wide distribution, the linear restriction of its habitat is a cause for concern. It may be under threat mainly because of enormous ongoing developmental activities on the coastal regions of the range countries. It is supposed to be common in Sundarbans of India and Bangladesh but good population estimates are not available.

Conservation measures undergoing: It is listed in Schedule IV of the Indian Wildlife (Protection) Act, 1972 and its hunting and trapping is banned.

RECOMMENDATIONS
1) Conduct search survey in the mangrove of Bhitarkanika specially for this species.
2) Depending upon the results of this survey, conduct ecological and behavioural research, particularly in Bhitarkanika where eight species of kingfishers are found.
3) Study its movement, if any, through colour banding and ringing.
4) Protect mangroves, particularly old growth preferred by this species.

Malabar Pied Hornbill *Anthracoceros coronatus* (Boddaert 1783)

PUTTURAJU K.

According to BirdLife International (2014), Malabar Pied Hornbill is considered Near Threatened as it has a moderately small population, and is likely to decline as a result of continuing habitat loss. It should be carefully monitored for any future increase in the rate of decline.

Field characters: The Malabar Pied Hornbill is a medium-sized hornbill, *c.* 92 cm in length. It has mainly black plumage, apart from its white belly, throat patch, tail sides and trailing edge to the wings. The bill is yellow with a large, mainly black casque. Female has white orbital skin, which is black in the male. There is no black on cutting edge of bill in male. The female lacks black at the rear end of casque. Juveniles lack the casque.

Distribution: This species occurs from southwest West Bengal and Bihar to northern Andhra Pradesh, Western Ghats, mainly along the eastern edge, south of southern Maharashtra (Ratnagiri) up to 300 m (Rasmussen & Anderton 2012).

In Odisha it is an uncommon resident but is locally common in certain suitable sites. It has been reported from **Barbara RF**, **Satkosia**, **Similipal** and parts of **Rayagada** district. Large groups are sometimes met with in fruiting *Ficus* in South Similipal. Breeding reliably known only from Similipal, where fledglings are regularly been rescued from local tribals.

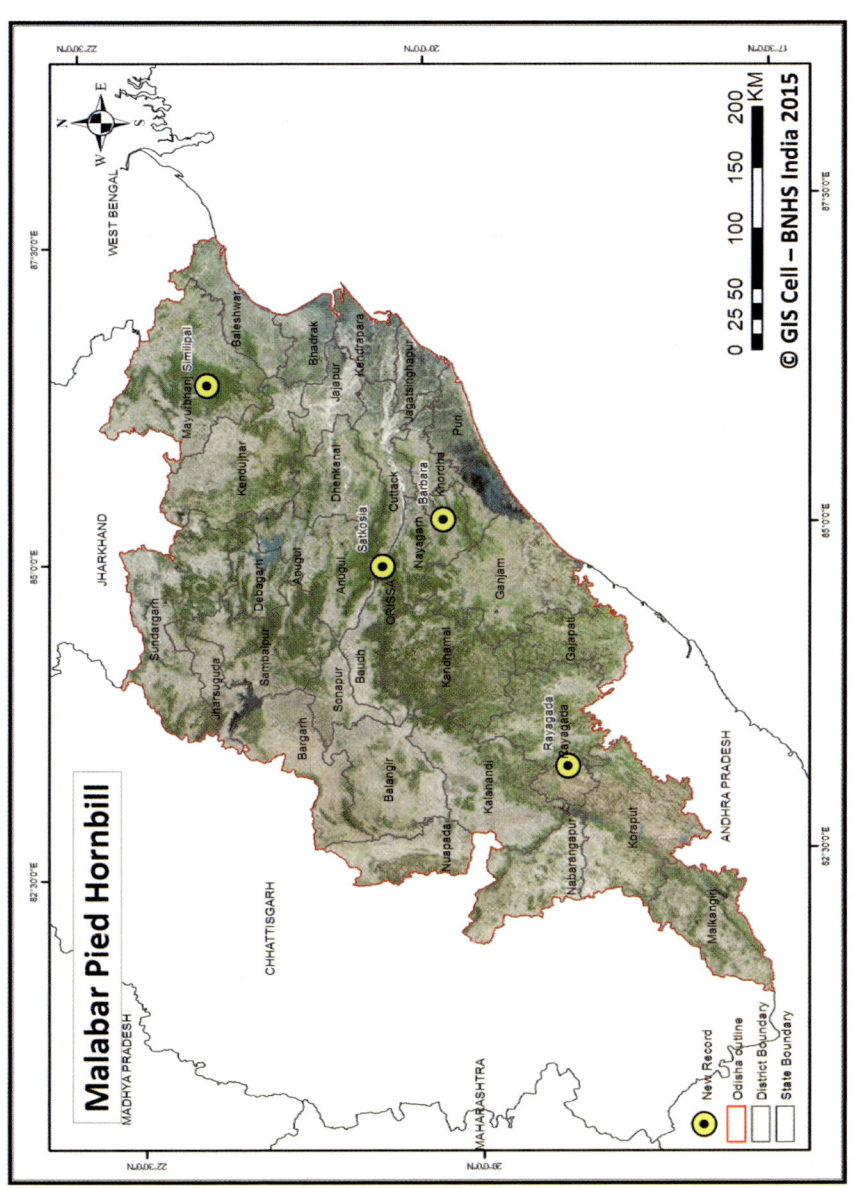

Malabar Pied Hornbill

The Barabara-Dhuanali Reserve Forests are a stronghold of the Malabar Pied Hornbill

Ecology: It usually feeds and roosts in small to medium-sized groups. It is primarily arboreal and frugivorous, but it can be omnivorous, taking fruits, small mammals, birds, small reptiles, and insects. It breeds in single pairs during March to September. Balasubramanian (2003) has conducted detailed studies on this species in the Western Ghats.

Conservation measures undergoing: It is listed in Schedule IV of the Indian Wildlife (Protection) Act, 1972 and its hunting and trapping is banned.

RECOMMENDATIONS

1) Conduct search survey in the whole state specially for this species.

2) Protect old growth forest, but particulary ficus trees

3) Study its movement, if any, through colour banding and ringing.

Alexandrine Parakeet *Psittacula eupatria*

SANJAY KUMAR

Although it remains common in some areas and the status is clouded by feral population, it is suspected to be undergoing a moderately rapid population decline owing to ongoing habitat loss, persecution and trapping pressure, therefore BirdLife International (2014) has listed it as a Near Threatened.

Field Character: A large parakeet (53 cm), bigger than Rose-ringed Parakeet, with huge red bill, maroon-shoulder patch in sexes and less yellow cheeks, mantle and breast. The upper side of the middle tail feathers is bluish-green, while the underside is yellow. The voice is loud and powerful.

Distribution: The Alexandrine Parakeet is widespread in South and Southeast Asia. In Odisha, it is a fairly widespread and breeding resident throughout the State. There are records from all forested Protected Areas including mangrove forests of Bhitarkanika.

Ecology: In India, it is a common species of orchards, gardens, plantations, roadside old avenue trees, agricultural areas and light-wooded forests, mainly below 900 msl, but reaching c. 1,600 msl locally (Juniper and Parr 1998). It feeds on a range of wild and cultivated seeds, flowers, flower buds, nectar, grain, fruit and vegetables (Juniper and Parr 1998). Along with Rose-ringed Parakeet, it can become an agriculture pest in some areas (e.g. Uttar Pradesh, Bihar). It nests in

Alexandrine Parakeet chicks are caught in large numbers for pet trade

tree cavities, palms and very rarely buildings, and generally breeds from January to April-May.

Threats: Trade and habitat loss are serious threats in many countries of its range (BirdLife International 2014). In India trade has been come down drastically after the ban, but it still occurs in a few areas. Large-scale trade of parrots, parakeets, munias etc. has been officially banned for the last 25 years in India but still occurs in some areas.

Conservation Actions Underway: Bird trade has been banned in India since the early 1990s. It is listed under CITES Appendix II and also under Indian Wildlife (Protection) Act, 1972.

RECOMMENDATIONS

1) Regular monitoring of its populations in Odisha.

2) Strict control on trade.

3) Conduct awareness-raising activities to discourage capture and trade.

4) Protection of old trees that provide it nesting and roosting sites.

Mangrove Pitta *Pitta megarhyncha*
Schlegel, 1863

BIJOY DAS

Birdlife International (2014) has recently included it in Near Threatened category as "this scarce species is restricted to a highly specialised and restricted habitat, and is therefore likely to have a moderately small global population. It is also suspected to be declining as a result of habitat loss and degradation."

Field Characters: It is a slightly larger version of Indian Pitta, but with much longer and heavier bill, and darker brown crown in adult birds. For details see Rasmussen and Anderton (2005).

Distribution: As the name indicates, the Mangrove Pitta is found in mangroves, so it has discontinuous linear distribution depending on the presence of mangroves. From Bangladesh east, it is widely distributed in Southeast Asia wherever suitable conditions occur. For a long time, it was doubtful whether it is found in the Indian territorial limits but now it is confirmed that it is fairly common and widespread in the mangroves of Sundarbans in West Bengal.

Within Odisha, this habitat specialist species is found only in the dense mangrove patches of **Bhitarkanika.** Though Pandav (1997) did not report it there, Gopi & Pandav (2007) considered it to be fairly common. However, breeding

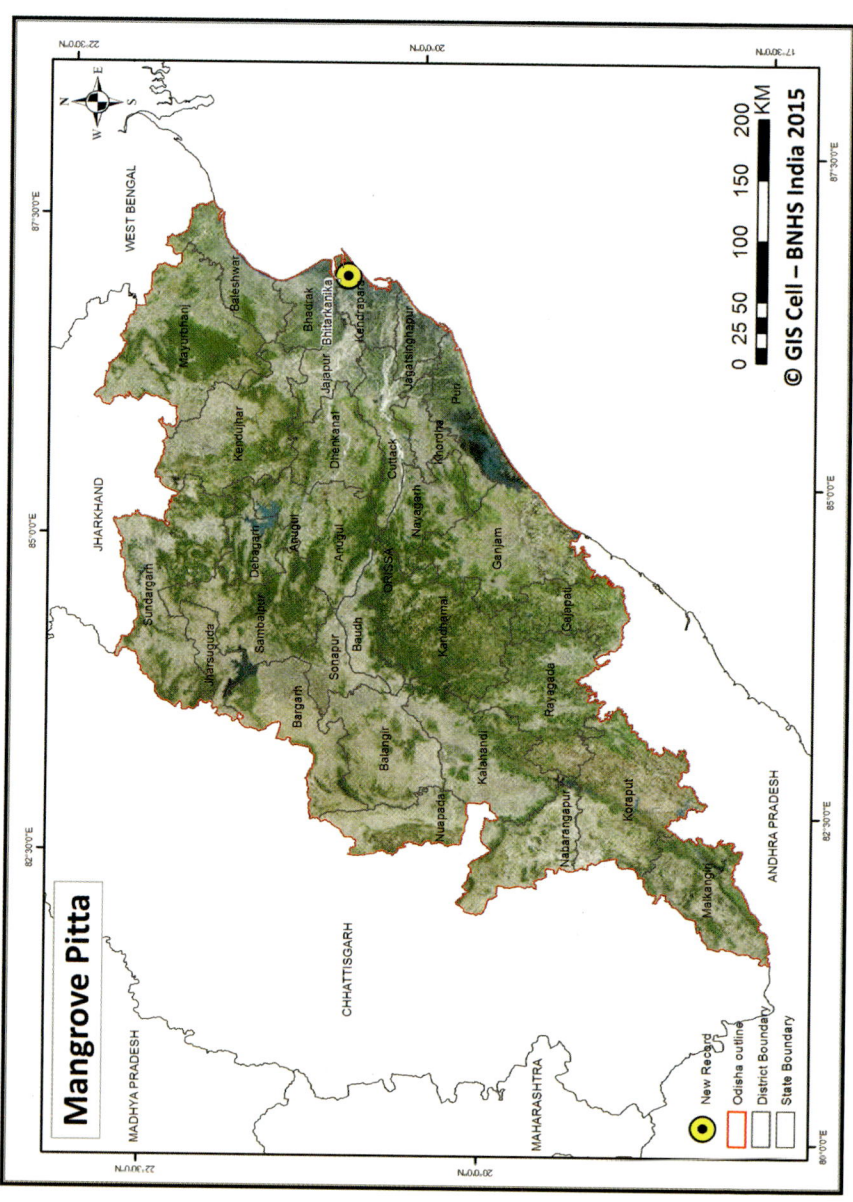

Mangrove Pitta

Threatened Birds of Odisha

Bhitarkanika WLS is a good area for studying ecology and
behaviour of Mangrove Pitta

was recorded only in 2014 (Nair *et al. in prep.*) where four nests were found in Dangmal area of Bhitarkanika Forest Block. A subsequent survey during 2014 and 2015 using callplayback located some 60 pairs in various forest blocks of the National Park area. Therefore, Bhitarkanika is possibly a globally significant site for this species (Nair *et al. in prep.*). The only other report of this species from Odisha is from **Dhamra**.

Ecology: It feeds on crustaceans, molluscs and terrestrial insects in drier mud at the bases of mangroves.

Threats: Coastal mangrove forests are suffering severe pressure through clearance for fuel-wood, charcoal production and construction materials, as well as fish and shrimp ponds.

RECOMMENDATIONS

(a) Conduct status surveys across the mangrove areas of the state.

(b) Campaign for the protection of remaining tracts of coastal mangrove woodland throughout the range.

REFERENCES

Ahmed, A. (1997) *Live bird trade in northern India*. TRAFFIC-India/WWF-India, New Delhi.

Ahmed, A. (1998) Some observations of the Green Munia in the Indian bird trade. *Oriental Bird Club Bulletin* 27: 21–25.

Ahmed, A. (1999) *Fraudulence in Indian live bird trade: An identification monograph for control of illegal trade*. TRAFFIC India/ WWF-India, New Delhi.

Ahmed, A. (2002) *Live Bird Trade in India*. TRAFFIC India/WWF-India, New Delhi. Unpubl.

Ahmed, A. (2008) Green Avadavat – A victim of illegal bird trade. TRAFFIC Post November Issue 5: 10–11.

Ahmed, A. (2009) Green Avadavat. WWF-India Newsletter 2(2): 8.

Ali S. and Abdulali, H. (1945) Addition to the birds of Bombay and Salsette and neighbourhood. *JBNHS* 45: 241–243.

Ali, S. (1981) Studies on the movement and population structure of Indian Avifauna. Annual Report. Bombay Natural History Society, Mumbai.

Ali, S. and Ripley, S.D. (1987) *Compact Edition of the Birds of India and Pakistan, Bangladesh, Nepal, Bhutan and Sri Lanka*. Oxford University Press, New Delhi.

Anon. (1991) New birds reported in Chilika. *Bihang Journal* 1(4): 7.

Anon. (1995) *Fauna of Tiger Reserves (Sunderbans, Palamau, Simlipal, Manas)*. Zoological Survey of India, Kolkata.

Anon. (2004) Report on the International South Asian Vulture Recovery Plan Workshop. *Buceros* 9 (1): 48.

Balachandran, S. and Sathiyaselvam, P. (2007) Further records of Great Knot *Calidris tenuirostris* and Red Knot *Calidris canutus* from the north-east coast of India. *JBNHS* 104 (3): 351–351.

Balachandran, S., Sathiyaselvam, P. and Panda, S. (2009) *Bird Atlas of Chilika*. Bombay Natural History Society, Mumbai and Chilika Development Authority, Bhubaneswar.

Balasubramanian, P. (2003) Habitat Utilization by Malabar Pied Hornbill in Athikadavu Valley, Western Ghats. SACON, Coimbatore, Unpubl.

Ball, V. (1877) Notes on birds observed in the region between the Mahanadi and Godavari rivers. *Stray Feathers* 5: 410–420.

Ball, V. (1878) From the Ganges to the Godaveri. On the distribution of birds, so far as it is at present known, throughout the hilly region which extends from the Rajmehal Hills to the Godaveri valley. *Stray Feathers* 7: 191–235.

Baral, H.S., Giri, J.B. and Virani, M.Z. (2005) On the decline of Oriental Whitebacked Vultures *Gyps bengalensis* in lowland Nepal. Pp. 215–219. In: Chancellor, R.D. and Meyburg, B.U. (Eds) *Raptors Worldwide. Proceedings of the 6th world conference on Birds of Prey and Owls*. WWGBP, Berlin and MME/Birdlife Hungary, Budapest.

Bhargava R. (1996) Notes on Green Munia. *JBNHS* 93: 588.

Bijlsma, R.G. and de Roder, F.E. (1986) Notes on Nordmann's Greenshank *Tringa guttifer* in Thailand. *Forktail* 2: 92–94.

Threatened Birds of Odisha

BirdLife International (2001) *Threatened Birds of Asia: The BirdLife International Red Data Book*. 2 Vols. BirdLife International, Cambridge, UK.

Bishop, K.D. (1999) Preliminary notes on some birds in Bhutan. *Forktail* 15: 87–91.

Cramp, S. & Simmons, K.E.L. (Eds). (1977) *Handbook of the Birds of Europe, the Middle East and North Africa. Vol. 1: Ostrich to Ducks.* Oxford University Press, Oxford, London and New York.

Cuthbert, R., Green, R.E., Ranade, S., Saravanan, S., Pain, D.J., Prakash, V. and Cunningham, A.A. (2006) Rapid population declines of Egyptian vulture (*Neophron percnopterus*) and red-headed vulture (*Sarcogyps calvus*) in India. *Animal Conservation* 9: 349–354.

Das, S.K., Dash, N. Ahmed, R.A. and Rout, S.D. (2010) Avifauna of Kuldiha Wildlife Sanctuary, Orissa, India. *Newsletter for Birdwatchers* 50: 49–54.

del Hoyo, J., Elliott, A. and Sargatal, J. (1992) *Handbook of the Birds of the World. Vol. 1: Ostrich to Ducks*. Lynx Edicions, Barcelona.

del Hoyo, J., Elliot, A. and Sargatal, J. (eds) (1994) *Handbook of the Birds of the World. Vol. 2: New World Vultures to Guineafowl*. Lynx edicions, Barcelona.

del Hoyo, J., A. Elliott and J. Sargatal (1996). *Handbook of the Birds of the World. Vol. 3: Hoatzin to Auks*. Lynx Edicions, Barcelona.

del Hoyo, J., Elliott, A. and Sagartal, J. (2001) *Handbook of the Birds of the World. Vol. 6. Mousebirds to Hornbills*. Lynx Edicions, Barcelona.

Dev, U.N. (1986) Checklist of the birds of Similipal. *Newsletter – Nature and Wildlife Conservation Society of Orissa* 4 (1 & 2): 1–57.

Dev, U.N. (2013) *A Field Guide to the birds of Chilika*. Odisha Forestry Sector Development Project, Bhubaneswar. Pp. 281.

Dutta, S.K. (2007) *Biodiversity assessment of Dhamra port site and surrounding areas, Orissa*. Greenpeace India, Bangalore. http://www.greenpeace.org/raw/content/india/press/reports/greenpeace-biodiversity.pdf

Dutta, S., Rahmani, A.R. and Jhala, Y.V. (2010) Running out of time? The Great Indian Bustard *Ardeotis nigriceps* – status, viability, and conservation strategies. *European Journal of Wildlife Research*. Published online November 24, 2010 on DOI 10.1007/s10344-010-0472-z.

Dutta, S., Rahmani, A., Gautam, P., Kasambe, R., Narwade, S., Narayan, G., and Jhala. Y. (2013) Guidelines for Preparation of State Action Plan for Resident Bustards' Recovery Programme. Ministry of Environment and Forests, Government of India. New Delhi. Pp. xi + 57.

Ferguson-Lees, J. and Christie, D.A. (2001) *Raptors of the World*. Christopher Helm, London.

Gaston A.J. and Mackrell J. (1980) Green Munia *Estrilda formosa* at Delhi and other interesting records for 1978. *JBNHS* 77(1): 144-145.

Gilbert, M., Watson, R.T., Virani, M.Z., Oaks, J.L., Ahmed, S., Chaudhry, M.J.I., Arshad, M. and Mahmood, S. (2006) Rapid population declines and mortality clusters in three Oriental white-backed vulture *Gyps bengalensis* colonies in Pakistan due to diclofenac poisoning. *Oryx* 40: 388–399.

Gopi, G.V. and Pandav, B. (2007) Avifauna of Bhitarkanika mangroves, India. *Zoos' Print Journal* 22: 2839–2847 (with web supplement).

Green, R.E., Newton, I., Shultz, S., Cunningham, A.A., Gilbert, M., Pain, D.J. and Prakash, V. (2004) Diclofenac poisoning as a cause of vulture population declines across the Indian subcontinent. *J. Appl. Ecol.* 41: 793–800.

Grewal, B. (1996) Bristled Grassbird *Chaetornis striatus* at Okhla, Delhi. *OBC Bulletin* 24: 43–44.

Grimmett, R., Inskipp, C. and Inskipp, T. (1998) *Birds of the Indian Subcontinent.* Helm Identification Guides. Christopher Helm, A & C Black. London. Pp. 888.

Ishtiaq, F. (1998) *Comparative ecology and behaviour of storks in Keoladeo National Park, Rajasthan, India.* Ph.D. Thesis. Aligarh Muslim University, Aligarh, India.

Ishtiaq, F. and Rahmani, A.R. (2000a) Further information on status and distribution of Forest Owlet (*Athene blewitti*). *Forktail* 16: 125–130.

Ishtiaq, F. and Rahmani, A.R. (2000b) Cronism in the Forest Owlet *Athene blewitti*. *Forktail* 16: 172–173.

Ishtiaq, F. and Rahmani, A.R. (2005) The Forest Owlet *Heteroglaux blewitti*: vocalization, breeding biology and conservation. *Ibis* 147(1): 197–205.

Ishtiaq, F., Javed, S., Coulter, M.C. and Rahmani A.R. (2010) Resource partitioning in three sympatric species of storks in Keoladeo National Park, India. *Waterbirds* 33(1): 41–49.

Ishtiaq, F., Rasmussen, P.C. and Rahmani, A.R. (2002) Ecology and behavior of the Forest Owlet. Pp. 80–88. In: Newton, I., Kavanagh, R. Osleon, J. and Taylor, I. (Eds) *Ecology and Conservation of Owls.* CSIRO Publishing, Australia.

Islam, M.Z. and Rahmani, A.R. (2004) *Important Birds Areas in India: Priority sites for conservation.* Indian Bird Conservation Network: Bombay Natural History Society and BirdLife International UK. Pp. xviii + 1133

Jathar, G.A. (2006) Ecology and behaviour of the Forest Owlet *Heteroglaux blewitti*. Ph.D. Thesis University of Mumbai, Mumbai.

Jathar, G. and Rahmani, A.R. (2010) Ecology of the Forest Owlet: A comprehensive study of the critically endangered Forest Owlet in Central India. Lambert Academic Publishing, USA. Pp. 197.

Jayakar, S.D. (1967) The Purple Wood Pigeon (*Columba punicea*, Blyth) and the Himalayan Tree Pie (*Dendrocitta formosae* Swinhoe) in Orissa. *JBNHS* 64: 109.

Johnsgard, P.A. (1981) *The Plovers, Sandpipers, and Snipes of the World.* University of Nebraska Press, USA.

Johnson, J.A., Lerner Heather R.L., Rasmussen, P.C. and Mindell, D.P. (2006) Systematics within *Gyps* vultures: a clade at risk. *BMC Evolutionary Biology* 6:65. doi:10.1186/1471-2148-6-65.

Juniper, T. and Parr, M. (1998) *Parrots: A Guide to the Parrots of the world.* Pica Press, Robertsbridge, UK.

Karuthedathu, D., Das, Vinay, Praveen J., Ramachandran, Vijay K. and Shurpali, Sachin (2014) Some significant avian records from Odisha. *Indian BIRDS* 9(1): 14—18.

Kasambe, R., Wadatkar, J., Bhusum, N.S., and Kasdekar, F. (2005) Forest Owlets *Heteroglaux blewitti* in Melghat Tiger Reserve, Dist. Amaravati, Maharashtra. *Newsletter for Birdwatchers* 45(3): 38–40.

Kaur, J. (2008) Impact of Land Use Changes on the Habitat, Behaviour and Breeding Biology of the Indian Sarus Crane (*Grus antigone antigone*) in the Semi-arid Tract of Rajasthan, India. Ph.D. Thesis. Forest Research Institute University, Dehra Dun.

Kaur, J. and Choudhury, B.C. (2002) Recognition of community involvement in Sarus Crane conservation in Kota, Rajasthan. *Mistnet* 3(4) October–December: 6.

Kaur, J., Nair, A. and Choudhury, B.C. (2008) Conservation of the vulnerable sarus crane *Grus antigone antigone* in Kota, Rajasthan, India: a case study of community involvement. *Oryx* 42: 452–455.

Khan, M.M.H. (2006) Spoon-billed Sandpiper *Calidris pygmeus* on the coast of Bangladesh. *BirdingASIA* 6: 84–85.

King, B.F. and Rasmussen, P.C. (1998) The rediscovery of the Forest Owlet *Athene* (*Heteroglaux*) *blewitti*. *Forktail* 14: 53–55.

Maheswaran, G. (1998) Ecology and behaviour of the Black-necked Stork *Ephippiorhynchus asiaticus* in Dudhwa National Park, Uttar Pradesh, India. Ph.D. Thesis. Aligarh Muslim University, Aligarh, India.

Majumdar, N. (1988) On a collection of birds from Koraput district, Orissa, India. *Records of the Zoological Survey of India, Miscellaneous Publications, Occasional Paper* 108: 53.

Manakadan, R. and Kannan, V. (2003) A study of Spot-billed Pelican *Pelecanus philippensis* with special reference to its conservation in southern India. Final Report. BNHS, Mumbai.

Manu, K. and Jolly, S. (2000). *Pelicans and People: The two-tier village of Kokkare-Bellur, Karnataka, India. Community based conservation in south Asia: Case Study No. 4.* Kalpavriksh and International Institute of Environment and Development, Pune.

Mehra S.P., Sharma S. and Mathur R. (2005) Munias of Mt. Abu (Rajasthan, India) with special emphasis on threatened Green Munia *Amandava formosa*. *Indian BIRDS*, 1(4): 77–79.

Mehta, P., Kulkarni, J. and Patil, D. (2010) A survey of the Critically Endangered Forest Owlet *Heteroglaux blewitti* in Central India. *BirdingASIA* 10: 77–87.

Mehta, P., Kulkarni, J., Patil, D., Kolte, P. and Khatavkar, P. (2007) A Survey of Critically Endangered Forest Owlet (*Heteroglaux blewitti*) in Central India. Final Report. Envirosearch, Pune. Pp. 60.

Mishra, A.K., Samantaray, R.K., Roy, P.K., Patnaik, A.K. and Ray, P. (2008) Rescue and rehabilitation of a Cinereous Vulture (*Aegypius monachus*) in Orissa. *e-planet* 6(2): 61

Mooney, H. F. (1934) Occurrence of the Purple Wood-Pigeon [*Alsocomus puniceus* (Tickell)] in Singhbhum Dist., Bihar and Orissa. *JBNHS* 37: 735.

Nagulu, V. (1983) Feeding and Breeding Biology of Grey Pelican at Nelapattu Bird Sanctuary in Andhra Pradesh, India. Ph.D. Thesis. Osmania University, Hyderabad.

Naidoo, V., Wolter, K., Cromarty, D., Diekmann, M., Duncan, N., Andrew, A.M., Taggart, M.A., Leon Venter, L. and Cuthbert, R. (2009) Toxicity of non-steroidal anti-inflammatory drugs to Gyps vultures: a new threat from ketoprofen. Biol. Lett. Published online. Electronic supplementary material is available at http://dx.doi.org/10. 1098/rsbl.2009.0818 or via http://rsbl.royalsocietypublishing.org.

Naik, S. (2015) Addition of Cinereous Vulture to the Checklist of the birds of Similipal Biosphere Reserve. http://satyeshnaik.blogspot.in/2015/03/addition-of-cinereous-vulture-to.html

Nair, M.V., Panda, S. and Pradhan, A.K. (2014) Hirakud Wetlands, Odisha: A little-known refuge and potential IBA for wintering waterfowl. Pp. 186–201. In: Gopi, G.V. and S.A. Hussain (eds.) *Waterbirds of India*, ENVIS Bulletin: Wildlife & Protected Areas. Vol 16. Wildlife Institute of India, Dehradun. Pp. 368.

Nair, M.V., Das, B., Sarkar, V., and Jani, C. (*in prep.*) Mangrove Pitta *Pitta megarhynchus* nesting in Bhitarkanika Mangrove—first breeding record from India.

Naoroji, R. (2007) *Birds of Prey of the Indian Subcontinent*. Om Books International, New Delhi.

Nath,I., Samantara, S. and Das, S. (2011) Rescue and rehabilitation of a Black Vulture (*Aegypius monachus*) in Orissa. *Zoos' Print* 26 (5): 15.

Nayak, A. K. (2003) Nesting ecology of resident birds in the Bhitarkanika Wildlife Sanctuary. *Cheetal* 41(3&4): 43–54.

Nayak, A.K and S.Naik (2014) *Birds of Similipal Biosphere Reserve*. Similipal Tiger Reserve, Odisha. Pp. 280.

Oaks, J.L., Gilbert, M., Virani, M.Z., Watson, R.T., Meteyer, C.U., Rideout, B., Shivaprasad, H.L., Ahmed, S., Chaudhry, M.J.I., Arshad, M., Mahmood, S., Ali, A. and Khan, A.A. (2004a) Diclofenac residues as the cause of vulture population decline in Pakistan. *Nature* 427: 630–633.

Oaks, J.L., Donahue, S.L., Rurangirwa, F.R., Rideout, B.A., Gilbert, M. and Virani, M.Z. (2004b) Identification of a novel mycoplasma species from an Oriental Whitebacked Vulture (Gyps bengalensis). *J. Clinical Microbiol.* 42: 5909–5912.

Pain, D.J., Cunningham, A.A., Donald, P.F., Duckworth, J.W., Houston, D.C., Katzner, T., Parry-Jones, J., Poole, C., Prakash, V., Round, P. and Timmins, R. (2003) Gyps vulture declines in Asia; temporospatial trends, causes and impacts. *Conserv. Biol.* 17: 661–671.

Pain, D.J., Bowden, C.G.R., Cunningham, A.A., Cuthbert, R., Das, D., Gilbert, M., Jakati, R.D., Jhala, Y., Khan, A.A., Naidoo, V., Oaks, J.L., Parry-Jones, J., Prakash, V., Rahmani, A., Ranade, S.P., Baral, H. S., Senacha, K.R. and Saravanan, S. (2008) The race to prevent the extinction of South Asian vultures. *Bird Conservation International* 18: 30–48.

Palei, H.S. (2012) Sighting of Green Avadavat *Amandava formosa* in Karlapat Wildlife Sanctuary, Odisha, India. *Zoo's Print Magazine* 27 (1): 25.

Palei, H.S., Mahapatra, P.P., Dutta, S.K., Singh, L.A.K., Sahu, H.K. and Rout, S.D. (2011) Avifauna of Karlapat Wildlife Sanctuary, southern Orissa, India. *Indian Forester* 137: 1197–1202.

Palei, H.S. and Mohapatra, P.P. (2011) Sighting of Black-bellied Tern in Samal Reservoir of Angul District, Odisha. *Newsletter for Birdwatchers* 51: 61.

Pandav, B. (1997) Birds of Bhitarkanika mangroves, eastern India. *Forktail* 12: 7–17.

Prakash, V. (1989) Lesser Spotted Eagle (*Aquila pomarina hastata*) Nesting in Keoladeo National Park, Bharatpur. *JBNHS* 85: 614.

Prakash, V. (1999) Status of vultures in Keoladeo National Park, Bharatpur, Rajasthan, with special reference to population crash in *Gyps* species. *JBNHS* 96(3): 365–378.

Prakash, V., Pain, D.J., Cunningham, A.A., Donald, P.F., Prakash, N., Verma, A., Gargi, R., Sivakumar, S., Rahmani, A.R. (2003) Catastrophic collapse of Indian White-backed *Gyps bengalensis* and Long-billed *Gyps indicus* vulture populations. *Biological Conservation* 109 (3): 381–390.

Prakash, V., Green, R.E., Pain, D.J., Ranade, S.P., Saravanan, S., Prakash, N., Venkitachalam, R., Cuthbert, R., Rahmani, A., and Cunningham, A.A. (2007) Recent changes in populations of resident *Gyps* vultures in India. *JBNHS* 104 (2): 127–133.

Rahmani, A.R. (1989) The Great Indian Bustard: Final Report. Bombay Natural History Society, Bombay.

Rahmani, A.R. (2012) *Threatened Birds of India: Their Conservation Requirements*. Indian Bird Conservation Network, Bombay Natural History Society, Royal Society for the Protection of Birds and BirdLife International. Oxford University Press. Pp xvi + 864.

Rahmani, A.R. and Islam, M.Z. (2008) *Ducks, Geese and Swans of India*. Indian Bird Conservation Network, Bombay Natural History Society, Royal Society for the Protection of Birds and BirdLife International. Oxford University Press, Delhi. Pp. 374.

Rahmani, A.R. and Manakadan, R. (1990) The past and present distribution of the Great Indian Bustard *Ardeotis nigriceps* (Vigors) in India. *JBNHS* 87: 175–194.

Rasmussen, P.C. and Anderton, J.C. (2005) *Birds of South Asia: the Ripley guide*. Vols 1 & 2. Smithsonian Institution and Lynx Edicions, Washington D.C. and Barcelona.

Rasmussen, P.C. and Anderton, J.C. (2012) *Birds of South Asia: The Ripley Guide*. Vols 1 & 2. 2nd edn. National Museum of Natural History, Smithsonian Institution, Michigan State University and Lynx Edicions, Washington D.C., Michigan and Barcelona.

Rasmussen, P.C. and Collar, N.J. (1998) Identification, distribution and status of Forest Owlet *Athene* (*Heteroglaux*) *blewitti*. *Forktail* 14: 41–49.

Rath, D.P. and Mohanty-Hejmadi, P. (1996) Birds of the Chandaka Sanctuary, Orissa, India. Unpubl.

Roberts, T.J. (1991) *The Birds of Pakistan*. Vol. I. Oxford University Press, Karachi.

Sankaran, R., Rahmani, A.R. and Ganguli-Lachungpa, U. (1992) The distribution and status of the Lesser Florican Sypheotides indica (J.F. Miller) in the Indian subcontinent. *JBNHS* 89: 156–179.

Senacha, K.R., Taggart, M.A., Rahmani, A.R., Jhala, Y.V., Cuthbert, R., Pain, D.J. and Green, R.E. (2008) Diclofenac levels in livestocks carcasses in India before the 2006 "ban". *JBNHS* 105(2): 148–161.

Shultz, S., Baral, H.S., Charman, S., Cunningham, A.A. , Das, D., Ghalsasi, D.R., Goudar, M.S., Green, R.E. , Jones, A., Nighot, P., Pain, D.J. and Prakash, V. (2004) Diclofenac poisoning is widespread in declining vulture populations across the Indian subcontinent. *Proceedings of the Royal Society of London*, B (Supplement), 271: 458–460.

Sugathan, R. (1985) Observations on Spoonbilled Sandpiper (*Eurynorhynchus pygmeus*) in its wintering ground at Point Calimere, Thanjavur District, Tamil Nadu. *JBNHS* 82: 407–408.

Sundar, K.S.G. (2003) Notes on the breeding biology of the Black-necked Stork *Ephippiorhynchus asiaticus* in Etawah and Mainpuri districts, Uttar Pradesh, India. *Forktail* 19: 15–20.

Sundar, K.S.G. (2009) Are rice paddies suboptimal breeding habitat for Sarus Cranes in Uttar Pradesh, India? *The Condor* 111: 611–623.

Swan, G.E., Cuthbert, R., Quevedo, M., Green, R.E., Pain, D.J., Bartels, P., Cunningham, A. A., Duncan, N., Meharg, A.A., Oaks, J.L., Parry-Jones, J., Taggart, M.A., Verdoorn, G. and Wolter, K. (2006b) Toxicity of diclofenac to Gyps vultures. *Biol. Lett.* 279–282.

Syroechkovskiy, E.E., Zockler, C. and Bird, J.P. (2009) Spoon-billed Sandpiper *Eurynorhynchus pygmeus*: last chance to save. *BirdingASIA* 12: 109–111.

Taggart, M.A., Cuthbert, R., Das, D., Pain, D.J., Green, R.E., Shultz, S., Cunningham, A.A. and Meharg, A.A. (2006) Diclofenac disposition in Indian cow and goat with reference to *Gyps* vulture population declines. *Environ. Pollut.* 147: 6065.

Taylor, J.H. (1887) Letter about the game birds of Khorda, Orissa. *Stray Feathers* 10: 526–531.

Tiwari, S.K., Alfred, J.R.B. and Dutta, S.K. (2002) *Vertebrate fauna of Chandaka-Dampara Wildlife Sanctuary, Orissa*. Conservation Area Series 14. Zoological Survey of India, Kolkata. Pp. 126.

Whistler, H. and Kinnear, N.B. (1933) The Vernay Scientific Survey of the Eastern Ghats (Ornithological Section). Part 6. *JBNHS* 36: 832–844.

Yosef, R., Pande, S., Pawashe, A., Kasambe, R. and Mitchell, L. (2010) Inter-specific interactions of the critically endangered Forest Owlet (*Athene blewitti*). *Acta Ethologica* 13: 63–69.

Zockler, C., Syroechkovskiy, E.E. and Bunting, G. (2008) The Spoon-billed Sandpiper: an International Species Action Plan. CMS and BirdLife International, UK.

Link: Ukil, P.M (2013) An ode to the Pink-headed Duck, http://www.kolkatabirds.com/pinkheadedduck.htm#sthash.h8gqHmaL.dpuf

■ ■ ■

Index of Common Names

Index of Scientific Names

ABOUT THE BOMBAY NATURAL HISTORY SOCIETY

The BNHS was founded in 1883 and today it is the prime non-governmental conservation organisation in the Subcontinent. We work towards the conservation of nature and natural resources, education and research in natural history, and have members in over 20 countries.

Membership Activities and Benefits

- Nature camps to wildlife places both in and outside India.
- Treks, walks and field trips at weekends.
- Excellent audio-visuals presented by experts regularly.
- Seminars, workshops and correspondence courses on specific natural history subjects.
- Members receive *Hornbill*, a quarterly magazine.
- Subscription to the *Journal* is optional to members.
- Up to 15% discount on BNHS publications.
- 10% discount on BNHS products.
- Access to the finest collection of books on natural history.
- Voluntary Nature Education and Conservation activities.

Publications

BNHS Publications have been the standard reference works on the natural history of the Indian subcontinent since 1886. They are essential acquisitions for naturalists, amateurs and professionals throughout the country and abroad. Published uninterrupted since 1886, the *Journal of the Bombay Natural History Society* is acknowledged to be one of the finest scientific natural history sources for the Oriental Region. The popular quarterly magazine *Hornbill*, published since 1976, caters to a varied readership of all ages.

To become a member or for other details contact:

Bombay Natural History Society
Hornbill House, S.B. Singh Road, Mumbai 400 001, Maharashtra, India.
Tel.: +91-22-2282 1811 Fax: +91-22-2283 7615
Email: info@bnhs.org Website: www.bnhs.org

THE SOCIETY'S PUBLICATIONS

40.	Understanding the Sea	
	by B.F. Chhapgar	Rs. 500
41.	Sea Shells of India –	
	An Illustrated Guide to Common Gastropods	
	by Deepak Apte	Rs. 600
42.	Treasures of Indian Wildlife	
	edited by A.S. Kothari & B.F. Chhapgar	Rs. 1900
43.	Living Jewels from the Indian Jungle	
	edited by A.S. Kothari & B.F. Chhapgar	Rs. 1600
44.	Wildlife of the Himalayas and the Terai Region	
	edited by A.S. Kothari & B.F. Chhapgar	Rs. 1250
45.	Natural History and the Indian Army	
	by J.C. Daniel & Lt. Gen. Baljit Singh (Retd.)	Rs. 1200
46.	Capturing Wildlife Moments in India	
	by Ashok Mahindra	Rs. 1450
47.	Walking the Western Ghats	
	by A.J.T. Johnsingh	Rs. 450
48.	Cassandra of Conservation	
	edited by J.C. Daniel	Rs. 200
49.	National Parks and Sanctuaries in Maharashtra Vol. I & II	
	by Pratibha Pande	Rs. 500
50.	In Harmony with Nature – A Teacher's Handbook	
	by BNHS Conservation Education Centre	Rs. 350
51.	Maitri Nisargashi – A Teacher's Handbook (Marathi)	
	by BNHS Conservation Education Centre	Rs. 350
52.	Green Guide for Teachers (English)	
	by CEC team, Goregaon	Rs. 350
53.	Nisarg Margdarshak for Teachers (Marathi)	
	by CEC team, Goregaon	Rs. 350
54.	100 Volumes of JBNHS (DVD)	Rs. 1000
55.	Indian Bird Calls (DVD)	Rs. 500

■ ■ ■